Rethinking Pedagogy for a Digital Age

E-learning is no longer seen as a technical and administrative tool, existing simply to deliver content. Practitioners continue to seek guidance on pedagogically sound, learner-focused and accessible learning activities, and learning contexts are increasingly rich in electronic and mobile technologies. This book examines different perspectives on effectively designing and delivering learning activities to ensure that future development is driven by pedagogy.

Rethinking Pedagogy for a Digital Age is a critical discussion of the issues surrounding the design, sharing and reuse of learning activities. It offers tools that practitioners can apply to their own concerns and incorporates a variety of contexts including face-to-face, self-directed, blended and distance learning modes, as well as a range of theories of learning and roles of technology. Topics discussed include:

- specific activities for achieving learning outcomes
- technologies' uses for learning and their role in educational design
- current systems and future developments
- learners' competencies and approaches
- designing for mobile technologies
- practitioner development
- sustainability, organizational barriers and learning communities.

Aiming to bring the insights of learning design into the edu~ ~ocess, and to extend the repertoire of tools and techniques in ever~ ~king *Pedagogy for a Digital Age* is an essential guide to eff~ ~mentation of sound e-learning activities. It is illustr~ disciplines and includes helpful appendices of ~ ~or researchers, practitioners and teachers in high~

Helen Beetham is an independent consulta~ ~orking for the UK Joint Information Systems Committee's (~ ~ng and Pedagogy programme.

Rhona Sharpe is a staff and educational developer in the Oxford Centre for Staff and Learning Development (OCSLD) at Oxford Brookes University, UK.

Rethinking Pedagogy for a Digital Age

Designing and delivering e-learning

Edited by Helen Beetham and Rhona Sharpe

Routledge
Taylor & Francis Group

LONDON AND NEW YORK

First published 2007
by Routledge
2 Park Square, Milton Park, Abingdon, Oxon OX14 4RN

Simultaneously published in the USA and Canada
by Routledge
270 Madison Ave, New York, NY 10016

Transferred to Digital Printing 2008

Routledge is an imprint of the Taylor & Francis Group, an informa business

© 2007 Edited by Helen Beetham and Rhona Sharpe

Typeset in Times New Roman by
Florence Production Ltd, Stoodleigh, Devon
Printed and bound in Great Britain by
Antony Rowe Ltd, Chippenham, Wiltshire

British Library Cataloguing in Publication Data
A catalogue record for this book is available from the British Library

Library of Congress Cataloging in Publication Data
Rethinking pedagogy for a digital age: designing and delivering
e-learning/edited by Helen Beetham and Rhona Sharpe.
       p. cm.
    Includes bibliographical references and index.
  1. Computer-assisted instruction – Curricula – Planning.
  I. Beetham, Helen, 1967–   II. Sharpe, Rhona, 1969–
  LB1028.5.R44 2007
  371.33′4–dc22   2006035710

ISBN10: 0–415–40873–3 (hbk)
ISBN10: 0–415–40874–1 (pbk)
ISBN10: 0–203–96168–4 (ebk)

ISBN13: 978–0–415–40873–8 (hbk)
ISBN13: 978–0–415–40874–5 (pbk)
ISBN13: 978–0–203–96168–1 (ebk)

Contents

PART III
Resources   219

Appendices

Illustrations

Figures

Tables

Boxes

Notes on contributors

Shirley Agostinho has spent the past ten years researching in the field of educational technology. She has expertise in design and development, evaluation and research of learning environments supported by the use of information communication technologies. She is currently employed as a Research Fellow at the Faculty of Education at Wollongong University where she has a research focus on developments in online learning standards and technologies and in particular, exploring how the concept of 'learning design' can be used to support online learning practitioners.

Helen Beetham is a Research Consultant to the JISC e-Learning Programme, in which role she develops and supports the JISC's activities in e-learning and pedagogy. Previously a Research Fellow in e-Learning at the Open University, she is widely published and a regular speaker at conferences in the UK and abroad.

Sandy Britain is currently based at Tairawhiti Polytechnic on the East Cape of New Zealand, having worked in the field of learning technology since 1996. He is also a senior advisor to the New Zealand Ministry of Education on strategic e-learning matters. In this role, he represents New Zealand's interests in interoperability standards development and adoption. Prior to moving to New Zealand in 2004, Sandy was based at the University of Wales in Bangor.

Gráinne Conole is Professor of e-Learning at the Open University, with research interests in the use, integration and evaluation of information and communication technologies and e-learning. She has published and presented extensively and is editor of the journal, *ALT-J* (*Association for Learning Technology Journal, Research in Learning*). Recent work includes co-editing *Contemporary Perspectives on e-Learning Research*, published by RoutledgeFalmer.

John Cook is Centre Manager for the Reusable Learning Objects CETL at London Metropolitan University. He has published over one hundred refereed articles in the area of e-learning and conducts review work for the ESRC, EU and Science Foundation of Ireland. He was President of the Association for Learning Technology (2005–6).

James Dalziel is Professor of Learning Technology and Director of the Macquarie e-Learning Centre of Excellence (MELCOE) at Macquarie University in Sydney, Australia. James leads a number of projects including: LAMS (Learning Activity Management System), including roles as a Director of the LAMS Foundation and LAMS International Pty Ltd; MAMS; RAMP; and ASK-OSS.

Rachel Ellaway is the e-Learning Manager for the College of Medicine and Veterinary Medicine at the University of Edinburgh. Her work in developing and implementing profession-focused VLEs was recognized in the award of one of the Queen's Anniversary Prizes for Higher and Further Education in 2005.

Chris Fowler is Director of Chimera, the Institute of Social and Technical Research at the University of Essex. His research interests include the development of innovative user needs elicitation and evaluation tools and techniques, conceptual frameworks that bridge technology and pedagogy, and understanding and managing the innovation process.

Sara de Freitas currently works as a Senior Research Fellow and Manager at the London Knowledge Lab, Institute of Education, University of London. She is also a consultant for the JISC e-Learning Programme and founded the UK Lab Group, which brings the research and development community together to create stronger links between industrial and academic research.

Michael Gardner is Deputy Director of Chimera, the Institute of Social and Technical Research at the University of Essex, and leads their Applied Technologies Lab. He is also co-director of the University's Digital Lifestyles Centre. His current research interests are focused on personalization within pervasive computing environments, user and domain modelling, and socio-technical implications of intelligent inhabited environments.

Peter Goodyear is Professor of Education at the University of Sydney, where he also co-directs CoCo (the Centre for Research on Computer-Supported Learning and Cognition). He has been carrying out research on learning and teaching with technology since the late 1970s. He has a strong interest in educational design.

Derek Harding began by teaching Modern History, Social Science and Politics and in the early 1990s began using computers to support his teaching. He directed the TLTP-funded Courseware for History Implementation Consortium project and has been involved with the Association for History and Computing for many years. A member of the History Advisory Panel for the History Classics & Archaeology Subject Centre, he is currently a Learning and Teaching Consultant at the University of Teesside.

Barry Harper's research focuses on the theory, design, development, implementation and evaluation of multimedia learning environments. He is Director of the Educational Media Laboratory within the Faculty of Education at Wollongong University which has won over twenty national and international awards for innovation and excellence for research and commercial products, including European Multimedia Association awards, Australian Interactive Media Industry Association awards, and a British Academy Award (BAFTA).

John G Hedberg is Millennium Innovations Chair in ICT and Education, and Director of the Macquarie ICT Innovations Centre at Macquarie University, Sydney, Australia. He has been Professor of Learning Sciences and Technologies at Nanyang Technological University in Singapore where he directed several research projects exploring the role of technologies in engaging students in Mathematics, Science, History and Geography classrooms. He is also the Editor-in-chief of Educational Media International and President of the International Council for Educational Media.

Joy van Helvert is a Senior Researcher at Chimera, the Institute of Social and Technical Research at the University of Essex, with extensive experience of business analysis, user requirements and research in diverse business environments. Her work within Chimera has included learning research, intercultural research and future product consultancy. It also includes development of scenario-based methodologies for collaborative product visualization and requirements capture.

Bruce Ingraham is a Teaching Fellow at the University of Teesside. With more than thirty years of experience in higher education, he began his career as a literary semiotician. For the last fifteen years he has specialized in the semiotics of multimedia and in the production of online learning resources. His current research interests include the impact of multimedia on the conduct of scholarly discourse and the role of e-books in higher education.

Christopher R. Jones is a Reader in the Institute of Educational Technology at the Open University, UK. His main research interests lie in the study of networked learning and e-learning in tertiary education. Chris teaches on the Masters programme in Online and Distance Education and the Doctorate in Education.

Agnes Kukulska-Hulme is a Senior Lecturer in Educational Technology, Deputy Director of the Open University's Institute of Educational Technology, and Convener of the Telelearning Research Group. She co-edited *Mobile Learning: A Handbook for Educators and Trainers* (Routledge, 2005). Agnes's background is in linguistics and foreign language learning.

Diana Laurillard is Professor of Learning with Digital Technologies at the London Knowledge Lab, Institute of Education, University of London. She was previously Head of the e-Learning Strategy Unit at the UK Government's Department for Education and Skills, and prior to that, held two terms of office as Pro-Vice-Chancellor for Learning Technologies and Teaching at the Open University.

Patrick McAndrew is a Senior Lecturer in the Institute of Educational Technology at the Open University where he teaches and researches on ways to support learning online. His interests include software systems to support the use of learning design and methods for the research and evaluation of open content.

Liz Masterman currently works as a Researcher and Evaluation Specialist with the Learning Technologies Group, Oxford University Computing Services. She has been involved in a number of JISC-funded investigations into design for learning, and also has a keen interest in the application of sociocultural theories to the design and evaluation of e-learning.

Terry Mayes is an Emeritus Professor at Glasgow Caledonian University. He has a long experience as researcher, author and practitioner in the pedagogical aspects of learning technology in which area he has collaborated in many research projects. Recently he has acted in a variety of advisory roles for the higher education sector.

Martin Oliver works as a Senior Lecturer in the London Knowledge Lab, Institute of Education, University of London. He is course leader for the ICT in Education MA. His research focuses on understanding the use of technology in education, including course design, evaluation and the way in which peoples' roles change when technology is introduced.

Ron Oliver is Professor of Multimedia at Edith Cowan University, Perth, Western Australia, and has wide experience in the design, development, implementation and evaluation of technology-mediated and online learning materials. He uses technology extensively in his own teaching and his ideas and activities are all grounded in practical applications. Ron has won a number of awards for his innovative teaching and research including the inaugural Australian Award for University Teaching for the use of multimedia in university teaching.

Andrew Ravenscroft is Deputy Director and Principal Research Fellow at the Learning Technology Research Institute (LTRI) of London Metropolitan University. He has published over ninety articles in interactive learning and has led or collaborated on a broad range of research and development projects funded by national and international agencies.

John Scott is a Senior Researcher at Chimera, the Institute of Social and Technical Research at the University of Essex. He has a background in computer science and is a trained teacher. For much of his early career he was involved in training delivery and management. He then moved into learning research with particular responsibility for system requirement definition and developing concept demonstrators and prototypes.

Rhona Sharpe is Principal Lecturer in Educational Development in the Oxford Centre for Staff and Learning Development, Oxford Brookes University. Previously Staff Tutor for the Open University's Institute of Educational Technology, she is a registered practitioner of the Higher Education Academy and Fellow of the Staff and Educational Development Association.

John Traxler is Reader in Mobile Technology for e-Learning at the University of Wolverhampton and works with the University's Centre of Excellence using innovative technologies to support non-traditional students and with its Centre for International Training and Development exploiting sustainable and appropriate technologies for learning in Africa. John is co-editor with Agnes Kukulska-Hulme of *Mobile Learning: A Handbook for Educators and Trainers* (Routledge, 2005).

Mira Vogel is a Learning Technologist and Researcher. Her interests include disciplinary differences in learning and research methodologies. Her educational development activities involve working with Goldsmiths' e-Learning Fellows, planning and evaluating institutional provision of online learning, and raising institutional awareness of advances in technology with its accompanying issues of educational approach, access and usability.

Sandra Wills, from the University of Wollongong, has authored over two hundred publications and educational products spanning thirty years and attracted $12 million in grants. Elected Fellow of Australian Computer Society (1991) and Fellow of Australian Council for Computers in Education (2002), she has also received an International Federation for Information Processing Silver Core Award (1995), Education Innovation Award (1990) and ACS Lecturer of the Year Award (1980).

Foreword

Education is in an interesting transitional phase between its 'ICT-free' past and its 'ICT-aware' future. That it is in such a transition is a fairly safe claim. Over the centuries prior to digital technology, education evolved into a system that used paper technology in a variety of highly sophisticated ways to fulfil its mission to develop and accredit knowledge and skills. Its future must certainly be one in which it extends this capacity to a sophisticated use of digital technology. Like every modern enterprise, education is currently learning and adapting to the opportunities afforded by information and communication technologies, albeit slowly. Learning technologists make it their business to accelerate the process because the learning cycles of the education system are long, while those of its immediate environment – youth culture, employment demands, scientific knowledge – are short, and changing ever more rapidly.

Leaders in the education system know that it derives its support from the communities that recognize its value, but have been slow to realize that this increasingly depends on how well it exploits the transformational potential of digital technology. All our educational ambitions for the post-compulsory sector are challenging: personalized learning, higher attainment standards, wider participation and improved retention in further and higher education, closer relationships between education and the workplace, lifelong learning, a more highly skilled workforce for our knowledge economy. We do not lack ambition. Achieving these ambitions, or even significant progress towards them, would have enormous value for the communities served by education. Every one of them requires the improved quality and economies of scale that proper use of technology will confer. Yet so many of our institutional and organizational strategies for education consign digital technology to the merely incremental tasks involved in improving our current systems supporting education, not to the transformational task of changing them.

What are we doing? In teaching and learning currently, we tend to use technology to support traditional modes of teaching – improving the quality of lecture presentations using interactive whiteboards, making lecture notes readable in PowerPoint and available online, extending the library by providing access to digital resources and libraries, recreating face-to-face tutorial discussions asynchronously online – all of them good, incremental improvements in quality and flexibility, but nowhere near being transformational.

What might we be doing? Let's look at it through the lens of the learner, and embrace all those vaulting ambitions in considering how they could combine to transform the educational experience of one individual. How can a young person who has always hated study, who believes further education is not for them, with few skills and low self esteem be persuaded to achieve their learning potential? The ambitions are right – their combined effect would certainly be to bring motivation, opportunity and support to that young person. But look at what it takes to achieve that: the processes of teaching and learning have to engage their attention so that they enjoy study; the knowledge and skills they need must link to their interests so they are motivated to study; they need constant personalized support and encouragement at the pace and level to keep them engaged; the content and process of learning must be compatible with their social culture; they need to be able to see the long-term value in the hard work of study – every teacher with a vocation to teach wants to provide all this, but in a non-elitist system this level of personalization cannot be offered for every student. The promise of new technology is that it can, for every one of those learner needs. It is an engaging and highly responsive medium; it can gather content according to interest; it can respond to individual needs of pace and level; it fits with the style and forms of youth culture; it can link the classroom to the workplace and in doing so enables teachers to provide much more of what only they can do for their students. Wherever we find an impossible challenge to inclusive educational provision, there is usually a way in which digital technology could make a significant difference.

But we focus the majority of technology provision on what we already understand – information systems, data gathering, communication processes, presentation – rather than using it to tackle the really difficult problems presented by our ambitions for universal and effective education. Imaginative use of digital technologies could be transformational for teaching and learning, taking us well beyond the incremental value of more accessible lecture presentations. The problem is that transformation is more about the human and organizational aspects of teaching and learning than it is about the use of technology. We have the ambition. We have the technology. What is missing is what connects the two. If education leaders were fully engaged with this, it would be strategy, and we would have a top-down change process. If practitioners were fully engaged it would be experimental innovation, and we would have a bottom-up change process. Better to have both, but too many educational institutions still lack serious leadership engagement with the innovative application of digital technologies. In any case, innovation in the pedagogical aspects of teaching and learning should be coming from the academic community. That is the focus here.

In this book, learning technologists from the UK and further afield pool their ideas around one way of accelerating the exploitation of digital technology: bringing its creative use within the capability of the individual teaching professional. By setting out to explore the design of learning activities in educational contexts already rich in electronic and mobile technologies, the authors show us what a technology-aware future for education would be like.

When our education system is making sophisticated use of e-learning it will pervade everything we do, just as paper technology does. Lecturers will count it as part of their professional responsibility to 'design for learning', using a variety of forms of digital technology. We will have discarded the idea that the problem of pedagogic innovation can be left to the commercial suppliers, and instead see their role as being the provision of the tools and environments that lecturers can use in all the creative, innovative and scholarly ways they currently use paper technologies. We don't expect the publishers to write the textbooks, we shouldn't expect them to create the educational software for us either. The authors collaborating on this book are providing the means for this to be possible, researching and developing the forms of learning activity, the tools for pedagogic design, the environments for collaborative practice, the conceptual frameworks, all of which will contribute to building the bridges between what digital technologies make possible, and what our educational ambitions require.

Diana Laurillard,
London Knowledge Lab,
Institute of Education,
University of London, UK

Acknowledgements

The editors and authors would like to acknowledge the support of the UK Joint Information Systems Committee (JISC) in the writing of this book. The JISC funded the original work on which many chapters in the book are based, and that has supported the writing process. In particular, the following chapters were developed from research originally funded by the JISC: Chapter 1 (Mayes and de Freitas), Chapter 2 (Beetham), Chapter 4 (Masterman and Vogel), Chapter 6 (Conole), Chapter 7 (McAndrew and Goodyear), Chapter 9 (Sharpe and Oliver), Chapter 14 (Kukulska-Hulme and Traxler) and Chapter 16 (Ravenscroft and Cock).

The material presented in this book has in many cases been developed in consultation with expert practitioners, who contributed to the Pedagogy Experts Group meetings of the JISC e-learning and Pedagogy programme, and helped to refine materials during a series of JISC and Higher Education Academy workshops in 2004–5. We are deeply indebted to those practitioners.

Abbreviations

AUTC	Australian University Teaching Committee
CAA	computer-aided (or computer-assisted) assessment
CETL	Centre for Excellence in Teaching and Learning
CGfL	Community Grid for Learning
CHIC	Courseware for History Implementation Consortium
CMC	computer-mediated communication
CMS	courseware management system
CoP	Community of Practice
CPD	continuing and professional development
CSALT	Centre for Studies of Advanced Learning Technology
CSCL	Computer Supported Collaborative Learning
DNER	Distributed National Electronic Resource
DUS	Device Unification Service
EASA	European Academic Software Award
ELT	Embedding Learning Technology
EML	Educational Modelling Language
ESRC	Economic and Social Research Council
FAQ	frequently asked question
FPP	Ferl Practitioners Programme
GLO	generative learning object
GPS	Global Positioning System
ICT	information and communication technology
ISD	Instructional Systems Design
IT	information technology
IUG	Islamic University Gaza
JISC	Joint Information Systems Committee
LAA	learning activity authoring
LAMS	Learning Activity Management System
LAR	learning activity realization
LOM	Learning Object Metadata
LOMS	learning object management system
LOR	Learning Object Repository

LRC	Learning Resources Centre
NCWBLP	National Centre of Work Based Learning Partnership
OCSLD	Oxford Centre for Staff and Learning Development
ODL	Open and Distance Learner
OUNL	Open University of the Netherlands
OOD	Object-Orientated Design
OSCE	objective standard clinical examination
OSID	Open Service Interface Definition
PAT	Pattern Analysis Template
PDA	personal digital assistant
Q&A	question(s) and answer(s)
RAE	Research Assessment Exercise
RLO	Reusable Learning Object
SCORM	Shareable Courseware Object Reference Model
SOSIG	Social Science Information Gateway
SUNA	Scenario-based User Needs Analysis
TESEP	Transforming and Enhancing the Student Experience through Pedagogy
TLTP	Teaching and Learning Technology Programme
UML	Unified Modelling Language
UOL	Unit of Learning
URL	universal resource locator
VAP	Value Attribution Process
VLE	virtual learning environment
WEA	Workers Educational Association
XML	Extensible Markup Language

An introduction to rethinking pedagogy for a digital age

Helen Beetham and Rhona Sharpe

In her foreword, Laurillard encourages us to build bridges between the technologies we have at our disposal and the ambitions we have to transform post-compulsory education. Throughout this book we argue that this can be achieved by a reconsideration of the pedagogical practices that underpin education. As learning contexts are increasingly rich in electronic and mobile technologies, so research into e-learning has more to offer the mainstream of educational practice. The chapters collected here offer a critical discussion of the issues surrounding the design, sharing and reuse of learning activities, and offer tools that practitioners can apply to their own concerns and contexts. The aim is to bring the insights of learning design into the educational process, and to extend the repertoire of tools and techniques in everyday use.

What is pedagogy?

The term 'pedagogy' is not without its critics, particularly in the field of post-compulsory education from which many of the ideas and practices of this book originate. Malcolm Knowles, for example (1990), notes that the term derives from the ancient Greek word *paidagogos*, meaning the slave who led children to school, and argues that this makes it inappropriate for the years beyond school in which learners gain in self-direction and self-reliance. Others have found the usual definition of pedagogy as the 'art or science of teaching' at odds with their preferred emphasis on the activity of learning. In a truly learner-centred environment, they suggest, teaching should not be the focus of concern.

These debates and difficulties are in fact one reason why we have chosen to foreground the term 'pedagogy' in this book. First, despite its etymological connection with children (*paidia*), contemporary use of the term has lost its exclusive reference to childhood while retaining the original sense of leading or guiding to learn. We observe that the need for guidance is not confined to childhood, and that even the most self-directed of adult learners can benefit from the support of others. The UK universities' Research Assessment Exercise (RAE), for example, makes extensive use of the term 'pedagogy' to refer to the processes, experiences, contexts, outcomes and relationships of teaching and learning in higher education

(RAE 2006). At a time when learning is increasingly seen as a lifelong project, it makes sense that the associated 'art or science' of guidance should extend its scope into adulthood. And as – in the West at least – the boundaries are becoming blurred between school and college, formal and informal education, learning *for* work and learning *at* work, it also makes sense to consider the continuities across different contexts of learning. How people learn, and how they can best be guided to learn, are no longer concerns that belong behind school gates.

Second, the word 'pedagogy' embraces an essential dialogue between teaching and learning. This is particularly significant in a context of educational discourse in which the two terms have come to be used in tension and even in opposition to one another. In extreme cases, the term 'teaching' is seen as denying the active nature of learning and individuals' unique capacities to learn (see for example the review by Alexander 2002). How are we to make sense of this apparent contradiction?

In the last century, a series of educational thinkers in the West sought to reinstate 'learning' as the central concern of pedagogy, arguing that undue emphasis had been placed on the content of what was taught, and that this had led to rigid and unhelpful habits of instruction. These trends in pedagogical thinking are discussed in more detail in Chapter 1: taken together they amount to a new emphasis on the individual capacities and needs of learners. Learners are no longer seen as passive recipients of knowledge and skills but as active participants in the learning process. Fields such as psychology and cognitive science have contributed to our understanding of how this process takes place, and how it can differ from one learner to another. Social scientists have demonstrated the impact that social and cultural contexts have on people's engagement with learning. Rightly, there is excitement about these advances, and eagerness to ensure that they are set at the heart of educational practice.

One of the ways in which this revolution has been acknowledged is in the privileging of the term 'learning' over 'teaching' in educational discourse. Throughout this book, we use the term 'pedagogy' in the original sense of guidance to learn: learning in the context of teaching, and teaching that has learning as its goal. We believe that guiding others to learn is a unique, skilful, creative and demanding human activity that deserves scholarship in its own right. We will not be afraid to use the term 'teaching' as well as 'learning' in this volume, recognizing that education concerns not only how people learn 'naturally' from their environment but also the social interactions that support learning, and the institutions and practices that have grown up around them. In fact, the essential dialogue between these two activities is at the heart of what we mean by 'pedagogy', and helps us to reclaim the idea of teaching from negative associations with dominant, unresponsive or even repressive forms of instruction.

It will be seen from this discussion that there is a further complexity to the term 'pedagogy'. As well as referring to the activities of learning and teaching, it is also used to describe how we think and talk about, plan and structure those activities when we are not actually engaged in them. From the time of Plato at least, thinkers have proposed specific theories of – as well as methods for – education. Pedagogy, then, involves ways of knowing as well as ways of doing. Like other applied disciplines, it is centrally concerned with how we understand practice (the 'evidence base' for theory), and how we apply that theoretical understanding *in* practice once again.

Ironically, the establishment of education as a field of study in its own right has helped to divide these two elements, so that within the same institution there may be professionals 'doing' teaching and professionals researching, thinking and writing about teaching who never have contact with one another. Educational developers, following the example of Schön (1987), have established the ideal of *reflective practice* as one means of re-connecting the two aspects of the discipline. Practitioners are encouraged to continuously evaluate the impact of their own pedagogical approaches and choices on their learners. At the same time, educational researchers and thinkers have used the term *scholarship of teaching* to describe the body of theory they have developed and the ways in which it can be applied (Trigwell *et al.* 2000). In fact the techniques used by reflective practitioners and by scholars focused on the pragmatics of teaching – such as evaluative methodologies, conceptual toolkits and model teaching approaches – often resemble one another quite closely. In using the term 'pedagogy' we are therefore initiating a dialogue between theory and practice, as well as between learning and teaching, which draws consciously on these traditions.

If we are serious about this dialogue, we must acknowledge that pedagogy needs to be 're-done' at the same time as it needs to be 're-thought'. Throughout this book we have tried to keep theoretical arguments and real-life examples of practice in alignment with one another. Many creative and innovative teachers have been involved in providing ideas for this book so that our theories can be rooted in the practical business of guiding learners to learn. We have also included practical tools for teachers in the hope that they will help translate some of the ideas discussed in this book into new thoughtful practices for the future. Our understanding is that neither of these two activities – the doing or the thinking – makes sense in isolation from the other.

The digital age

If the last century did so much to reinvent the art or science of teaching, why does pedagogy need to be re-thought again just now? This is a particularly urgent question in relation to the new digital technologies, because teachers who are excited about these technologies are often accused of using them regardless of whether or not they are pedagogically effective, and even in ignorance of the long tradition of pedagogical evidence and thought. 'Pedagogy before technology' is a common catchphrase of reflective practitioners in this field, suggesting that – far from trying to create pedagogy anew – we should be in the business of locating the new technologies within proven practices and models of teaching.

A second aspect of this argument is that there is nothing new about technologies for learning. Papyrus and paper, chalk and print, overhead projectors, educational toys and television, even the basic technologies of writing were innovations once. The networked digital computer and its more recent mobile and wireless counterparts are just the latest outcomes of human ingenuity that we have at our disposal. Like previous innovations, they can be assimilated to pedagogical practice without altering the fundamental truths about how people learn. While this book will situate discussions about the new technologies for learning firmly within established educational discourse, we also contend that these technologies represent a paradigm shift with specific and multiple impacts on the nature of knowledge in society, and therefore on the nature of learning. In rethinking pedagogy we are not trying to define some new aspect or area of the discipline: we are trying to rearticulate the entire discipline in this new context.

So how do digital technologies constitute a new context for learning and teaching? The technical advances are relatively easy to identify. The latest figures for access to the Internet in the UK are 83 per cent of the 16–24 age group (NSA 2006): in the same year UK schools spent £426.3m on information and communication technology (ICT) resources (Shaw 2006). Personal web pages, blogs, podcasts and wikis are democratizing the creation of information; social software is allowing participation in online communities that define and share the information they need for themselves. Individuals have access to processing power in personal applications that even five years ago would have been confined to specialist institutions. Personal mobile and wireless devices are increasingly integrated with the global computer network to provide seamless, location-independent access to information services. Chapters 14 and 16 deal with some of these technologies in terms of their specific impacts on, and benefits for, learning.

But what of the social and cultural changes that have accompanied these technical developments? The phrase 'information age' was coined by Manual Castells (1996) to describe a period in which the movement of information through networks would overtake the circulation of goods as the primary source of value in society. Some of the social and cultural reorganization that he predicted can already be traced in the ways that the contexts of education are changing.

Epistemologically, for example, what counts as useful knowledge is increasingly biased towards what can be represented in digital form. Many scientific and research enterprises now depend on data being shared in the almost instantaneous fashion enabled by the Internet. Vast libraries are being digitized, and disputes over access to this information look likely to determine the face of the Internet over the next few years. Academic institutions have a central role to play in these disputes and in how the conflict between digital commons and digital consumerism is played out. However, less thought has been given to the knowledge that is forgotten or lost in the process of digitization: practical skills, know-how that is deeply embedded in the context of use, and other tacit knowledge associated with habits of practice (Dreyfus and Dreyfus 1986). Ironically, it may be exactly this kind of knowledge that is drawn on by effective teachers, and by effective learners too.

The nature of work in Western societies is also changing out of all recognition, and learning institutions have changed their offering in response. As more and more jobs demand information literacy, higher education has become a goal for 50 per cent of the young population in the UK, rather than the 5 per cent who attended a generation ago. Learning has been refigured as the acquisition of information skills – new forms of literacy and numeracy, adaptability, problem solving, communication – rather than the acquisition of a stable body of knowledge. And as the job market demands ever more flexibility and currency, post-compulsory education has been reorganized around a model of constant updating of competence, also called continuous professional development. These changes have usually been driven by education department directives, or the demands of professional bodies and employers, rather than by learners themselves; nevertheless the underlying rationale is the preparation of learners for work in the new information economy.

Technology has also had a profound impact on educational organizations themselves. Schools and colleges are being networked in a learning grid that cuts across traditional institutional and even sectoral divides. Learners have increasing opportunities to take their learning from place to place, in the form of e-portfolios and learning records, and to make choices about how, when and where they participate in education. They are also likely to interact differently with those institutions once enrolled: they may use a public web site to find out about courses, contact tutors by email, access resources through an information portal or virtual learning environment (VLE), and take examinations via a computer-based assessment system. The wholly virtual learning experience is still a minority choice, and most such courses are provided by specialist institutions such as the Open Universities of the UK and the Netherlands, or Phoenix University in the US. But institutions of this kind are now competing with more traditional universities and colleges for market share, and this is having an impact on the way that all educational institutions relate to their learners and to potential learners in their communities.

Finally, those learners are changing. Most young people in Western societies make routine use of the Internet and email, text messaging and social software, and their familiarity with these new forms of exchange are carried over into their learning. Whether or not they use the 'e-learning' facilities provided by their institution, learners will use the communication and information tools they have around them to help manage their learning. Some of the habits of mind associated with these technologies are regarded by teachers as unhelpful, particularly the often uncritical attitude to Internet-based information, and the cut-and-paste mentality of a generation raised on editing tools rather than pen and paper. The brevity of chat and text pose a challenge to traditional standards of spelling and grammar, and there is no doubt that the use of personal technologies creates new inequalities among learners. Teachers should be free to respond critically as well as creatively to these new technologies, but they cannot afford to ignore them if they want to engage with their learners.

This is not a book about social change – many others have covered this terrain – but it does take change within and beyond the educational organization as essential background for understanding the new pressures on learning and teaching. Against the argument that new technologies make 'no significant difference' (Russell 2001), we contend that learning is a set of personal and interpersonal activities, deeply rooted in specific social and cultural contexts. When those contexts change, how people learn changes also. We do not intend by this argument to suggest that educational practice is determined by technology. The developments outlined in this section were not pre-destined when the first two computers were networked by Thomas Merrill and Lawrence G. Roberts in 1965. Such events may dictate that our society and its relationship with knowledge will change, but not what form or direction those changes will take. Otherwise there would be little point in a book such as this one, in which we lay out some of the alternative possibilities over which we, as human actors, have decisions to make. Understood as a social and cultural phenomenon, technology cannot but influence the ways in which people learn, and therefore what makes for effective learning and effective pedagogy.

The idea of 'effectiveness' in this discussion should alert us to the fact that pedagogy and technology also involve issues of value. Just as the impact of technology is changing how knowledge is valued in our society, so it is changing how we value different kinds of learning and achievement and different models of the learning organization. Some values, such as the values of the marketplace and the values of the traditional academic institution, are brought into conflict by the effects of technology. Though different contributors to this book have different perspectives on these debates, we will be explicit about the alternatives wherever we find conflicts over value arising.

Design for learning

If 'pedagogy' helps to locate this book within a tradition of thinking about learning and teaching, 'design' helps to identify what is different and new about the ideas we are proposing. Why is 'design' a good term around which to reclaim the scholarship of teaching, and to rethink pedagogy for the digital age? First, like pedagogy, design is a term that bridges theory and practice. It encompasses both a systematic approach with rules based on evidence, and a set of contextualized practices that are constantly adapting to circumstances. It is a skilful, creative activity that can be improved on with reflection and scholarship.

Second, 'design' is a highly valued activity in the new information economy, and a discipline that has come into its own in the digital age. We have already touched on the impact that new information technologies have had on what counts as valuable knowledge. This change has been variously characterized by commentators as a 'postmodern turn' (e.g. Hassan 1988) or as a shift from 'mode 1 to mode 2' knowledge (Gibbons *et al.* 1994). In either case, knowledge comes to be seen as provisional, contextualized, culturally specific, constructed rather than discovered. This shift is not without its critics, particularly from within the natural sciences and other 'enlightenment' disciplines of the academy. It can seem at odds with the academic values of disinterested, independent investigation. Nevertheless, even within these disciplines, knowledge is understood to have specific uses and users, and the ways in which it is communicated to those users have become an essential aspect of what is known. Design has therefore become a paradigmatic discipline for the digital age.

The process of design involves:

- Investigation: Who are my users and what do they need? What principles and theories are relevant?
- Application: How should these principles be applied in this case?
- Representation or modelling: What solution will best meet users' needs? How can this be communicated to developers and/or directly to users?
- Iteration: How does the design stand up to the demands of development? How useful is it in practice? What changes are needed?

Teaching has always involved some element of 'design' in the process of preparation and planning. With e-learning, however, the need for intentional design becomes more obvious and pressing. Classroom teaching with minimal equipment allows us to tailor our approach to the immediate needs of learners. Tutors can quickly ascertain how learners are performing, rearrange groups and reassign activities, phrase explanations differently to help learners understand them better, guide discussion and ask questions that challenge learners appropriately. With the use of digital technologies, all of these pedagogical activities require forethought and an explicit representation of what learners and teachers will do. An interesting and unforeseen consequence of the greater reliance on technologies in education has been this opportunity for teachers to reconsider how courses and learning activities are structured: new technologies make visible aspects of their pedagogic practice that were previously taken for granted.

Quality assurance and professionalization of teaching have also meant an increasingly formal approach to design. 'Designs' in the form of lesson plans, module validation documents and pro-formas are routinely produced as evidence of the teaching process, for example for quality assurance and review. And as class sizes have risen, and other economic pressures been brought to bear on the teaching process, it has become increasingly important that effective pedagogical approaches can be shared and reused, to offset the investment of time and expertise that has gone into their development. One aim of design in all its forms is to generalize across cases, streamlining the process of future design by offering general principles of application or even universal patterns. In the case of education, some general principles can certainly be offered, but it is an open question whether universal patterns exist that make sense across a wide range of different learning contexts. Individual contributors to this book have different views on this question.

'Design for learning' is a phrase we have coined for the process by which teachers – and others involved in the support of learning – arrive at a plan or structure or design for a learning situation. The situation may be as small as a single task or as large as a degree course. In a learning situation, any of the following may be designed with a specific pedagogic intention: learning resources and materials; the learning environment; tools and equipment; learning activities; the learning programme or curriculum. However, in this book we are mainly concerned with the design of learning activities and curricula. For practitioners, who are rarely involved in the design of the technologies and environments they are offered as pedagogically useful, the crucial questions are: how can I choose from, use, adapt and integrate what is available to me to provide a coherent experience for my learners? Our aim is to focus on design as a holistic process based around the learning activity, in which the 'already designed' elements such as materials and environments are only one aspect.

When we talk about design for learning we are viewing design as an intentional and systematic, but also a creative and responsive, approach to these challenges. We recognize that in reality learners and learning situations are unpredictable: as teachers, we encourage learners to engage in dialogue with us, to respond individually to learning opportunities, and to take increasing responsibility for their own learning. The use of digital technologies should not alter this fundamental relationship between learner and teacher. We acknowledge, then, that learning can never be wholly designed, only designed *for* (i.e. planned in advance) with an awareness of the contingent nature of learning as it actually takes place. This contingency demands constant dialogue with learners, recognizing that effective designs will evolve only through cycles of practice, evaluation and reflection. Also in this book, 'learning designs' will be used to mean representations of the design process and its outcomes, allowing for aspects of design to be shared.

Although the terminology may be relatively new, there are widely shared principles for effective pedagogic design that we will draw on in this book. We know that for learners to learn well we need to set clear expectations and provide engaging activities, which should include the key elements of practice, feedback and time for consolidation. We know that these activities should be at the centre of the design process, and that they should be carefully aligned with the desired learning outcomes and with processes of assessment and review. Traditions of pedagogical thought that are important to specific chapters of this book include constructivism (see e.g. Jonassen *et al.* 1999), social constructivism (Vygotsky 1986), activity theory (Engeström *et al.* 1999) and theories of experiential learning (Kolb 1984). Many more insights are drawn from the newer traditions associated with 'e-learning' or 'networked learning', for example from instructional design (Gagné *et al.* 2004), theories of networked learning and computer-supported collaborative work (McConnell 2000), and various forms of pedagogic evaluation.

In using the term 'design for learning' we are conscious that 'Learning Design' is a discipline in its own right, with its own specific protocols and modelling language (Jochems *et al.* 2004). Historically, Learning Design has emerged from instructional design, but with a focus on learning activity as the central concern of the design process. The theoretical scope of Learning Design, and particularly its goal of providing a generalized language for describing and sharing learning activities, is clearly relevant to our project. However, we consider it an open question how far – and in what situations – learning can be treated as a set of generic activities to be instantiated in particular contexts. The goal of a pedagogical meta-model, while it has many attractions, is in tension with a view of learning as culturally situated, negotiated between participants, and specifically contextualized. Chapters 7 and 8 discuss this tension, and the Learning Design specification itself, more fully.

Reading this book

As we have outlined, a number of approaches – theoretical, practical and research-led – are relevant to effective design for learning. Part I of this book, Models of learning, outlines our current understanding of how people learn and of how planned, purposeful activities can help them to learn more effectively. Chapter 1 looks in detail at the principles and theories that are relevant to pedagogic design, while Chapter 2 suggests how these might be applied to the design of specific learning activities. Broader considerations for the design of curricula and learning environments are dealt with in Chapter 3. Moving on from theory to practice, Chapter 4 presents evidence that how practitioners actually design for learning may be a much less rational – and more responsive – process than design protocols allow. The challenge of representing and sharing real designs for learning is addressed in different ways by the authors of Chapters 5, 6 and 7, while Chapter 8 considers how such designs are represented in the technical systems that are increasingly used to support designers in their practice.

Chapter 9 bridges the book's two halves by asking how shared representations can help designers to understand and develop their own practice. Specific contexts are given more detailed consideration in Part II, The practice of design. We include here discussions of specific disciplinary aspects of design, recognizing not only that there are many differences in pedagogical cultures between the subject areas (see for example Meyer and Land 2002), but also that the discipline of educational design itself has different faces and draws on different traditions. We also include consideration of specific technical advances, including mobile and wireless computing (Chapter 14), not simply to illustrate general points made in the first half of the book but as an intrinsic part of our exploration of what 'design for learning' means. The final two chapters look to the future of design, in which active communities of designers will be able to share their expertise, and in which learners' experiences and contexts are the focus of design practice.

Each chapter opens with a brief introduction from us, the editors, to help guide your reading. Part III provides a range of conceptual tools that we hope you will find useful in your own communities and contexts of working.

References

Alexander, R.J. (2002) 'Dichotomous pedagogies and the promise of comparative research', paper presented at the American Educational Research Association Annual Conference, New Orleans, April 2002.

Castells, M. (1996) *The Rise of the Network Society, The Information Age: Economy, Society and Culture*, Oxford: Blackwell.

Dreyfus, H.L. and Dreyfus, S.E. (1986) *Mind Over Machine: The Power of Human Intuition and Expertise in the Age of the Machine*, Oxford: Basil Blackwell.

Engeström, Y., Miettinen, R. and Punamaki, R.-L. (eds) (1999) *Perspectives on Activity Theory*, Cambridge: Cambridge University Press.

Gagné, R., Wager, W., Golas, K. and Keller, J.M. (2004) *Principles of Instructional Design*, 5th edn, Belmont, CA: Wadsworth.

Gibbons, M., Limoges, C., Nowotny, H., Schwartzman, S., Scott, P. and Trow, M. (1994) *The New Production of Knowledge*, London: Sage.

Hassan, I. (1988) *The Postmodern Turn: Essays in Postmodern Theory and Culture*, Ohio: Ohio State University Press.

Jochems, W., van Merrienboer, J. and Koper, R. (2004) *Integrated e-Learning: Implications for Pedagogy, Technology and Organization*, London: Taylor & Francis.

Jonassen, D.H., Peck, K. and Wilson, B.G. (1999) *Learning with Technology: A Constructivist Perspective*. Columbus, OH: Merrill/Prentice-Hall.

Knowles, M.S. (1990) *The Adult Learner: A Neglected Species*, 4th edn, Houston, TX: Gulf Publishing.

Kolb, D. (1984) *Experiential Learning*, Englewood Cliffs, NJ: Prentice Hall.

McConnell, D. (2000) *Implementing Computer Supported Cooperative Learning*, 2nd edn, London: Kogan Page.

Meyer, J.H.F. and Land, R. (2002) 'Threshold concepts and troublesome knowledge: linkages to ways of thinking and practising within the disciplines', paper presented to the Educational Research Conference, Brussels, September 2002.

National Statistics Agency (NSA) (2006) *Internet Access: Households and Individuals*. Online. Available www.statistics.gov.uk/pdfdir/inta0806.pdf (accessed 6 October 2006).

RAE (2006) 'Generic statement on criteria and working methods'. Online. Available www.rae.ac.uk/pubs/2006/01/docs/genstate.pdf (accessed 29 September 2006).

Russell, T.L. (2001) *No Significant Difference Phenomenon: A Comparative Research Annotated Bibliography on Technology for Distance Education*, International Distance Education Certification Center. Online. Available www.nosignificantdifference.com (accessed 29 September 2006).

Schön, D.A. (1987) *Educating the Reflective Practitioner*, San Francisco: Jossey-Bass.

Shaw, M. (2006) 'Exam bill soars', *Times Education Supplement* (24 February 2006).

Trigwell, K., Martin, E., Benjamin, J. and Prosser, M. (2000) 'Scholarship of teaching: a model', *Higher Education Research and Development*, 19: 155–68.

UK National Statistics Agency (2006) *Internet Access: Households and Individuals*. Online. Available www.statistics.gov.uk/pdfdir/inta0806.pdf (accessed 6 October 2006).

Vygotsky, L.S. (1986) *Thought and Language*, A. Kozulin (trans.), Cambridge, MA: MIT Press.

Part I

Models of learning

Chapter 1

Learning and e-learning

The role of theory

Terry Mayes and Sara de Freitas

EDITORS' INTRODUCTION

Mayes and de Freitas argue that design decisions need to be based on clear theoretical principles. While there is consensus on many theoretical issues in pedagogy, the authors identify three broadly different perspectives on learning and three sets of pedagogic priorities that arise from them. They go on to suggest that each of these perspectives is incomplete, and that a principled approach to e-learning requires an understanding of all three as distinct viewpoints on the learning process.

Introduction

It is arguable that there are really no models of e-learning per se – only e-enhancements of existing models of learning. Technology can play an important role in the achievement of learning outcomes but it is not necessary to explain this enhancement with a special account of learning. Rather, the challenge is to describe how the technology allows underlying processes common to all learning to function effectively. A true model of e-learning would need to demonstrate on what new learning principles the added value of the 'e' was operating. Where, for example, the 'e' allows remote learners to interact with each other and with the representations of the subject matter in a form that could simply not be achieved for those learners without the technology, then we may have a genuine example of added value. However, in this example the role of the technology may be primarily to get remote learners into a position to learn as favourably as if they were campus-based, rather than offering a new learning method. In such a case the enhancement is an educational one, though the underlying learning theory explains both campus-based and distance learning with the same theoretical constructs.

Even something that looks like a new paradigm for achieving learning outcomes, a peer-to-peer learner-matching tool, for example, will also not need a new account of learning, though its educational value may be enormous if it could be exploited through an infrastructure that integrated its use with quality assurance methods. We will argue in this chapter that in the powerful new learning opportunities that are being facilitated in an entirely new way through the Internet, we are beginning to witness a new model of education, rather than a new model of learning.

The need for theory

Biggs (1999) describes the task of good pedagogical design as one of ensuring that there are absolutely no inconsistencies between the curriculum we teach, the teaching methods we use, the learning environment we choose, and the assessment procedures we adopt. To achieve complete consistency, we need to examine very carefully what assumptions we are making at each stage and to align those. Thus, we need to start with carefully defined intended learning outcomes, we then need to choose learning and teaching activities that stand a good chance of allowing the students to achieve that learning, then we need to design assessment tasks that will genuinely test whether the outcomes have been reached. This process is easy to state, but very hard to achieve in an informed way. Biggs' book is largely about how the task of making the design decisions can be made more straightforward by adopting the assumptions of a constructivist pedagogical approach, where the focus is always on what the learner is actually doing: placing the learning activities at the heart of the process. Thus, Biggs uses the term 'constructive alignment' to indicate that in his view the guiding assumptions about learning should be based on constructivist theory. The relevant point is that the alignment process cannot proceed without first examining the underlying assumptions about learning, and then adopting teaching methods that align with those assumptions.

The main purpose of this chapter is to outline the theoretical underpinning of e-learning, and to argue that, to be comprehensive, e-learning design must consider three fundamental perspectives, each of which leads to a particular view of what matters in pedagogy. The intention is to show how e-learning can be approached in a principled way, which means uncovering the implicit assumptions about e-pedagogy, and then asking the right questions. We thus try to place e-learning models within the design framework described above. But the crucial step is the one Biggs made when he adopted a constructivist approach to ground the design decisions: there must be guidance on how to judge whether the learning and teaching processes adopted will really achieve the intended learning outcomes. For good pedagogical design, there is simply no escaping the need to adopt a theory of learning, and to understand how the pedagogy that is suggested by the theory follows naturally from its assumptions about what is important. Even when defining a learning outcome there are implicit assumptions about what is important. Is the learning to demonstrate smooth performance – applying a clinical procedure, say? Or is it to demonstrate the deep understanding of a principle – so that it can be explained clearly to someone else? Or is it being able to make appropriate judgements in a difficult social situation? Each of these intended outcomes would require a different kind of theoretical perspective and a different pedagogical approach.

Learning theory and pedagogical design

There are distinct traditions in educational theory that derive from different perspectives about the nature of learning itself. Although learning theory is often presented as though there is a large set of competing accounts for the same phenomena, it is more accurate to think of theory as a set of quite compatible explanations for a large range of different phenomena. In fact it is probably true to say that never before has there been such agreement about the psychological fundamentals (Jonassen and Land 2000). Here, we follow the approach of Greeno *et al.* (1996) in identifying three clusters or broad perspectives that make fundamentally different assumptions about what is being explained.

The associationist perspective

The associationist approach models learning as the gradual building of patterns of associations and skill components. Learning occurs through the process of connecting the elementary mental or behavioural units, through sequences of activity followed by feedback. This view encompasses the research traditions of associationism, behaviourism and connectionism (neural networks). Associationist theory requires subject matter to be analysed as specific associations, expressed as behavioural objectives. This kind of analysis was developed by Gagné (1985) into an elaborate system of instructional task analysis of discriminations, classifications and response sequences. Learning tasks are arranged in sequences based on their relative complexity according to a task analysis, with simpler components as prerequisites for more complex tasks.

Neural network theory (Hinton 1992) can also be regarded as following the associationist tradition in the way that it models knowledge states as patterns of activation in a network of elementary units. This approach has not yet been applied widely to educational issues, but is potentially significant. It suggests an analysis of knowledge in terms of attunement to patterns of activities, rather than in terms of task components as traditional task analysis requires.

Robert Gagné (1985) set out the psychological principles on which the dominant approach to training has subsequently been based. The instructional approach known as Instructional Systems Design (ISD) is essentially a recursive decomposition of knowledge and skill. Much of what is termed e-learning is still based in the training departments of organizations within a training philosophy that is traditional ISD. The intellectual base for this consists of principles that are widely accepted within the organizational training culture and which derive essentially from associationism.

The basic principle of ISD is that competence in advanced and complex tasks is built step by step from simpler units of knowledge or skill, finally adding coordination to the whole structure. Gagné argued that successful instruction depends on placing constraints on the amount of new structure that must be added at any one stage. So ISD consists of several steps:

- Analyse the domain into a hierarchy of small units.
- Sequence the units so that a combination of units is not taught until its component units are grasped individually.
- Design an instructional approach for each unit in the sequence.

Analysis of complex tasks into Gagné's learning hierarchies – the decomposition hypothesis – involves the assumption that knowledge and skill need to be taught from the bottom up. This assumption has been the subject of long controversy (e.g. Resnick and Resnick 1991), but is still prevalent in e-learning. Combining this approach with immediate feedback, and with the individualizing of instruction – through allowing multiple paths to successful performance where each student is provided with the next problem contingent on their response to the previous one – led to the development of programmed instruction. This approach, ideally suited to automation through simple technology, came to be widely discredited along with the excesses of 'behavioural modification' in a crude application of behaviourist theory to education. However, it is worth underlining the point made by, for example, Wilson and Myers (2000), that although behaviourism is currently widely dismissed when offered as a serious theoretical basis for education, and mistakenly often associated with a teacher-centred model of learning, this view is seriously wide of the mark. Behaviourism was centrally concerned to emphasize active learning-by-doing with immediate feedback on success, the careful analysis of learning outcomes, and above all with the alignment of learning objectives, instructional strategies and methods used to assess learning outcomes. Many of the methods with the label 'constructivist' – constituting the currently accepted consensus on pedagogy among educational developers – are indistinguishable from those derived from the associationist tradition.

The cognitive perspective

As part of a general shift in theoretical positioning in psychology starting in the 1960s, learning, as well as perception, thinking, language and reasoning became seen as the output of an individual's attention, memory and concept formation processes. This approach provided a basis for analysing concepts and procedures of subject matter curricula in terms of information structures, and gave rise to new approaches to pedagogy.

Within this broad perspective, certain sub-areas of cognitive research can be highlighted as particularly influential, e.g. schema theory, information processing theories of problem-solving and reasoning, levels of processing in memory, general competencies for thinking, mental models, and metacognitive processes. The underlying theme for learning is to model the processes of interpreting and constructing meaning, and a particular emphasis was placed on the instantiation of models of knowledge acquisition in the form of computer programmes (e.g. Anderson and Lebiere 1998). Knowledge acquisition was viewed as the outcome of an interaction between new experiences and the structures for understanding that have already been created. So building a framework for understanding becomes the learner's key cognitive challenge. This kind of thinking stood in sharp contrast to the model of learning as the strengthening of associations.

The cognitive account saw knowledge acquisition as proceeding from a declarative form to a procedural, compiled form. As performance becomes more expert-like and fluent so the component skills become automatized. Thus, conscious attention is no longer required to monitor the low-level aspects of performance and cognitive resources are available for more strategic levels of processing. The computer tutors developed by Anderson and co-workers (Anderson *et al.* 1995) are all based on this 'expertise' view of learning.

Increasingly, mainstream cognitive approaches to learning and teaching have emphasized the assumptions of constructivism that understanding is gained through an active process of creating hypotheses and building new forms of understanding through activity. In school-level educational research the influence of Piaget has been very significant, in particular his assumption that conceptual development occurs through intellectual activity rather than by the absorption of information. Piaget's constructivist theory of knowledge (1970) was based on the assumption that learners do not copy or absorb ideas from the external world, but must construct their concepts through active and personal experimentation and observation. This led Piaget to oppose the direct teaching of disciplinary content – although he was arguing against the behaviourist bottom-up variety, rather than the kind of meaningful learning advocated by Bruner (1960).

Collins *et al.* (1989) argued that we should consider concepts as tools, to be understood through use, rather than as self-contained entities to be delivered through instruction. This is the essence of the constructivist approach in which the learners' search for meaning through activity is central. Nevertheless, it is rather too simplistic to argue that constructivism has emerged directly from a cognitive perspective. In fact, in its emphasis on learning-by-doing, and the importance of feedback, it leans partly towards the behaviourist tradition. In its emphasis on authentic tasks, it takes much of the situativity position. The emergence of situated cognition was itself partly dependent on the influence on mainstream cognitive theory of Lave's socio-anthropological work (Lave 1988). Vygotsky's (1978) emphasis on the importance of social interaction for the development of higher cognitive functions continues to influence constructivist pedagogy. Duffy and Cunningham (1996) distinguish between cognitive constructivism (deriving from the Piagetian tradition), and socio-cultural constructivism (deriving from the Vygotskian approach).

A challenge for the design of curricula in higher and further education continues an unresolved theme in pedagogy – the fundamental tension between what Newell (1980) called weak methods, a focus on generic skills, and strong methods, which are domain specific. Many studies have shown that students' abilities to understand something new depends on what they already know. Educators cannot build expertise by having learners memorize experts' knowledge. New knowledge must be built on the foundations of already existing frameworks, through problem-solving activity and feedback.

Activities of constructing understanding have two main aspects:

- Interactions with material systems and concepts in the domain.
- Interactions in which learners discuss their developing understanding and competence.

The emphasis on task-based learning and reflection can be seen as a reaction to the rapid development of multimedia and hypermedia in the 1980s and early 1990s, in which a tendency for technology-based practice to resurrect traditional instructionist approaches was evident. Here the main focus was on the delivery of materials in which information can be more effectively transmitted by teachers and understood by learners. Indeed, for a while in the early 1990s, these trends were working in opposite directions: the research community was uniting around some key ideas of learning that emphasized the importance of the task-based and social context, while the policy makers were seizing on the potential of e-learning to generate efficiencies through powerful methods of delivering information. There are recent signs that, while still not perfectly congruent, these are no longer in opposition. Since the development of the Web, both have converged on communication as a key-enabling construct.

The situative perspective

The social perspective on learning has received a major boost from the gradual re-conceptualization of all learning as 'situated'. A learner will always be subjected to influences from the social and cultural setting in which the learning occurs, which will also, at least partly, define the learning outcomes. This view of learning focuses on the way knowledge is distributed socially. When knowledge is seen as situated in the practices of communities then the outcomes of learning involve the abilities of individuals to participate in those practices successfully. The focus shifts right away from analyses of components of subtasks, and onto the patterns of successful practice. This can be seen as a necessary correction to theories of learning in which both the behavioural and cognitive levels of analysis had become disconnected from the social. Underlying both the situated learning and constructivist perspectives is the assumption that learning must be personally meaningful, and that this has very little to do with the informational characteristics of a learning environment. Activity, motivation and learning are all related to a need for a positive sense of identity (or positive self-esteem), shaped by social forces.

Barab and Duffy (2000) have distinguished two rather different accounts of situated learning. The first can be regarded as a socio-psychological view of situativity. This emphasizes the importance of context-dependent learning in informal settings and leads to the design of constructivist tasks in which every effort is made to make the learning activity authentic to the social context in which the skills or knowledge are normally embedded ('practice fields'). Examples of this approach are problem-based learning (Savery and Duffy 1996) and cognitive apprenticeship (Collins et al. 1989; Jarvela 1995). Here, the main design emphasis is on the relationship between the nature of the learning task in educational or training environments, and its characteristics when situated in real use.

The second idea is that with the concept of a community of practice comes an emphasis on the individual's relationship with a group of people rather than the relationship of an activity itself to the wider practice, even though it is the practice itself that identifies the community. This provides a different perspective on what is 'situated'. Lave and Wenger (1991) characterized learning of practices as processes of participation in which beginners are initially relatively peripheral in the activities of a community and as they learn the practices their participation becomes more central. For Wenger (1998), it is not just the meaning to be attached to an activity that is derived from a community of practice: the individual's identity as a learner is shaped by the relationship to the community itself. The concept of vicarious learning (Mayes *et al.* 2001) is also based on the idea of learning through relating to others. Strictly, this occurs through observing others' learning, as for example in a master class. A great deal of conventional classroom-based learning is vicarious, and there are obvious ways in which this kind of learning is enhanced through computer-mediated communication (CMC).

There are perhaps three levels at which it is useful to think of learning being situated. At the top level is the social-anthropological or cultural perspective that emphasizes the need to learn to achieve a desired form of participation in a wider community. The essence of a community of practice is that, through joint engagement in some activity, an aggregation of people comes to develop and share practices. This is usually interpreted as a stable and relatively enduring group, scientists for example, whose practices involve the development of a constellation of beliefs, attitudes, values and specific knowledge built up over many years. Yet a community of practice can be built around a common endeavour that has a much shorter time span. Greeno *et al.* (1998) give examples of communities of practice that more closely resemble the groups studied in the social identity literature (e.g. Ellemers *et al.* 1999). Some examples are a garage band, an engineering team, a day care cooperative, a research group or a kindergarten class. It is worth noting that these are exactly the kind of groups described as activity systems in the approach that has come to be known as activity theory (Cole and Engeström 1993; Jonassen and Rohrer-Murphy 1999).

For long-term stable communities there are two different ways in which the community will influence learning. First, there is the sense most directly addressed by Wenger – someone aspires to become a legitimate participant of a community defined by expertise or competence in some field of application. The learning in this case is the learning of the practice that defines the community. This is the learning involved in becoming an accredited member of a community by reaching a demonstrated level of expertise, and then the learning involved in continuous professional development. This may be formal, as in medicine, or informal, by being accepted as a wine buff or a political activist. The second sense is that of a community of learners, for whom the practice is learning per se. That is, a very broad community identified by a shared high value placed on the process of continuous intellectual development.

At the next level of situatedness is the learning group. Almost all learning is itself embedded in a social context – the classroom, or the tutorial group, or the virtual computer-mediated communication discussion group or even the year group. The learner will usually have a strong sense of identifying with such groups, and a strong need to participate as a full member. Such groups can have the characteristics of a community of practice but here the practice is the learning itself, in a particular educational or training setting. Or rather it is educational practice, which may or may not be centred on learning. While there have been many studies of learning in informal settings (e.g. Resnick 1987), there are comparatively few ethnographic studies of real groups in educational settings to compare with the many studies of group dynamics in work organizations (see Greeno *et al.* 1998).

Finally, learning is experienced through individual relationships. Most learning that is motivated by the other levels will actually be mediated through relationships with individual members of the communities or groups in question. The social categorization of these individuals will vary according to the context and nature of particular dialogues. Sometimes their membership of a group will be most salient, in other situations their personal characteristics will be perceived as more important. Such relationships will vary according to the characteristics of the groups involved, the context within which they operate and the strength of the relationships (Fowler and Mayes 1999). Over the last few years e-learning has begun to place more and more emphasis on a pedagogy based on learning relationships. Such an approach supports the development of discussion boards, chat rooms, instant messaging and forms of communication that include the more exotic web-based tools that are collectively referred to as 'social software'.

E-learning and the learning cycle

It is possible to view these differing perspectives as analysing learning at different levels of aggregation. An associationist analysis describes the overt activities, and the outcomes of these activities, for individual learners. A cognitive analysis attempts a level of analysis that describes the detailed structures and processes that underlie individual performance. The situative perspective aggregates at the level of groups of learners, describing activity systems in which individuals participate as members of communities. There will be few current examples of approaches that derive from taking just one level of analysis and neglecting the others. Most implementations of e-learning will include blended elements that emphasize all three levels: learning as behaviour, learning as the construction of knowledge and meaning, and learning as social practice.

We conclude that each of the three perspectives described above are integral to learning. It seems appropriate to regard them as perspectives rather than theories, since each is incomplete as an account of learning. It is tempting to regard them not as competing accounts but as stages in a cycle (cf. Mayes and Fowler 1999). The three perspectives address different aspects of the progression towards mastery of knowledge or skill, with the situative perspective addressing the learner's motivation, the associative perspective focusing on the detailed nature of perform-ance, and the cognitive on the role of understanding and reflecting on action. Each of these perspectives is associated with a particular kind of pedagogy, and each is capable of being enhanced through e-learning. A handout summarizing the three perspectives and their implications for teaching and assessment is provided in Appendix 1.

There is quite a long tradition of describing learning as a cycle through stages, with each cycle focusing in turn on different perspectives (Fitts and Posner 1968; Rumelhart and Norman 1978; Kolb 1984; Mayes and Fowler 1999). Such a representation of learning also carries the advantage of describing learning as iterative. Welford (1968), for example, reports work that demonstrated that practice will lead to performance improvements that proceed almost indefinitely even on simple perceptual-motor tasks. Learning should not be thought of as being completed when an assessment has been successfully passed. However, as it proceeds from novice to expert, the nature of learning changes profoundly and the pedagogy based on one stage will be inappropriate for another. Depicting our three perspectives as a cycle invites the e-learning designer to consider what kind of technology is most effective at what stage of learning. Fowler and Mayes (1999) attempted to map broad pedagogies onto types of technology, distinguishing between the technology of presenting information (primary), the technology of supporting active learning tasks and feedback (secondary), and the technology of supporting dialogue about the application of the new learning (tertiary). Such a model is attractive as a design framework since it gives maximum scope for using technology strategically: addressing different pedagogical goals in different ways.

When we consider the current landscape of e-learning another kind of model suggests itself, based perhaps on a simple dimension of locus of control. At one end of this dimension we have institutional virtual learning environments (VLEs), with their emphasis on standardization. These are at the institution-in-control end of this dimension. At the other end is an environment that empowers learners to take responsibility for their own learning to the point where they make their own design decisions. The currently popular notion of the personalization of learning environments moves us part of the way along this dimension, although it depends whether the personal choices offered allow the learner to shape the learning environment in a way that really influences pedagogic control. Some of the rapidly developing web tools for learning (Web 2.0) do provide the fully empowered e-learner with great flexibility in control of their own learning through processes allowing rich dialogue with others with whom the learner can identify (see Box 1.1). More than any previous educational technology, current tools allow the rapid identification of like-minded others, and allow learning relationships to drive both direct communication and the sharing of relevant information.

We might bring these ideas together in the following way. The stages represent a cycle that starts with the social. Motivation to start and continue learning will be derived from communities and peers. This represents the situative perspective and it is served by the various technologies that allow the identification of, and communication with, others who will share in, or contribute to in some way, the learning experience. Gradually, personal ownership of the learning activities becomes necessary for the derivation of meaning and the construction of understanding. Learning tasks come into play. These will involve the production of outputs that can

---

Box 1.1 The TESEP project

TESEP (Transforming and Enhancing the Student Experience through Pedagogy) is a Scottish e-learning transformation project that is attempting to show how institutions can use e-learning effectively through the application of a pedagogy that puts 'learners in control'. It is attempting to drive the development of e-learning partly through a 'demand-side' philosophy that first tries to fully empower the learners by raising their awareness and skill level in Internet-based learning. It places learners as far as possible in the role of teachers of their peers, expecting them to locate and tailor, with guidance and feedback from their tutors, appropriate learning objects. Teaching staff engage with the transformation through a cascading process of staff development, where the same principles of pedagogy that encourage us to view learners as teachers apply to teachers as learners.

---

only be achieved through understanding. This brings the cognitive perspective into focus. The learner will interact with subject matter, but in a way that manipulates it actively. What are usually regarded as the pedagogical inputs, learning objects, should rather be outputs, created by the learner. To reach this point, however, it will at times be necessary to subject oneself as a learner to the discipline of bottom-up mastery of the components of a task, so an associationist perspective will underpin pedagogy at key moments. As learning progresses, so the learner will benefit from checking progress with peers, and engaging in dialogue about the refinements of the developing understanding, and the associated skills, so the cycle can continue for as long as necessary.

Other chapters in this book offer a range of different approaches to learning design underpinned by the general principles discussed here. In Chapter 5, Oliver *et al.* take the notion of constructive alignment and use it to explore learning designs where activities are designed to support learning outcomes that involve conceptual change. In Chapter 6, Conole uses the three perspectives described here in a taxonomy for describing and designing learning activities.

Conclusions

We have offered a mapping of theoretical accounts of learning onto pedagogical principles for design. We have attempted to frame this account within a familiar curriculum design model, with the following stages: describing intended learning outcomes; designing teaching methods and learning environments to achieve them; making assessments to measure how well they have been achieved; and making an evaluation of whether the stages are properly aligned. Most of this will now be familiar territory. For the training of skills we adopt an associative account, with its emphasis on task analysis and practice; for deep learning of concepts a constructivist pedagogy is emphasized, with a learner actively involved in the design of his or her own learning activity. Giving meaning to the whole process is an engagement with the social setting and peer culture surrounding it.

As our understanding of e-learning matures, so our appreciation of the importance of theory deepens. This view is one that rather challenges the conventional rationale of learning design. For most educational outcomes, theory points us clearly in a particular direction. Learners, in communities and other groups, but also individually, should be encouraged to take responsibility for the achievement of their own learning outcomes. As e-learning tools become truly powerful in their capability, and global in their scope, so it becomes more feasible to remodel the educational enterprise as a process of empowering learners to take reflective control of their own learning. This view challenges current assumptions about how far institutions can put a boundary around a learning experience.

A VLE may be seen as representing a twentieth-century instantiation of the role of institutions in attempting to manage the process. In peer-to-peer social networks we see a glimpse of a twenty-first-century view. Now that peer-to-peer learning is facilitated in a powerful way, and on a global scale, through new social networking tools such as blogs, wikis, social bookmarking and folksonomy, we see how learning can be socially situated in a way never previously possible. The Internet gives every course in every institution a potentially global span. Learning theory emphasizes the importance of this, but it does not provide us with a clear understanding of how to exploit it efficiently within the context of a mature educational infrastructure. Positioning empowered individual learners at the centre of the e-learning design process will clearly impact on the role of the educator but it is not yet clear how that role will evolve. What is clear is that theory and practice must be aligned within a coherent and workable model of education.

References

Anderson, J.R. and Lebiere, C. (1998) *The Atomic Components of Thought*, Mahwah, NJ: Lawrence Erlbaum.

Anderson, J.R., Corbett, A.T., Koedinger, K.R. and Pelletier, R. (1995) 'Cognitive tutors: lessons learned', *Journal of the Learning Sciences*, 4 (2): 167–207.

Barab, S.A. and Duffy, T.M. (2000) 'From practice fields to communities of practice', in D.H. Jonassen and S.M. Land (eds) *Theoretical Foundations of Learning Environments*, Mahwah, NJ: Lawrence Erlbaum.

Biggs, J. (1999) *Teaching for Quality Learning at University*, Buckingham: Society for Research in Higher Education and Open University Press.

Bruner, J. (1960) *The Process of Education*, Cambridge, MA: Harvard University Press.

Cole, M. and Engeström, Y. (1993) 'A cultural-historical approach to distributed cognition', in G. Salomon (ed.) *Distributed Cognitions: Psychological and Educational Considerations*, New York: Cambridge University Press.

Collins, A., Brown, J.S. and Newman, S.E. (1989) 'Cognitive apprenticeship: teaching the crafts of reading, writing and mathematics', in R.B. Resnick (ed.) *Knowing, Learning and Instruction: Essays in Honour of Robert Glaser*, Mahwah, NJ: Lawrence Erlbaum.

Duffy, T.M. and Cunningham, D.J. (1996) 'Constructivism: implications for design and delivery of instruction', in D.H. Jonassen (ed.) *Educational Communications and Technology*, New York: Simon & Schuster Macmillan.

Ellemers, N., Spears, R. and Doosje, B. (eds) (1999) *Social Identity: Context, Commitment, Content*, Malden, MA: Blackwell.

Fitts, P. and Posner, M.I. (1967) *Human Performance*, Monterey, CA: Brooks/Cole.

Fowler, C.J.H. and Mayes, J.T. (1999) 'Learning relationships: from theory to design', *Association for Learning Technology Journal*, 7 (3): 6–16.

Gagné, R. (1985) *The Conditions of Learning*, New York: Holt, Rinehart & Winston.

Greeno, J.G., Collins, A.M. and Resnick, L. (1996) 'Cognition and learning', in D.C. Berliner and R.C. Calfee (eds) *Handbook of Educational Psychology*, New York: Simon & Schuster/Macmillan.

Greeno, J.G., Eckert, P., Stucky, S.U., Sachs, P. and Wenger, E. (1998) 'Learning in and for participation in work and society', paper presented at US Dept of Education and OECD Conference on How Adults Learn, Washington DC, April 1998.

Hinton, G.E. (1992) 'How neural networks learn from experience', *Scientific American*, 267 (3): 144–51.

Jarvela, S. (1995) 'The cognitive apprenticeship model in a technologically rich learning environment: interpreting the learning interaction', *Learning and Instruction*, 5 (3): 237–59.

Jonassen, D.H. and Land, S.M. (2000) *Theoretical Foundations of Learning Environments*, Mahwah, NJ: Lawrence Erlbaum.

Jonassen, D.H. and Rohrer-Murphy, L. (1999) 'Activity theory as a framework for designing constructivist learning environments', *Educational Technology Research and Development*, 47 (1): 61–80.

Kolb, D.A. (1984) *Experiential Learning: Experience as the Source of Learning and Development*, Englewood Cliffs, NJ: Prentice-Hall.

Lave, J. (1988) *Cognition in Practice: Mind, Mathematics and Culture in Everyday Life*, Cambridge: Cambridge University Press.

Lave, J. and Wenger, E. (1991) *Situated Learning: Legitimate Peripheral Participation*, Cambridge: Cambridge University Press.

Mayes, J.T. and Fowler, C.J.H. (1999) 'Learning technology and usability: a framework for understanding courseware', *Interacting with Computers*, 11: 485–97.

Mayes, J.T., Dineen, F., McKendree, J. and Lee, J. (2001) 'Learning from watching others learn', in C. Steeples and C. Jones (eds) *Networked Learning: Perspectives and Issues*, London: Springer.

Newell, A. (1980) 'One final word', in D.T. Tuma and F. Reif (eds) *Problem Solving and Education: Issues in Teaching and Research*, Mahwah, NJ: Lawrence Erlbaum.

Piaget, J. (1970) *Science of Education and the Psychology of the Child*, New York: Orion Press.

Resnick, L.B. (1987) 'Learning in school and out', *Educational Researcher*, 16: 13–20.

Resnick, L.B. and Resnick, D.P. (1991) 'Assessing the thinking curriculum: new tools for education reform', in B.R. Gifford and M.C. O'Connor (eds) *Changing Assessment: Alternative Views of Aptitude, Achievement and Instruction*, Boston: Kluwer.

Rumelhart, D.E. and Norman, D.A. (1978) 'Accretion, tuning and structuring: three modes of learning', in J.W. Cotton and R.L. Klatzky (eds) *Semantic Factors in Cognition*, Hillsdale, NJ: Erlbaum.

Savery, J.R. and Duffy, T.M. (1996) 'Problem-based learning: an instructional model and its constructivist framework', in B.G. Wilson (ed.) *Constructivist Learning Environments: Case Studies in Instructional Design*, Mahwah, NJ: Educational Technology Publications.

Vygotsky, L.S. (1978) *Mind in Society*, Cambridge, MA: Harvard University Press.

Welford, A.T. (1968) *Fundamentals of Skill*, London: Methuen.

Wenger, E. (1998) *Communities of Practice: Learning, Meaning, and Identity*, Cambridge: Cambridge University Press.

Wilson, B.G. and Myers, K.M. (2000) 'Situated cognition in theoretical and practical context', in D.H. Jonassen and S.M. Land (eds) *Theoretical Foundations of Learning Environments*, Mahwah, NJ: Lawrence Erlbaum.

Chapter 2

An approach to learning activity design

Helen Beetham

EDITORS' INTRODUCTION

In the Introduction we stated that good design applies theoretical principles to specific cases of use. This chapter considers how design principles have been developed from theories of how people learn (see Mayes and de Freitas, Chapter 1) and how these can be applied to learning with digital technologies. A model of learning activity design is presented, and a range of tools to support design for learning are introduced (the tools themselves can be found in the appendices in Part III).

Introduction

What design principles can be derived from the theoretical discussions of the previous chapter? All three approaches – which I will term associative, constructive and situative – emphasize the central importance of activity on the part of the learner. Several decades of research support the view that it is the activity that the learner engages in, and the outcomes of that activity, that are significant for learning (e.g. Tergan 1997). There is no reason why the introduction of digital tools and materials should change this emphasis, and indeed the emergence of Learning Design as a dominant paradigm can be taken as a sign that activity is being reinstated as the focus of concern. Design for learning should therefore focus primarily on the activities undertaken by learners, and only secondarily on (for example) the tools or materials that support them.

It is useful to distinguish activities from tasks (see also Jones, Chapter 13). In a formal educational setting, tasks are required *of* learners by the demands of the curriculum. Activities are engaged in *by* learners in response to the demands of a task. Although good teachers will provide direction as to how tasks should be carried out, and may scaffold learners' activities quite rigidly, different learners will still have their own ways of proceeding. This is particularly true during the period of consolidation or practice that is another common principle of all three theoretical approaches. Learners need opportunities to make a newly acquired concept or skill their own: to draw on their own strengths and preferences, and to extend their repertoire of approaches to task requirements.

Theorists also stress the need for integration across activities, whether associatively (building component skills into extended performance), constructively (integrating skills and knowledge, planning and reflecting), or situatively (developing identities and roles). The two principles of consolidation and integration help us to understand why a learning activity is not a given entity, but depends on the capabilities of the learner. A postgraduate student may consider it a simple task to read and prepare notes on a journal article, or to derive a set of experimental data. For a college student, the same skills will almost certainly need to be practised through component tasks with support and feedback on each one. A learning activity, therefore, is an entity that is meaningful to the learner, given his or her current level of expertise.

It is precisely because of their contingent nature, learning activities are the most pedagogically meaningful focus of design for learning. Reviews of the use of virtual learning environments (VLEs) consistently find that they promote design approaches that are either based on the content of materials or on non-pedagogical aspects of course administration (e.g. Britain and Liber 2004). Systems are now emerging that allow practitioners to design from an activity-based standpoint (see Britain, Chapter 8), but a focus on activity enables all kinds of technology to be integrated effectively into the learning and teaching process.

Different theories: different emphases

If there are many agreed design principles (consolidation, integration, feedback etc.), as Chapter 1 has indicated, there are also substantially different theories about how people learn. Associative, constructive and situative learning are not necessarily at odds with one another – in different contexts people do learn in these different ways – but they do emphasize different issues in activity design. These can be briefly summarized as follows.

- *Authenticity of the activity*: Apprenticeship and work-based learning depend on activities arising 'naturally' from a highly authentic context (situative learning). Lab and field activities are designed to mimic 'authentic' research tasks and so develop complex skills (constructive learning), but the context is artificially created and the methods and outcomes are anticipated in advance. Associative learning depends not on authenticity but on rehearsing skills and concepts in a highly structured way (see next point).
- *Formality and structure*: Learning activities may be highly structured and carefully sequenced – perhaps because this format has been shown to help fast and accurate learning. Or they may be poorly defined, allowing learners to develop their own approaches. Highly structured activities can often be expressed as a sequence or 'narrative' (see Britain, Chapter 8) while open-ended activities will more likely be represented as a cluster of possibilities.

- *Retention/reproduction versus reflection/internalization*: When the focus is on accuracy of reproduction, learners will be given opportunities to practise the required concept or skill until they can reproduce it exactly as taught. When the focus is on internalization, learners will be given opportunities to integrate a concept or skill with their existing beliefs and capabilities, to reflect on what it means to them, and to make sense of it in a variety of contexts.
- *The role and importance of other people*: Most learning involves dialogue with a more expert other person, but the role of this person – instructor, mentor, facilitator – differs considerably among the different approaches. Peer learners also have different roles to play, with some approaches (e.g. social constructivism) emphasizing the value of collaboration, and others emphasizing the development of self-reliance.
- *Locus of control*: A related issue is how decisions about the learning activity are made. Who decides when a learning activity is completed? Who controls the timing of and criteria for assessment? Some approaches favour strong tutor control, giving learners the security to focus on the skill or concept at hand, while others insist on giving learners more autonomy. An ideal is perhaps that learners should progress from situations in which they are strongly guided to situations in which they are more responsible for their own and other people's learning.

The approach outlined in the rest of this chapter indicates the decisions that have to be made in learning activity design. Designers may approach these decisions already committed to a specific theoretical approach, or already decided on how the issues of authenticity, formality etc. will play out in a specific context. On the other hand, their priorities may only emerge as they reflect on the decisions they have taken.

Defining a learning activity

We are interested here to define a learning activity in a way that supports the design process, including the design decisions to be made, the information to support these decisions, and how theories or principles can be applied. From this perspective, a learning activity can helpfully be defined as *a specific interaction of learner(s) with other(s) using specific tools and resources, orientated towards specific outcomes*. Examples of learning activities might include solving problems, comparing and evaluating arguments, presenting facts or negotiating goals.

Figure 2.1 shows an outline for a learning activity with its component elements in place. When practitioners were consulted about their own design practice, these were the elements they considered it necessary to share (JISC 2004). There is a close match between these and the elements defined in the IMS Learning Design specification (IMS 2005) and they also provide a useful checklist against which learning activities can be evaluated (Masterman *et al*. 2005). The specific arrangement of elements in this figure is loosely derived from activity theory (see

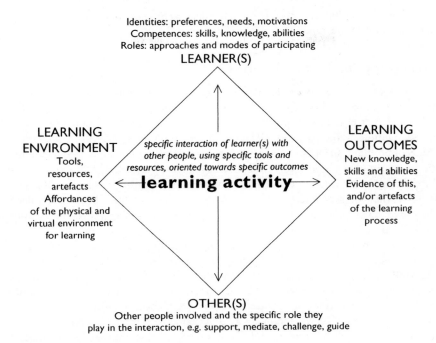

Identities: preferences, needs, motivations
Competences: skills, knowledge, abilities
Roles: approaches and modes of participating
LEARNER(S)

LEARNING ENVIRONMENT
Tools,
resources,
artefacts
Affordances
of the physical and
virtual environment
for learning

*specific interaction of learner(s) with
other people, using specific tools and
resources, oriented towards specific outcomes*
←**learning activity**→

LEARNING OUTCOMES
New knowledge,
skills and abilities
Evidence of this,
and/or artefacts
of the learning
process

OTHER(S)
Other people involved and the specific role they
play in the interaction, e.g. support, mediate, challenge, guide

Figure 2.1 An outline for a learning activity

e.g. Engeström 1999), an approach that has proved productive for learning technology researchers in recent years (e.g. Issroff and Scanlon 2002).

Jonassen (2000) classifies activities as rule-based, incident-based, strategy-based or role-based. Drawing on the insights of Chapter 1, we can see that associative learning is highly rule-based, with activities that help learners to recall the rules of a skill set or conceptual framework. Constructive learning focuses on incidents and strategies: activities enable learners to discover their own rules and devise their own strategies for increasingly complex situations. Role-based activities are inherently situative. Jonassen's distinction is discussed more thoroughly by Oliver *et al.* in Chapter 5.

Because a learning activity – or interaction – emerges as the learner engages in a task, the elements identified here are in practice highly interdependent and can only finally be defined as the activity is completed. Nevertheless, practitioners have found it helpful to consider these elements separately when undertaking the design process. In highly learner-centred contexts such as research projects or key skills acquisition, the needs and goals of the learner will be of first concern. There are pragmatic situations in which access to specific technologies are limited, or in which an important other person (e.g. expert or mentor) is available only at a certain time. In these situations, access will predominate over other considerations. On the whole though, in curriculum-based education, the desired learning outcome(s) will be the starting point for design.

Designing for learning outcomes

A learning outcome is some identifiable change that is anticipated in the learner. In associative learning this might be the performance of a new skill or the expression of a new concept. In constructive learning there might be evidence of a new understanding on the part of the learner, for example in a capacity to solve new kinds of problem. In situative learning the learner will be able to participate in new situations, or play a more expert role. We have already argued that an activity must be meaningful to the learner, and it is the nature of the learning outcome that makes it so. Learners must be interested in achieving the outcome, either because it reflects their own developmental goals, or because they see its place in a wider curriculum to which they have committed themselves.

In line with the focus on activity, learning outcomes are typically expressed in the form *learners will be able to [verb] [qualification]* where the verb describes the kind of activity that learners will undertake (e.g. solve, describe) and the qualification describes the context, scope or method to be used (e.g. solve equations of the type x; describe the impact of recent legislation on childcare services). Outcomes can even be written in a way that defines different levels of attainment and how these will be graded: indeed this level of description is advocated by instructional designers (see e.g. Dick and Carey 1990). Verbs for learning outcomes – and by extension for relevant tasks – are often chosen from an educational taxonomy such as Bloom's (1956) or Biggs' (2002). Appendix 7 includes a taxonomy of outcomes similar to Bloom's. While designers are often encouraged to consider separately those outcomes that concern knowledge, skills and values, it seems likely that concepts and the conceptual skills required to handle them are acquired in parallel, and that neither can be divorced from the values of the community in which they are practised.

Criticism of outcomes-based design centres on the fact that it expects learners to adhere very closely to a curriculum and its assessment goals. In doing so, it may even foster a strategic approach, with learners valuing only those tasks that lead transparently to assessment outcomes (Hussey and Smith 2003). Written outcomes usually focus on aspects of learning that are easy to assess, neglecting, for example, learners' developing values, their capacities to learn, and subtler skills. However, outcomes can be written to focus on the capability (verb), giving learners room to demonstrate this in a variety of ways and so supporting constructive and situative learning more effectively. Assessing the activity process as well as the end-product is another way of helping learners to capture unanticipated outcomes, and to value their different approaches to the task at hand.

It has been argued that the current generation of digital technologies is better suited to open-ended outcomes than the technologies of the Instructional Design era. Simulations and virtual environments are used to foster exploration rather than a linear progression through materials. Individual learning logs and e-portfolios allow learners to collate evidence towards broadly defined learning goals, and to reflect on their progress. Collaborative technologies and VLEs can be used to capture dialogue, bringing to light the processes as well as the outcomes of learning. However, more broadly defined outcomes will always mean that a wider range of activities needs to receive support and feedback. The resulting designs may be highly learner-centred, but only if there are sufficient teaching resources to support them effectively.

Designing for learners

An outcomes-based or curriculum-led design deals with differences among learners very simply. At the outset, learners are directed towards the tasks that are appropriate for their current level of attainment. On completion, they are assessed against an average to determine their level of performance, one aim being to reproduce learner differences as a tidy assessment curve. Learners are assumed to respond to instruction in similar ways, and differences that are not related to performance on task are generally ignored. In contrast to this, current educational practice is widely described as 'learner centred' (Lea *et al.* 2003). Learners are understood to have different priorities, preferences and approaches to learning, and different requirements for support. Accessibility and inclusion are also issues that have moved beyond the 'special needs' agenda. Now the aim is to make all learning facilities adaptive to individual needs (Dagger *et al.* 2005).

There are two challenges involved in taking a learner-centred approach, and both have new aspects in a technology-rich environment. The first is to know, among the many ways learners can vary from one another, which ones are significant to the learning at hand. The second is to deal with this variance in ways that are supportive of individual learners. Depending on the task and context, it may be necessary to consider learners':

- subject-specific experience, knowledge and competence;
- access needs, including any physical and sensory disabilities;
- motives for learning, and expectations of the learning situation;
- prior experience of learning, including the specific mode (e.g. online);
- preferred approaches to learning (see Box 2.1);
- social and interpersonal skills;
- confidence and competence in the use of information and communication technology (ICT).

Appendix 2 outlines some design considerations arising from specific learner differences, but does not deal with the complex ways in which these differences interact. Even ICT competence is not a stand-alone issue but can impact on a wide range of other factors, including learners' confidence, choice of location and support requirements (Lockitt 2004). A recent review of individual differences in e-learning

---

Box 2.1 The learning styles debate

There is no doubt that learners can gain insights into their own processes of learning, and that teaching improves when differences in learners' approaches are recognized. Of particular interest in learning design has been evidence that learners prefer different representational formats – holistic versus serial, for example (Pask 1988), or linguistic versus spatial (Gardner 1993). There is controversy, however, over the wholesale use of 'learning style' inventories to categorize learners as having a particular set of learning needs. Coffield *et al.* (2004), in a comprehensive review, highlight the lack of reliable evidence that stable learning styles exist independently of the contexts in which they are expressed, and the lack of consensus about how teaching ought to be organized in light of these apparent differences.

It seems safe to state that learners have stable or slowly changing characteristics such as their identities, lifelong motivations and experiences of learning, physical and sensory access requirements, and related personal preferences, e.g. for particular kinds of information. But learners also have characteristics that develop in the process of learning, and that are dependent on the context in which they find themselves. Indeed, learning can involve fundamental changes in a person's outlook, values, social role and identity. This is learning as self-actualization (Maslow 1970).

(Sharpe *et al.* 2005) concluded that, as well as ICT skills, key issues were learners' emotional relationship to the technologies they were offered – especially feelings of frustration and alienation – and issues around time management. The same review found evidence that the use of technologies can compound existing differences among learners due to their gender, culture and first language. Learners cannot therefore be treated as a bundle of disparate needs: they are actors, not factors, in the learning situation. They make sense of the tasks they are set in terms of their own goals and perspectives, and they may experience tasks quite differently if digital technologies – with all the social and cultural meanings that they carry – are involved.

The second challenge in learner-centred design is dealing effectively with learner variance. For many years Instructional Design has aimed to provide individualized or adaptive learning, matching materials to learners' performance on set tasks. Diagnostic tools now offer the possibility that materials might be adapted to other learner characteristics such as their 'style' or preferred approach to learning. The benefits of such an approach remain controversial. It is not clear, for example, that learners should be accommodated in their preferences rather than challenged to try alternatives (Beetham 2005). Individualized instruction banishes the frustrations of cohort learning, but also its many advantages. And technologies that diagnose learners' needs *for* them do not help them to understand and take responsibility for their own learning process.

An alternative route is the provision of *flexible* learning, in which learners make their own choices over issues such as the tasks they undertake, the mediational means they use, and the evidence they provide for assessment. Digital technologies are increasingly used to increase learner choice in this way (see, e.g. Luckin *et al.* 2005). Hypermedia and adaptive tutorials allow learners to select their own routes through materials. Search engines and portals give a far wider choice of resources, and e-portfolios allow learners to collate evidence of their achievements in a way that is highly personal. For this flexibility to enable learning, however, learners must be supported in all the different choices they make. This is why, despite the capacity of technology to present a wider range of options, the limiting factor remains the availability of skilled practitioners to provide relevant feedback and support.

Designing with digital resources and technologies

The Introduction to this book argued that the use of digital technologies changes the meaning of a learning activity, subtly or profoundly. The technologies available in the learning environment, and how learners are encouraged to use them for specific activities, are therefore essential aspects of design.

In this section we are concerned with designed objects (artefacts) such as digital cameras and microscopes, electronic whiteboards, mobile devices, laptop computers and web pages. These tend to be visible in the learning environment, and may have design features that make clear how they are intended to be used for learning. Less obviously, the environment includes other features that can influence learning: the layout of a seminar room affects how learners interact, while different kinds of learning are possible in a fieldwork situation, laboratory or workplace. Digital environments similarly help to structure learners' time and space, and they support – or constrain – learners' interactions. The design of whole environments for learning is dealt with in Sharpe and Oliver (Chapter 3) and Kukulska-Hulme and Traxler (Chapter 14).

Properties of designed artefacts are often referred to as their 'affordances' for a particular use: in this case their affordances for learning (after Gibson 1979). Here, however, we will talk about tools and resources in terms of how they *mediate* learning (see Box 2.2). This emphasizes that artefacts can have different meanings in different activity contexts.

Resources are content-based artefacts that use various representational media such as text, images, moving images and sound. It is now understood that the medium used can have a profound effect on how content is assimilated and remembered, and that different learners have different capacities with different media. A choice of medium, or the opportunity to experience two media in parallel – for example a spoken text and a visual diagram – have been shown to be particularly effective for learning (Bereiter and Scardamalia 1996).

Box 2.2 A note on affordances

Norman (1999, cited in Oliver 2006) states that 'affordances reflect the possible relationships among actors and objects'. This is an intuitively helpful concept to bring into the activity diagram. However, Norman goes on to state that affordances are not in fact properties of the relationship between user and object: 'they are properties of the world'. The use of the term 'affordance' in the context of learning technologies has received criticism recently (see, e.g. McGrenere and Ho 2000, and Oliver 2006) because of this emphasis on the properties of objects – especially their design features – rather than on the varied ways in which people experience those properties and adopt them for their own ends. Effective learners will glean something from the most unpromising materials: teachers will use technologies 'against the grain' of their designers' intentions. We need to see a designed object as a place where the intentions of its designers and its users converge, whose meaning is not fixed but emerges as it is used. As designers for learning, we need to make choices about technologies in a way that takes account both of how they support the learning task and of how they will be experienced by individual learners – the different 'possible relationships' between task and learner that they might mediate.

Learning designers have in the past paid great attention to information design: aligning the representation of knowledge with what is believed to be its logical structure (e.g. through conceptual hierarchies, key words, linear progressions). These skills need not be discarded in activity-based design, but designers may prefer to support the development of conceptual skills through varieties of representation, rather than by offering a single 'best' version of content.

Many claims have been made about the inherent advantages of digital media for learning – for example that they are more motivating or 'interactive' – but the evidence is that any such advantages are largely contextual. When first introduced, digital media had the advantage of novelty; now they enjoy familiarity and ubiquity. For today's 'digital natives' (Prensky 2001) online research and the capacity to manage multiple forms of information are essential life skills, and this alone makes their use in education desirable. The main intrinsic benefits of digital resources are their greater flexibility of access, reproduction and manipulation. Simply being able to study at a time, place and pace to suit them can profoundly change learners' relationships with conceptual material.

Resources can communicate simple information or instruction to learners, for example in associative sequences, but for deeper learning they need to be embedded in appropriate conceptual tasks. The nature of these tasks is highly dependent on the content to be learned, and this relationship between varieties of knowledge and varieties of conceptual activity is the main reason why designing for learning is a subject-specific skill. However, most subjects require learners to engage in *research* tasks (such as searching databases, evaluating online resources) and in *comprehension* tasks (such as answering questions, note-taking and mind-mapping).

Digital tools are now routinely used to support these activities. 'Tool' here is used to designate an artefact designed to support a specific task function rather than to represent content, though as we will see this distinction is becoming blurred.

Tools for *creating* representations in different media – e.g. PowerPoint, web editors, video and animation software, digital cameras – are all too often regarded as the prerogative of the learning designer, but there is no reason why they should not be used by learners to create their own representations of subject matter. Applications can even be shared to enable collaborative representations to be built, as happens face to face with electronic whiteboards, and with wikis online. Learners' representations can of course be used for assessment but they can also be re-integrated into the learning situation for reflection and peer review, or even as learning materials for future cohorts. The portability of digital representations is particularly valuable in this respect. Digital editing and analysis tools have also changed learners' relationships with content resources, automating routine activities and freeing up time for more demanding tasks such as evaluation, comparison and reflection. There is evidence from higher education that students' approaches to writing and argumentation have changed radically since the advent of the Internet and word processing software (Brindley 2000; Wegerif 2002).

Tasks of *analysis* are likely to be very subject-specific and there is a wide range of digital tools – diagnostics, infomatics, design and manufacturing systems, specific analytical software – with which learners may need to become familiar. Tasks that closely mirror authentic professional practice are called for here. In many subjects, analytical tasks are carried out not only on content but also on material that is found in 'the real world' of the laboratory or the field. This is almost always the case for tasks of *experimentation* and *discovery*. These are activities that may still be mediated by digital tools and instruments, and as a result the distinction between content-based and 'real-world' tasks is less than clear-cut. Computing power is the potential of artefacts based on information (software) to be used as tools. With these tools as mediators, learning activities can take place in an entirely represented space: for example using models, simulations and complex digital environments (e.g. the Visible Human Project, National Library of Medicine 2006). As we live and work in an increasingly designed, artefactual environment, this kind of learning becomes arguably more relevant and 'real'.

An entirely different set of tools is used to support *communicative* activities, and these are discussed more fully in the following section.

Diana Laurillard's Conversational Theory of Learning (Laurillard 2002; Sharpe and Oliver, Chapter 3) has been particularly influential on thinking about the choice and use of digital technologies for learning. Laurillard distinguishes five different media 'types' – narrative, communicative, interactive, productive and adaptive – with different capacities to mediate learning. Appendix 3 offers a version of this classification system, showing how media types can support the different tasks discussed in this section, and suggesting reasons for choosing and using digital artefacts in each category. With the rise of networked computing, consideration of digital *services* must stand alongside consideration of digital *artefacts* when designing for learning. Wilson (2005) examines how the new generation of services can be harnessed to the different pedagogical approaches we have discussed.

No technologies should be introduced to the learning situation without consideration of learners' confidence and competence in their use. Ideally designs should also extend that competence, for example by having learners explore different functions, make choices about use of a tool, and integrate it with other tools in their environment. Designers should also take account of learners' own technologies, including mobile phones, email, instant messaging and personal digital assistants (PDAs), digital TV and radio, and social software. The use of such 'private' technologies is an essential aspect of the construction of personal identity (Turkle 1995) and there are preliminary findings that it can help learners bridge the gap between their existing skills and the kinds of ICT literacy required in formal education (Attewell 2005). Yet learners may feel that these technologies are not relevant to their learning, and may even hide these practices for fear that they are outside the 'rules' implied by the provision of institutional technologies.

Designing for interaction with others

Most learning involves interaction with a more expert other person. Associative learning demands a teacher who is skilled not only in the subject matter but also in guiding learners through structured activities. Situative learners need a sympathetic mentor with insight into their context and the ability to support their developing role. Teachers committed to a constructive approach require a wide range of facilitative skills – negotiating outcomes, supporting learner discussion, giving relevant feedback – and the ability to respond to learners' different needs. Dialogue with peer learners is also highly valued by many theorists. Vygotsky (1986) argued that learning is a socially mediated activity in the first instance, with concepts and skills being internalized only after they have been mastered in a collaborative context.

Constructivists following Piaget (2001), and in computer-mediated learning, Papert (1993), give dialogue a secondary role but agree that it can support the individual processes of reflection and abstraction. There is in fact evidence that some learners prefer to learn alone, but this is typically at advanced levels when they have already mastered the relevant skills in more supportive contexts. Opportunities for dialogue are considered crucial in most approaches to learning design. Some or all of these interactions can now take place through computer-mediated communication (CMC) systems.

Many e-learning developments, particularly in higher education, have focused on the use of CMC. Although increasing use is being made of video conferencing in some subject areas, and of mobile and wireless audio in others (see Kukulska-

Hulme and Traxler, Chapter 14), text-based media are by far the most widespread. There is evidence that the use of such media changes the roles of learners considerably (McConnell 2005). For example, expertise need no longer be 'handed out' by the teacher from the front of the class, but can be contributed more equitably. Turn-taking becomes less significant (everyone can 'talk' at once), and many face-to-face markers of difference are removed. Participation also becomes more explicit, and the content of discussion becomes available for reflection and review – many online courses routinely assess participation (Macdonald 2004). The explicit nature of online dialogue makes it particularly good for negotiating and building shared understanding in collaborative tasks. Perhaps the main advantage of these new media, however, is the ability to participate with a much wider range of other people (e.g. remote experts, learners in other institutions and countries) and at a time and place to suit the learner.

Managing the transition to a more facilitative role is demanding for tutors (Fox and MacKeogh 2003), but text-based CMC also requires new skills from learners. The explicit nature of communication favours a more reflective approach than face-to-face dialogue, demands keyboard skills and good standards of written language, and also requires the motivation to participate without the support of a live social context. There are studies that report students being uncomfortable with these demands, for example, struggling with the learner locus of control (Crook 2002) or with the use of peer review and feedback (Ramsey 2003). Designing for effective collaboration is discussed in more detail in Jones (Chapter 13) and Ravenscroft and Cook (Chapter 16). Here it is important to note that designing with CMC requires attention to participants' roles, and to the rules and structures of the interaction. In face-to-face contexts these tend to emerge spontaneously, though highly constrained by participants' expectations; CMC offers opportunities both to break with established modes of discourse, and to make explicit the ground rules and structures of power that exist.

Conclusions

This chapter has outlined considerations for design that arise from theories about how people learn (see Mayes and de Freitas, Chapter 1) and the experience of applying these theories to learning with digital technologies. Many of the considerations discussed in this chapter are expanded in the Appendices, including a learning activity design checklist (Appendix 4). But 'good' design does not always move in a linear fashion from theory to principle to practice. It can evolve from a range of practical examples without ever being formally articulated (see Sharpe and Oliver, Chapter 9), remaining a kind of shared expertise, or 'theory-in-use' (Argyris 1997). The application of 'sound' principles is therefore only one facet of the design process: it is also important to understand how practitioners actually *do* design for learning (see Masterman and Vogel, Chapter 4), to evaluate what is being done (see Sharpe and Oliver, Chapter 3), and to describe and share effective designs with others (see Oliver *et al.*, Chapter 5 and Dalziel, Chapter 15). This is particularly true in a rapidly changing situation such as the use of digital technologies, where new opportunities and threats – including new kinds of learner and learning organization – are continually challenging established practices of design.

Acknowledgements

Some of the content of this chapter was developed in collaboration with educational innovators who were invited to share aspects of their practice during a series of workshops (JISC 2004). Thanks to Martin Oliver for advice on the affordances discussion in Box 2.2.

References

Argyris, C. (1997) 'Learning and teaching: a theory of action perspective', *Journal of Management Education*, 21 (1): 9–27.

Attewell, J. (2005) *Mobile Technologies and Learning: A Technology Update and M-learning Project Summary*, London: Learning and Skills Development Agency. Online. Available www.m-learning.org/reports.shtml (accessed 6 September 2006).

Beetham, H. (2005) 'Personalization in the curriculum: a view from learning theory', in C. Yapp and S. de Freitas (eds) *Personalizing Learning in the 21st Century*, London: Network Education Press, pp. 17–24.

Bereiter, C. and Scardamalia, M. (1996) 'Rethinking learning', in D. Olson and N. Torrance (eds) *Handbook of Education and Human Development*, Cambridge: Blackwell, pp. 485–513.

Biggs, J. (2002) *Aligning the Curriculum to Promote Good Learning, Symposium Paper*, London: Learning and Teaching Support Network Generic Centre. Online. Available www.ltsn.ac.uk/genericcentre/index.asp?docid=17269 (accessed 6 September 2006).

Bloom, B.S. (ed.) (1956) *Taxonomy of Educational Objectives: The Classification of Educational Goals*, New York: MacKay.

Brindley, S. (2000) 'ICT and literacy', in N. Gamble and N. Easingwood (eds) *ICT and Literacy*, London: Continuum, pp. 11–18.

Britain, S. and Liber, O. (2004) *Framework for the Pedagogical Evaluation of Virtual Learning Tools (Revised)*, Bristol: JISC. Online. Available www.jisc.ac.uk/index.cfm?name=project_pedagogical_vle (accessed 6 September 2006).

Coffield, F., Moseley, D., Hall E. and Eccleston, K. (2004) *Learning Styles and Pedagogy in Post-16 Learning: A Systematic and Critical Review*, Learning and Skills Development Agency.

Crook, C. (2002) 'The campus experience of networked learning', in C. Steeples and C. Jones (eds) *Networked Learning: Perspectives and Issues*, London: Springer-Verlag, pp. 293–308.

Dagger, D., Wade, V. and Conlan, O. (2005) 'Personalization for all: making adaptive course composition easy', *Educational Technology and Society: Special Issue on Authoring of Adaptive Hypermedia*, 8 (3): 9–25.

Dick, W. and Carey, L. (1990) *The Systematic Design of Instruction,* 3rd edn, New York: Harper Collins.

Fox, S. and MacKeogh, K. (2003) 'Can e-learning promote higher order learning without tutor overload?', *Open Learning*, 18 (2): 121–34.

Engeström, Y. (1999) 'Activity theory and individual and social transformation', in Y. Engeström, R. Miettinen and R.-L. Punamaki (eds) *Perspectives on Activity Theory*, Cambridge: Cambridge University Press, pp. 19–38.

Gardner, H. (1993) *Frames of Mind: The Theory of Multiple Intelligences*, London: Fontana Press.

Gibson, J. (1979) *The Ecological Approach to Visual Perception*, Boston: Houghton Mifflin.

Hussey, T. and Smith, P. (2003) 'The uses of learning outcomes', *Teaching in Higher Education*, 8 (3): 357–68.

IMS (2005) *Learning Design Specification. Version 1.0 Final Specification*, IMS Global. Online. Available www.imsglobal.org/specifications.html (accessed 30 September 2006).

Issroff, K. and Scanlon, E. (2002) 'Activity theory and enhancing learning: using technology in higher education', *Journal of Computers and Learning*, 18 (1): 77–83.

JISC (2004) 'Effective practice with e-learning, workshop series'. Online. Available www.jisc.ac.uk/index.cfm?name=elp_practice> (accessed 30 September 2006).

Jonassen, D. (2000) 'Toward a design theory of problem solving', *Educational Technology Research and Development*, 48 (4): 63–85.

Laurillard, D. (2002) *Rethinking University Teaching: A Conversational Framework for the Effective Use of Learning Technologies*, 2nd edn, London: Routledge.

Lea, S.J., Stephenson, D. and Troy, J. (2003) 'Higher education students' attitudes to student-centred learning: beyond "educational bulimia?"', *Studies in Higher Education*, 28 (3): 321–34.

Lockitt, B. (2004) *Adult, Community and Work Based Learning: E-learning*. Cheadle: 3T Productions.

Luckin, R., du Boulay, B., Smith, H., Underwood, J., Fitzpatrick, G. *et al.* (2005) 'Using mobile technology to create flexible learning contexts', *Journal of Interactive Media in Education*. Online. Available http://jime.open.ac.uk/2005/22 (accessed 6 September 2006).

McConnell, D. (2005) 'Examining the dynamics of networked e-learning groups and communities'. *Studies in Higher Education*, 30 (1): 25–42.

MacDonald, J. (2004) 'Developing competent e-learners: the role of assessment', *Assessment and Evaluation in Higher Education*, 29 (2): 215–26.

McGrenere, J. and Ho, W. (2000) 'Affordances: clarifying and evolving a concept', Proceedings of Graphics Interface 2000, Montreal, May 2000. Online. Available www.graphicsinterface.org/cgi-bin/DownloadPaper?name=2000/177/PDFpaper177.pdf (accessed 6 September 2006).

Maslow, A.H. (1970) *Motivation and Personality*, 2nd edn, New York: Harper and Row.

Masterman, L., Lee, S., Beetham, H., Knight, S. and Francis, R. (2005) 'Supporting effective practice in learning design: an evaluation of the Learning Activity Management System (LAMS)', paper presented at Computer Assisted Learning: Virtual Learning, Bristol, April 2005.

National Library of Medicine (2006) 'The Visible Human Project'. Online. Available www.nlm.nih.gov/research/visible/visible_human.html (accessed 6 September 2006).

Norman, D. (1999) 'Affordances, conventions and design', *Interactions*, May: 38–43. Online. Available www.jnd.org (accessed 6 September 2006).

Oliver, M. (2006) 'The problems with affordance', *E-Learning*, 2 (4): 402–13.

Papert, S. (1993) *Mindstorms: Children, Computers and Powerful Ideas*, New York: Perseus.

Pask, G. (1988) 'Learning strategies, teaching strategies, and conceptual or learning style', in R. Schmeck (ed.) *Learning Strategies and Learning Styles*, New York: Plenum Press.

Piaget, J. (2001) *The Language and Thought of the Child*, London: Routledge Modern Classics.

Prensky, M. (2001) *Digital Game-based Learning*, New York: McGraw-Hill.

Ramsey, C. (2003) 'Using virtual learning environments to facilitate new relationships', *International Journal of Management Education*, 3 (2): 31–41.

Sharpe, R., Benfield, G., Lessner, E. and de Cicco, E. (2005) *Scoping Study for the Pedagogy strand of the JISC e-Learning Programme,* Bristol: JISC. Online. Available www. jisc.ac.uk/index.cfm?name=elearning_pedagogy (accessed 6 September 2006).

Tergan, S. (1997) 'Misleading theoretical assumptions in hypertext/hypermedia research', *Journal of Educational Multimedia and Hypermedia*, 6 (3–4): 257–83.

Turkle, S. (1995) *Life on the Screen: Identity in the Age of the Internet*, New York: Simon & Schuster.

Vygotsky, L. (1986) *Thought and Language*, Cambridge, MA: MIT Press.

Wegerif, R. (2002) *Thinking Skills, Technology and Learning, Literature Review,* Bristol: FutureLab. Online. Available www.futurelab.org.uk/research/reviews (accessed 6 September 2006).

Wilson, S. (2005) *Can Web Service Technology Really Help Enable 'Coherent Diversity' in E-learning?* Bristol: JISC. Online. Available www.elearning.ac.uk/features/pedagandws/view?searchterm=services%20pedagogy%20Wilson (accessed 29 September 2006).

Chapter 3

Designing courses for e-learning

Rhona Sharpe and Martin Oliver

EDITORS' INTRODUCTION

In the previous chapter, the design of learning activities was located within the wider context of the learning organization and curriculum. This chapter picks up where that chapter left off, at the level of the course and curriculum design. Starting with the generic teaching and learning literature, the authors outline established approaches to course design and go on to discuss the evidence for how these approaches work within e-learning contexts. The chapter emphasizes the power of the transformative course design and presents a series of examples of courses designed for learning, and a set of tools to support practitioners in this task.

Approaches to course design

The idea that technology can help learning begs the question of how that technology should be used. However, the process of course design is complicated, and often remains a private, tacit process. In order to impose some sort of explicit structure onto this practice, researchers have developed a wide selection of models that prescribe how to design courses. Whether formalized as a 'model' or not, most of these focus on rational planning and logical sequencing starting with writing aims and learning outcomes and going on to identifying and sequencing topics, selecting teaching methods and resources, planning assessments and finally, evaluating the design (e.g. Ramsden 1992; D'Andrea 1999; Turner 2002). As discussed in Chapter 2, the learning outcomes are often given as the starting point as they can be used to

- define students' knowledge, understanding, intellectual and subject specific skills at each level;
- clarify the purpose of the course;
- identify and prioritize which topics to teach, and in what depth;
- select appropriate teaching and learning strategies; and
- specify how students demonstrate their learning through purposeful assessment tasks.

Having specified these outcomes with sufficient clarity, practical decisions are then taken about how best to lead learners towards meeting these criteria. One approach has taken these practical concerns and turned them into something more systematic: constructive alignment. John Biggs (1999) coined the term constructive alignment to describe the way that effective teaching strategies deliberately align outcomes, activities and assessment tasks: 'In aligned teaching there is maximum consistency throughout the system . . . . The students are "entrapped" in this web of consistency, optimizing the likelihood that they will engage the appropriate learning activities' (Biggs 1999: 26).

However, Biggs' approach has received criticism. For example, the discussion of learning activity design in Chapter 2 indicates that effective design also takes account of the needs and preferences of individual learners, and of how they participate with others. Others have also raised questions about the appropriateness or even the morality of 'entrapping' learners who are supposed to be mature, responsible and self-directed, particularly given the increasing number of mature students in higher education.

Biggs' work is particularly useful though in highlighting the power of assessment to shape students' experiences. Although unanticipated outcomes frequently occur in learning – and ideally also receive feedback – it is essential that learners receive feedback on their performance in relation to the anticipated outcome. Of course, while an ideal learner is hungry for feedback of any kind, results that contribute to a final assessment are particularly motivating. Paul Ramsden has observed that 'from our students' point of view, assessment always defines the actual curriculum' (Ramsden 1992: 187). Ensuring assessment strategies are constructively aligned with the learning objectives seems to be particularly important in e-learning contexts. Here it is often noted that e-learning resources or activities need to be integrated into the assessment in order to be used regularly be students. For example, Stubbs *et al.* (2006) and Boyle *et al.* (2003) have both aligned blended e-learning activities with the assessment in undergraduate computing courses. Online materials included samples of code that could be assembled to form a working model like the ones the students had to build for their individual assessment. This alignment encouraged the use of the web materials. In the Boyle *et al.* (2003) example, the course design explicitly took a spiral approach where each topic was introduced early and revisited and elaborated on later.

Drawing on the classification of learning theories from Chapter 1, it is possible to see how ideas about how students learn have underpinned course designs for e-learning. Rationales to enhance learning through an associative approach often start with the recognition that there are problem areas either in students' achievement in specific parts of the course or overall course pass levels (see for example the introduction of computer-aided assessment (CAA) introduced to improve pass rates in Box 3.1).

Box 3.1   Computer-aided assessments into an introductory chemistry course

The course team recognized that there was a problem in the course with a 73 per cent overall pass mark and 'weaker students failing to grasp some of the basics of the subject matter and only scraping a pass mark' (Morris and Walker 2006: 1). The students had complained about the time lag for feedback on the eight practical reports and the inconsistency in quality of feedback and grading between the ten markers.

The course was redesigned to include both high and low stakes CAAs. The low stakes assessments were made available for a week, students were allowed unlimited attempts and their best mark was recorded. High stakes assessments were unseen and conducted under examination invigilation conditions in computer labs.

The pass rate improved to 93 per cent and student feedback and analysis of logs identified the low stakes assessments as being critical. Students completed each of the five low stakes assessments on average three or four times and received instant feedback that provided clues to the answer, but not the actual answer.

Student feedback was extremely positive and students identified the multiple attempts with feedback as highly motivating and helpful: 'The ability to re-do tests and assignments again once you have already done it is good. It enables you to continue learning the more you try it' (Morris and Walker 2006: 5).

Reviews of the pedagogic literature in the UK and Australia confirm that constructivism is the dominant model of learning influencing school and post-compulsory education (Cullen *et al.* 2002; Eklund *et al.* 2003). For example, Clark and James (2005) present a coherent rationale for their blended design based on principles of 'guided construction'. They describe the redesign of an introductory soil science module at the University of South Australia. Here weekly online readings with question prompts replaced the course textbook. There were two lectures every week. The first lecture was of a traditional type, at the end of which that week's course readings and questions were released. Students were expected to use the online discussion forum to work collaboratively on their answers before the next lecture, which was run in a question and answer format.

Designs to promote situative learning are most commonly seen in professional and vocational education (see Ellaway, Chapter 12) where courses have a clear rationale to develop the skills, attitudes and behaviours of practitioners in the subject's profession. The professional skills might be quite specific to the discipline, including developing differential diagnosis in veterinarian science (Ellis *et al*. 2005), writing guidelines for users in computing (Oliver 2006), or negotiating and bargaining in world trade economics (Carr *et al*. 2004).

Models guiding course designs

Designing in the context of e-learning raises particular questions about how to incorporate technology into teaching. Diana Laurillard's conversational theory of learning has been influential on thinking about the choice and use of digital technologies for learning. Laurillard (2001) distinguishes five different media 'types' – narrative, productive, interactive, productive and adaptive – with different capacities to mediate learning. The properties of each media are analysed in relation to the conversational framework in order to highlight what elements of the teaching process each supports. Appendix 3 explains and extends this classification system, with suggestions for choosing and using technologies, and an indication of the advantages and disadvantages of digital artefacts in each category.

Laurillard identifies 12 types of interactions essential to learning. These take place within a conversational framework between teacher and student that involves description, adaptation, interaction and reflection. This would translate into the teacher attempting to describe some aspect of the subject and the student attempting to understand, the teacher setting a goal and both interacting and adjusting their actions and reflecting on them in the light of the feedback received.

A first step in choosing appropriate technologies is obviously to know what technology is available – but this is not enough. Mishra and Koehler (2006) point out that knowledge about technology is useless unless it is combined with knowledge about teaching and knowledge about the topic being taught. Good course design, they argue, requires an understanding of how technology is used to produce and share knowledge within the discipline, and then an appreciation of how these technologies can be used in the service of learning and teaching.

Conole and Oliver (2002), however, take a slightly different approach: rather than attribute the technology with the quality of supporting particular forms of learning and teaching, their approach involves requiring practitioners to describe their own uses of technology (giving a situated and provisional account) and then formalizing this, to help them decide whether they are using technology appropriately. No matter what the assumption about technology, however, all of these approaches involve practitioners representing their practice in a way that relates aspects of teaching onto technology use and maps this out over some period of time.

Another influential model within the field of e-learning is Gilly Salmon's model for e-moderating. This splits students' engagement with a course into five stages: access and motivation, online socialization, information exchange, knowledge construction, and development (Salmon 2004). This model has been very widely applied as a way of sequencing activities in courses that rely on collaborative computer-mediated discussions. See Box 3.2 for an example of a course designed according to this model.

Box 3.2 An example of a course designed according to Salmon's five-stage model

The students are postgraduate professionals, studying a blended course part time.

1   *Access and motivation*: Explore the virtual learning environment (VLE) and the course site.
2   *Online socialization*: Get into groups and share tips and advice on how to work collaboratively online.
3   *Information exchange*: Work together in groups to compile an annotated bibliography on one of four topic areas.
4   *Knowledge construction*: Work together in groups to identify an online course or materials of common interest and review them from the perspective of an educational theory or theories.
5   *Development*: Work on your individual assignment, searching the literature and producing an outline plan, and a draft.

(Provided by Sandra Windeatt, University of Northumbria at Newcastle)

Course design in practice

Although we can see that there has been plenty written on how academics ought to design curricula, less attention has been given to how they actually do so (Oliver 2003). Even when design practices are studied, it is inevitably in the context of change and innovation, rather than what might be considered to be 'normal' practice.

When routine curriculum design practice has been examined, the studies reveal the complexity and sensitivity of this part of academic work. Millen (1997), for example, demonstrated how the negotiation of content – such as which readings to put on the reading list – was an important way for academics to express their own professional identity in relation to the 'canon', contested or otherwise, that defined their field of study. Oliver (2003) showed further how academics held multiple notions of what the curriculum was, simultaneously. The simplest of these levels can be described as 'curriculum as syllabus', which was nested within a more sophisticated notion of 'curriculum as map' (relating modules or other teaching events), which in turn was located with a conception of the 'curriculum as plan', which was expressed in terms of ideas such as constructive alignment, discussed earlier.

Yet this was not the final layer; the idea of the planned curriculum was seen as being contained within something else: a hidden curriculum, reflecting the values and politics that surrounded the act of teaching. This social context, which is so important in framing the curriculum, is rarely analysed in higher education, although it has been more extensively studied within schools. Crucial here were issues such as approval by teaching committees (often seen as conservative), the difficulties of innovating on an inherited or co-taught course (especially for junior members of staff; this seemed particularly acutely felt by women) and the potential for 'treading on toes' when choosing what topics to include or exclude from a taught offering.

Additionally, there was a contrary conception of the curriculum, expressed by lecturers as the idea of 'curriculum as space' (or opportunity). Rather than something mechanical or planable, this saw the curriculum as something that was performed; students were provided with opportunities ('spaces'), and the curriculum – the 'lived' curriculum – emerged from the interactions of teachers and students as the course was enacted. This re-conception of the curriculum requires a different emphasis to be taken up when designing courses, highlighting the limits of design and the points at which professional artistry substitutes for mechanical analysis.

Rational models of course planning played no part in the process of course design, although some used them retrospectively to justify what they were doing, particularly if required to do so for a quality audit.

In a recent review of evaluations of blended e-learning implementations, we found that practitioners were often able to be explicit about the rationales for incorporating technology into their course redesigns (Sharpe *et al.* 2006b). Their rationales were overwhelmingly prompted by practical challenges they faced in their teaching, most frequently the implications of large group sizes. For example, Davies *et al.* (2005) introduced technology to the physiotherapy course at the University of Birmingham in response to an almost doubling of student numbers over two years that led to difficulties giving students access to patients. To support the development of observational skills with limited access to patients, the neurology module has introduced video clips of patients in combination with traditional group-based and practical classroom sessions. Over three successive years of course delivery the blend has been refined so that now the video clips are presented through the VLE and are available on CD-ROM. Observational skills are assessed by multiple choice and short answers presented through the VLE.

It is clear that higher education staff are developing a creative range of blended course designs to tackle problems created by large group sizes such as developing learning objects for difficult topics (Boyle *et al.* 2003), offering extension activities for some students (Oliver 2006), creating additional opportunities for feedback (Catley 2004), preparing students for practical work (Davies *et al.* 2005, see Box 3.3), promoting interactivity in class (Boyle and Nicol 2003), and creating opportunities for dialogue in smaller groups (Condron 2001).

Radical course redesign for transformative learning

It has long been recognized that technology needs to be integrated into courses in order for them to have an impact on the student experience (see for example Mason's (1998) framework for three types of online courses: content and support, wrap around, integrated). With the rise in the use of VLEs and the popularity of blended learning, traditionally taught courses are more frequently incorporating technology, and we are finding that it is those courses that have undergone some redesign that are creating sustainable and embedded blended courses. It appears that it is the course redesign process that is crucial for transforming the learning experience.

In our literature review of blended e-learning implementations, we identified transformative course level designs as one of the characterizations of successful blended e-learning (Sharpe *et al*. 2006b). Throughout the review, studies repeatedly identified that engaging in course design or redesign was critical to their success. This was particularly notable where studies described a blended course that had been developed in response to a real and relevant problem at the course level or with very clear design principles set in advance (see Box 3.3).

'Transformative' is a particularly important word in this context because, in spite of the assumptions made in rational planning modules of curriculum development, it is exceptional for a course to be created without drawing on some existing points of reference. Indeed, the majority of course design work could be better described as redesign: updating, replacing, copying and adapting form the basis for most of the curriculum work academics describe themselves as doing (Oliver 2004).

Box 3.3 Creating a coherent blended learning experience

The Emerging Technologies and Issues first year module in the Business School at Manchester Metropolitan University was redesigned to set students' expectations for university study. The course team used clear design principles to make explicit their intended outcomes and to inform the activities and assessment of the course.

One design principle was 'the tutor as expert of last resort'. This was designed in by allowing access to tutors only for those students who had engaged with the online environment. This was reinforced by showing usage data for online materials during the lectures. The students quickly grasped what was expected of them, e.g. 'Don't even bother asking – he knows you haven't had a go yet.' Tutors noted that peer support groups formed and that tutorials were 'intense experiences' of non-trivial problems.

Another design principle was that students engaged regularly. It was felt that routine was important in establishing good study patterns in this first year course. The course team booked ten hours of computer labs each week and scheduled students for one hour each, each week. A tutor was on hand for half an hour with each session. This encouraged students to work on their assignments regularly.

Described in full in Stubbs *et al*. (2006)

The process of course redesign

If it is the process of course design, or more accurately, redesign, that has the power to transform the student experience, then it is worth looking at the process more carefully. There are a number of studies that have helpfully described what their course design involved and which features they considered contributed to their success (see for example Box 3.4).

Studies of courses that have been designed to incorporate technology, highlight the following elements of their design as important to their success:

- Analysing the successful and less successful features of the current course, including student feedback (Boyle 2005). For example, Morris and Walker (2006) engaged in an honest appraisal of the current course identifying problems and targeting their use of technology in response to this (see Box 3.1). Stubbs *et al.* (2006: 174) conclude from their evaluation of such a radical redesign that evaluation should be improved through 'careful study of rich, longitudinal data'. An example of a tool to promote review of a current course is provided in Appendix 5.
- Undertaking the design as a team, ensuring that staff have the time to properly integrate face-to-face and online material (Aycock *et al.* 2002; Sharpe *et al.*

Box 3.4 The course redesign intensive at Oxford Brookes University

Teams of staff undertaking projects identified as being strategically important to their school are invited to come on the two-day course redesign intensive experience. These expanded course teams included their learning technologist and e-learning champion. The two-day event allows the programme team to work on their redesign with additional support and resources on hand in the form of learning technologists, educational developers and other innovators. The aim is to bring additional development resources into the picture for a team in a concentrated way to get a quick result. By the end of the day teams will have designed the basic structure of an online course for delivery in the institutional VLE and developed an action plan for development of the project.

This event recognizes that e-learning courses do need high levels of planning. Course teams are taken through a guided planning process supported by such tools as course design checklist (Appendix 5), prompts for blue skies thinking, storyboarding, risk assessment, and culminating in a questioning consultation with critical friends (see Appendix 6).

Described in full in Sharpe *et al.* (2006a)

2006a) such as by allowing staff to develop only part of a module in depth (Boyle *et al.* 2003).

- Designs that make explicit their underlying principles. These might be based on established pedagogical principles such as being sensitive to the needs of learners as individuals (Graff 2003), active learning (Hinterberger *et al.* 2004), repetition and elaboration (Boyle *et al.* 2003), the requirement for prompt and frequent feedback (Morris and Walker 2006) or design principles related to the course outcomes e.g. 'attention to detail' (Stubbs *et al.* 2006).
- Developing the course iteratively over a number of years. Studies that discussed course design as a success factor suggest that as many as three or four iterations of course design, development and implementation may be needed to complete the transition from traditional to blended e-learning course (Danchak and Huguet 2004; Ellem and McLaughlin 2005; Trevitt 2005).

Conclusions

E-learning is often talked about as a 'trojan mouse', which teachers let into their practice without realizing that it will require them to rethink not just how they use particular hardware or software, but all of what they do. This is clearly the case in course design. As has been shown in this chapter, to incorporate technology successfully requires the purpose of the course to be negotiated and made explicit. This process prompts reflection, negotiation and adaptation in what has, traditionally, been a private and tacit area of work.

This ongoing process of negotiation and re-negotiation, as designs are shared and evolve, reveals why the 'one off' processes of rational course design have been so problematic. However, this does not diminish the potential they have when reviewing existing courses or acting as a spur to further discussions. It does, however, suggest that attempts to follow these approaches in a simple, formulaic manner are unlikely to be successful.

Equally unsuccessful are those courses that simply treat technology as a 'bolt on', attempting to use it alongside everything that went before. Instead, the most productive approach involves an ongoing attempt to accommodate technology into a course, with continued discussion about its purposes and ethos, and the purposes that each form of teaching serves. This ongoing, transformative engagement with teaching serves a double purpose: it guides the use of technology, but at least as important, it provides academics with the incentive to reflect upon their teaching and learn from the problems that technology adoption can create.

Acknowledgements

Parts of this chapter have appeared previously in Sharpe *et al.* (2006b): a review of UK literature and practice undertaken for the Higher Education Academy and are reproduced here with permission.

References

Aycock, A., Garnham, C. and Kaleta, R. (2002) 'Lessons learned from the hybrid course project', *Teaching with Technology Today*, 8. Online. Available www.uwsa. edu/ttt/articles/garnham2.htm (accessed 25 August 2006).

Biggs, J. (1999) *Teaching for Quality Learning at University*, Buckingham: The Society for Research into Higher Education and Open University Press.

Boyle, J.T. and Nicol, D.J. (2003) 'Using classroom communication systems to support interaction and discussion in large class settings', *ALT-J, Research in Learning Technology*, 11 (3): 43–57.

Boyle, T. (2005) 'A dynamic, systematic method for developing blended learning', *Education, Communication and Information*, 5 (3): 221–32.

Boyle, T., Bradley, C., Chalk, P., Jones, R. and Pickard, P. (2003) 'Using blended learning to improve student success rates in learning to program', *Journal of Educational Media*, 28 (2–3): 165–78.

Carr, T., Cox, G., Eden, A. and Hanslo, M. (2004) 'From peripheral to full participation in a blended trade bargaining situation', *British Journal of Educational Technology*, 35 (2): 197–211.

Catley, P. (2004) 'One lecturer's experience of blending e-learning with traditional teaching or how to improve retention and progression by engaging students', *Brookes eJournal of Learning and Teaching*, 1 (2). Online. Available www.brookes.ac.uk/publications/bejlt/volume1issue2/academic/catley05_1.html! (accessed 25 August 2006).

Clark, I. and James, P. (2005) 'Blended learning: an approach to delivering science courses on-line', *UniServe Science Blended Learning Symposium Proceedings*. Online. Available http://science.uniserve.edu.au/pubs/procs/wshop10/index.html (accessed 25 August 2006).

Condron, F. (2001) 'Using electronic resources to support dialogue in undergraduate small-group teaching: the Aster project', *ALT-J, Research in Learning Technology*, 9 (2): 39–46.

Conole, G. and Oliver, M. (2002) 'Embedding theory into learning technology practice with toolkits', *Journal of Interactive Media in Education*. Online. Available www-jime. open.ac.uk/2002/8 (accessed 25 August 2006).

Cullen, J., Hadjivassiliou, K., Hamilton, E., Kelleher, J., Sommerlad, E. and Stern, E. (2002) 'Review of current pedagogic research and practice in the fields of post-compulsory education and lifelong learning', London: The Tavistock Institute. Online. Available www.tlrp.org/pub/acadpub/Tavistockreport.pdf (accessed 30 March 2006).

Danchak, M. and Huguet, M.P. (2004) 'Designing for the changing role of the instructor in blended learning', *IEEE Transactions on Professional Communication*, 47 (3): 200–10.

D'Andrea, V. (1999) 'Organizing teaching and learning: outcomes based planning', in H. Fry, S. Ketteridge and S. Marshall (eds) *A Handbook for Teaching and Learning in Higher Education*, London: Kogan Page, pp. 41–57.

Davies, A., Ramsay, J., Lindfield, H. and Couperthwaite, J. (2005) 'A blended approach to learning: added value and lesson learnt from students' use of computer-based materials for neurological analysis', *British Journal of Educational Technology*, 36 (5): 839–49.

Eklund, J., Kay, M. and Lynch, H. (2003) *E-learning: Emerging Issues and Key Trends*, Australian National Training Authority. Online. Available www.flexiblelearning.net.au/flx/webdav/site/flxsite/users/kjohnson/public/elearning250903final.pdf (accessed 25 August 2006)

Ellem, G.K. and McLaughlin, E.A. (2005) 'Tales from the coalface: from tragedy to triumph in a blended learning approach to the teaching of 1st year biology', *UniServe Science Blended Learning Symposium Proceedings*, University of Sydney, Australia. Online.

Available http://science.uniserve.edu.au/workshop/2005/index.html (accessed 25 August 2006).

Ellis, R.A., Marcus, G. and Taylor, R. (2005) 'Learning through inquiry: student difficulties with online course-based material', *Journal of Computer Assisted Learning*, 21: 239–52.

Graff, M. (2003) 'Individual differences in sense of classroom community in a blended learning environment', *Journal of Educational Media*, 28 (2–3): 203–10.

Hinterberger, H., Fässler, L. and Bauer-Messmer, B. (2004) 'From hybrid courses to blended learning: a case study', Proceedings of the International Conference on New Educational Environments, Neuchâtel, Switzerland, 27–30 September 2004.

Laurillard, D. (2001) *Rethinking University Teaching*, 2nd edn, London: RoutledgeFalmer.

Mason, R. (1998) 'Models of online courses', *Asynchronous Learning Networks Magazine*, 2 (2). Online. Available www.aln.org/alnweb/magazine/vol2_issue2/Masonfinal.htm (accessed 9 October 2006).

Millen, J. (1997) 'Par for the course: designing course outlines and feminist freedoms', *Curriculum Studies*, 5 (1): 9–27.

Mishra, P. and Koehler, M. (2006) 'Technological pedagogical content knowledge: a framework for teacher knowledge', *Teachers College Record*, 108 (6): 1017–54.

Morris, L. and Walker, D. (2006) 'CAA sparks chemical reaction: integrating CAA into a learning and teaching strategy', in *Flexible Delivery: Evaluation of the use of the virtual learning environment in higher education across Scotland*, The Quality Assurance Agency for Higher Education, Scotland. Online. Available www.enhancementthemes.ac.uk/documents/flexibleDelivery/Flexible_delivery_QAA_128.pdf (accessed 9 October 2006)

Oliver, M. (2003) 'Curriculum design as acquired social practice: a case study', paper presented at the 84th Annual Meeting of the American Educational Research Association, Chicago.

Oliver, M. (2004) 'Effective support for e-learning within institutions', unpublished project report, JISC practitioners research study project. Online. Available www.jisc.ac.uk/uploaded_documents/Effective%20support%20instit%20v2_Martin_Oliver.doc (accessed 9 October 2006).

Oliver, R. (2006) 'Exploring a technology-facilitated solution to cater for advanced students in large undergraduate classes', *Journal of Computer Assisted Learning*, 22 (1): 1–12.

Ramsden, P. (1992) *Learning to Teach in Higher Education*, London: Routledge.

Salmon, G. (2004) *E-moderating: The Key to Teaching and Learning Online*, 2nd edn, London: RoutledgeFarmer.

Sharpe, R., Benfield, G. and Francis, R. (2006a) 'Implementing a university e-learning strategy: levers for change within academic schools', *ALT-J, Research in Learning Technology*, 14 (2): 135–51.

Sharpe, R., Benfield, G., Roberts, G. and Francis, R. (2006b) 'The undergraduate experience of blended e-learning: a review of UK literature and practice undertaken for the Higher Education Academy'. Online. Available www.heacademy.ac.uk/4884.htm (accessed 9 October 2006).

Stubbs, M., Martin, I. and Endlar, L. (2006) 'The structuration of blending learning: putting holistic design principles into practice', *British Journal of Educational Technology*, 37 (2): 163–75.

Trevitt, C. (2005) 'Universities learning to learn? Inventing flexible (e)learning through first- and second-order action research', *Educational Action Research*, 13 (1): 57–83.

Turner, D. (2002) *Designing and Delivering Modules*, Oxford: Oxford Centre for Staff and Learning Development.

Chapter 4

Practices and processes of design for learning

Liz Masterman and Mira Vogel

EDITORS' INTRODUCTION

The previous two chapters looked at how educational theory and research have been applied to educational design, and put forward an updated approach for a context in which digital and mobile technologies are widely available. This chapter looks at current practice: what practitioners really do, or say they do, when they undertake design for learning at either the course or session level. The authors consider evidence from three research projects involving UK practitioners in further, higher and adult education and raise a series of provocative questions about how – and whether – the available technologies can really support effective pedagogic practice.

Introduction

In this chapter we draw together research from three projects in the Learning Design strand of JISC's e-Learning and Pedagogy programme, which focused on the tools used by teaching staff in the practice and process of design for learning. For the purposes of this chapter, we synthesize their findings in order to answer four questions in turn:

1 What are the key elements in the task of design for learning, how do they vary among practitioners, and how do they map to tool use?
2 To what extent is it possible to represent a learning design within a particular tool?
3 Which socio-cultural factors influence individual practice in design for learning?
4 What evidence is uncovered by these projects regarding the impact, real or potential, of the use of learning design tools on practitioners' underlying pedagogical approach?

The nature of our research – capturing a process which is often tacit ('in the head'), incremental and distributed – posed challenges vis-à-vis appropriate methodologies and, through the methods adopted, raised issues regarding the wider applicability of our findings. The account of these findings is followed by a reflection on the contribution of our work to the domain of design for learning.

Overview of projects

The projects, funded through JISC's e-Learning programme, shared a common aim: namely, to understand design practices in order to broaden the community's understanding of 'effective practice' in design for learning (JISC 2004), to inform the packaging and sharing of designs, and to elicit requirements for future learning design systems.

The Learning Design Tools Project: An Evaluation of Generic Tools Used in Design for Learning (Masterman 2006). The principal aim of the 'LD tools project' was to gather research-based information on post-compulsory practitioners' use of generic tools (e.g. word processing, presentation tools and mind-mapping software) in designing for learning: specifically, to identify the key elements of the task of learning activity authoring (LAA) that emerged in the task of planning an individual learning session. We explored how these may vary among practitioners, what tool(s) they use and how introducing a new tool might affect their pedagogy. Information was gathered through an online questionnaire and from interviews and lesson plans collected at specially convened workshops.

Evaluation of the Practitioner Trial of LAMS (Masterman and Lee 2005a). Our remit in the 'LAMS evaluation' was to investigate its acceptability to practition-ers as an activity-based tool for post-compulsory learning. The Learning Activity Management System (LAMS) is considered to represent the emergent generation of online managed learning environments (see James Dalziel, Chapter 15). Data were primarily collected from questionnaires and interviews.

Design for Learning in Virtual Learning Environments: Insider Perspectives (Vogel and Oliver 2006). The 'VLE project' explored the practice of designing and representing learning activities in virtual learning environments (VLEs). It aimed to enrich our understanding of the relationship between the educational role of a VLE (as opposed to its administrative function) and the context in which it is used. Data were collected from questionnaires, VLE course areas and interviews with e-learning leads, teachers and learners from a range of subject areas and post-compulsory settings.

Elements and tools in the task of design for learning

In considering the task of designing for learning, the LADIE Reference Model project distinguishes between LAA – 'the design and construction of learning activities and the discovery, specification, sequencing and packaging of content' – and learning activity realization (LAR) – 'the construction of the environ-ment in which learning activities are to take place and execution of the learning activities themselves' (LADIE 2005). This is, of course, an artificially rigid distinction, as we uncovered several instances of elision and overlap in the LD tools project (Masterman 2006). For example, within LAA, some practitioners start with pre-defined learning outcomes, while others structure their plan around a set of activities negotiated with their learners. Practitioners may also take different routes through the task, some mapping out learning materials while creating the plan and others creating all such learning materials afterwards. Ultimately, LAA can never be wholly dissociated from LAR, since a plan may need to be adapted 'on the fly' in response to contingencies that arise during the learning session, or a review may lead to components of the plan being added, modified or dropped.

The LD tools project also uncovered some evidence of separation in the use of generic tools: 'I made a sketch of concepts on paper. Wrote the lecture notes in Word. Then created the PowerPoint slides. Finally created the Web pages to make the notes, slides available to the students' (Masterman 2006: 15).

However, elision emerged strongly in the use of, for example, PowerPoint, which can function as both a design (sequencing) and presentation tool:

> I start with the summary slide (learning outcomes); I then build each outcome outwards. [S]lide sorter is used to shuffle them as needed or when it comes to customising to a different audience or to change it from level 2 to 3 or 4 or downwards.
>
> (Questionnaire response from tutor in Business Studies)

Elision can thus be viewed as an affordance of the tool, as well as a matter of individual approach. This affordance becomes more apparent as we move into the sphere of 'dedicated' e-learning tools, where LAA can continue even during LAR, or LAR can be 'rehearsed' as part of LAA (as in LAMS' Preview feature). The VLE project suggested that, as both design and delivery medium, VLEs invite this elision. As one participant, a lecturer in Management Studies, observed: 'The site doesn't stand still.'

Beyond the obvious convenience of using the same tool to author and realize a learning activity, what are the ramifications of this elision? Where a tool leaves each activity editable by the teacher – and, in the case of LAMS, learners – the design-for-learning space can remain open, allowing the design to evolve incrementally, continuously and reactively during and between learning sessions. Changes can then be saved into the learning design and carried forward to realization with the next cohort of learners.

Representing learning designs

Where planning constitutes a discrete activity within design for learning, it is often characterized by the successive production of a number of representations of all or part of a given learning experience. The LD tools project yielded a number of such artefacts, including draft sketches (textual and/or graphical), the completed course outline/lesson plan, and materials for learners such as reading lists, worksheets and online activities. The product of the design task, the learning design, is thus a 'dispersed' representation in the sense that it is spread over several of separate artefacts, although the gestalt may be summarized in a specification such as a course map or lesson plan. The LD tools project captured several examples of lesson plans: typically, tabular representations laid out in a format specified by the department or institution (see Figure 4.1).

However, where no view of the gestalt is constructed by the designer, the representation may be fragmented. For example, the VLE project illustrated how learning designs – even those for activities intended for within the VLE – are often either only partially represented or not represented at all in a form discernible by the outsider. Practitioners may even rely in part on ephemeral representations constructed during the learning session itself, such as spoken instructions delivered by the teacher to relate or sequence VLE elements for the benefit of the learners:

> I have a tendency to plan everything in my head. I . . . know what my objectives are, know what I'm trying to achieve and know how I'm going to do it . . . and I tend not to favour detailed schemes of work.
>
> (Vogel and Oliver 2006: 25)

Gloscat

Lesson Plan

Course: Parents in IT Action	**Module/unit:** Word		No of students: 8 - 10	Background information on students: Parents of Year 1 and Year 2 children at the school. Most have completed a FLNN course in Literacy.
Term: Summer 05	**Week:** 4	**Date:** 30 June 2005		
Time From.....9.15................ to ......11.15.................				

Essential / basic skills	IT	Communications/Literacy	Application of number/Numeracy
	Evidence ☐ Opportunity to develop ☐	Evidence ☐ Opportunity to develop ☐	Evidence ☐ Opportunity to develop ☐

Aim of the session
Completion of pictures and text for story books
Introduction to proofreadi
Objectives: By the end o
Must
State one feature of a para
Order text using linking w
Write sentences in story
Should
State 3 common errors me
Spot errors in given text
Could
Proofread own text
Write in paragraphs

Time	Topic / Activity	Teaching and learning activities (Remember to sign-post differentiation) Tutor / Student	Learning outcomes (students will be able to.....)	Assessment	Resources
9.15	Welcome and register	T – take register – collect in paragraph work for marking. Ask learners to work on learning logs.	Open and edit existing document Save existing document		Learning log on disc
9.25	Aims and Objectives of Session	T – to outline aims and objectives for session	State aims and objectives for session		Objectives handout Whiteboard
9.30	Recap on session 3	Learners to update tutor on previous week's session – lead into paragraphs – work at home completed? Each learner to contribute one feature of a paragraph. Tutor to record on whiteboard	State at least one key feature of a paragraph	Group recap	Whiteboard
9.40	Paragraphs – linking words	Discuss bathtime story again – are there any linking words to lead into next paragraph. Hand out laminated story (Pacemaker) – learners in pairs to put into correct order.	Order text into paragraphs using linking words as clues	Laminated/cut text exercise Group discussion – how did you know?	http://www.bbc.co.uk/skillswise/yourstories/2005/june/story_four.shtml
9.55	Storybook	Learners to continue work on Story books – creating total of 4/5 pages with pictures and simple text.	Use shapes and text boxes in publisher to create simple story book	Creation of story	
10.10	BREAK				

Figure 4.1 Lesson plan laid out in tabular format, showing aims and objectives of the session as a whole, as well as the timings, intended learning outcomes, assessment methods and resources for individual activities

Source: Reproduced by kind permission of Gloscat.

Without this explanatory commentary, a VLE course area may appear opaque to the outsider and give the impression of a 'design-less' repository of content, rather than a cohesive set of core resources and a highly structured and effective sequence of learning activities.

We have focused on the dispersal and fragmentation of learning designs, since they impinge on a key concern in design for learning: namely, the dissemination of effective practice through sharing not just individual resources (e.g. images, texts or activities) but also complete learning designs (as on the LAMS Community website (n.d.)). The issues at stake are threefold: whether the different representations that comprise the learning design are made available to the outsider (dispersal), the form chosen for representing the design, and what aspects of the design have been represented or, conversely, omitted (fragmentation). Collectively, they beg the question whether it is possible for a practitioner to apprehend a learning design authored by someone else sufficiently to decide on its reusability within his or her own context. We refer to this as the issue of 'manifestation'. A learning design that is represented in a relatively complete and explicit manner is said to be highly manifest; conversely, a fragmented or impenetrable design is said to be opaque (see Figure 4.2).

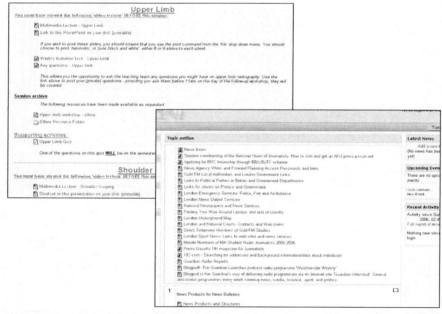

Figure 4.2 Degrees of design manifestation in hypothetical VLE course areas. Note the contrast between the explicit relationships between elements in the upper example – expressed in notation, special organization, colour-coding and repeating structure – and the undifferentiated listing in the lower example

Bringing together (packaging) the various components of a learning design into the same physical or virtual space is probably the most tractable of the manifestation issues. An example is the LAMS Community website (n.d.), where the requisite learning materials can be downloaded along with the learning design itself.

VLE areas offer another solution to dispersed representation; however, they can also impede other aspects of manifestation. For the outside observer (who may in fact be a learner), the degree to which a given VLE course area manifests the course or session can be unclear, and few of the participants in the VLE project had provided a gestalt representation. Yet – and here we move on to the issue of representational forms – in order to be apprehended, a design must show not only the components of a learning experience (e.g. resources, activities and instructions) but also the relationships between them: sequential, conditional, thematic etc. Conversely, it must also represent the absence of relationships between elements so that learners do not make incorrect inferences about them.

If the nature of relationships is not made explicit in the representational notation, then the learner must rely on conventions to interpret a given form, together with any prior knowledge that they have of the domain. Hence, the linear display of elements within a VLE area might imply an ordering that corresponds to the sequence in which learners must work through them, when in fact the order in which they appear may simply be a function of the order in which they were uploaded to the VLE. Using icons, colour-coding and spatial organization to signal relationships, as well as text annotation, can go some way to alleviate this problem. In this respect, it is unsurprising that participants in the LAMS evaluation cited as one of its most appealing features the graphical representation of the activity sequence and the ability 'to visualise activities required by a learning process and their relationships' (questionnaire response from learning technologist). Moreover, interview data from the LD tools project workshops suggest that it might even be advantageous to provide multiple perspectives on a learning design through alternative representations or 'views': say, to indicate learners' possible paths through activities or to highlight the 'mix' of activities (e.g. the balance between reading and discussion).

As we have seen, the fragmented representation of the learning design primarily affects blended VLE-supported courses where the offline, teacher-mediated, components are 'represented' as gaps in the VLE area. Although it may be possible to infer their presence through apparent discontinuities between online components, the observer remains in the dark about their structure and content. This has obvious implications for sharing. However, to insist that teachers explicitly represent every aspect of their learning design just so that other teachers can make an informed decision about the potential for reusing it is to impose an additional burden with no obvious personal benefit (Masterman and Lee 2005b). Little evidence emerged of an urge in teachers to share whole designs – either giving or receiving.

Collaboration and community aspects of design for learning

Data from the LD tools project on 'routine' practice suggest that LAA is frequently a collaborative activity, primarily between fellow practitioners but also between practitioners and learners. Three broad patterns of collaboration were identified: team-teaching; teaching different topics of the same course or teaching the same topic/course to separate cohorts and planning together; and teaching the same topic/course to separate cohorts but planning separately.

Some teams have a definite leader, while others negotiate the different responsibilities in a democratic manner: 'I meet with colleagues (telephone/F2F, email), establish the bottom-line objective, brainstorm a pathway to it, sketching on pencil and paper, or in Word/email as we go, agree who's doing what' (Masterman 2006: 21).

Collaboration can also provide opportunities for staff development: 'sometimes I delegate to help my colleagues to develop new skills' (ibid.).

The collaboration process itself may range from the highly structured: '1 Set up a course team; 2 arrange planning meeting; 3 use flipchart + notes or mind map; 4 allocate tasks; 5 email plans or put on collaborative site – Moodle' (ibid.) to the decidedly informal: 'We just sit down with a beer and think it over . . . there is no need to think about who decides what as we work together pretty well' (ibid.).

In contrast to the LD tools project participants, nearly all tutors participating in the VLE project reported being sole designers of their VLE area (and this is probably a factor in their opacity). Where present, imported designs constituted only a small proportion of a course area, and there was little indication that tutors perceived a need to make use of each other's designs.

Nevertheless, even when carried out in isolation, designing for learning is an inherently social act. Every teacher is part of at least one community, whether this is formally constituted (e.g. an institution or special interest group) or an informal grouping of people who share a common interest. Communities can overlap (in that someone may belong to both a university department and a society for subject-specialists), or be nested within each other (e.g. a department within an institution). They may be long-lived (as in colleges and universities) or convene for a short time only (e.g. a workshop to share effective practice).

Together, communities constitute the socio-cultural context in which designs for learning are created: for example, how they are prescribed (curriculum planning bodies), carried out (practitioners), enabled (support staff) or promoted ('communities of practice'). A panoply of policies, strategies, conventions, procedures, guidelines and norms – whether ratified or tacitly agreed – can be formulated by different groups within the community (or supra-community organizations such as governments) for different purposes. Within an institution, they may include curriculum planning and operational concerns such as timetabling, booking procedures for information technology (IT) facilities, software purchasing policies and student attendance. On the broader plane, they may extend to national information and communication technology (ICT) strategies, which will themselves impact on institutional practices. Regardless of their scope, their primary effect is to act as constraints on the educational practice design for learning, where 'constraint' is interpreted as the conditions necessary for successful accomplishment of the activity (cf. Greeno 1994). Some of these constraints may appear restrictive: for example, where an institution limits the tools available to practitioners on cost grounds. Other constraints may be seen as 'enabling': for example, the guidelines presented in the booklet *Effective Practice with E-learning* (JISC 2004).

The impact of learning design tools on pedagogy

Many online managed learning environments now include activities such as reflective journals or discussion forums that encourage students to be active agents in their own learning through engaging in independent and/or collaborative activities. In this they appear to foster a social-constructive model of learning that stands in contrast to the didactic, knowledge-transmission model exemplified by the traditional 50-minute university lecture.

Articulated from a Vygotskyan perspective on the mediational role of tools in human actions, this shift in models suggests that introducing a new tool has the potential to change the structure of the learning activity (cf. Vygotsky 1981a; 1981b; Säljö 1996). However, when investigating the impact of new tools on the practice of design for learning (and, in particular, looking for evidence of a move towards social constructivism) we must guard against the presupposition that, abstracted from the mechanics of the task, 'e-design for learning' differs radically from 'low-tech' design for learning, that change is necessarily concomitant with technological innovation, or that the new status quo is always superior to the preceding one.

There were few grounds for explicitly associating the use of LAMS with a shift in practitioners' underlying pedagogical approach. True one LAMS user commented that the range of activities available in LAMS 'made me question my use of pedagogy – was I wanting them to chat, or complete a poll?' (Masterman and Lee 2005a: 32) and another noted 'I think it has made me want to be less instructivist' (ibid.). However, a third person actually confessed that '[t]he ease of authoring probably encouraged me towards an excessively didactic/instructivist style that isn't really consistent with the aims of LAMS or good practice generally' (questionnaire response from university lecturer in Bioinformatics). An analysis of the project's 14 LAMS sequences showed a willingness to include discussion and idea-sharing activities (present in 13 sequences), but some reticence about allowing learners to pool web-based resources (present in 5 sequences only). However, with no comparison of previous practice and no follow-up investigation, it was impossible to determine whether these 'social-constructive' activities constituted a fundamental and lasting change in approach.

Several VLE project participants did not consider that their pedagogies had been revised through VLE use. One participant was adamant that 'I do it my own way, however I want to do it. And I . . . exploit the tools that suit me and ignore the ones that don't' (Vogel and Oliver 2006: 22), while another said that it had influenced his course but in a way 'convergent' with his existing aims (ibid.). A third (a course leader in Health and Social Care) likened his initial reaction to a 'child in a sweet shop', setting up activities just because the tools to do so existed. Even so, after this initial experimental phase conservatism set in, and he later advised peers to use the VLE as it fitted in with their existing practice.

However, further analysis suggests that VLEs might indeed have an impact on pedagogy, but that it might be an unconscious one emerging from the phenomenon of 'design blindness', or the unconscious restriction of e-learning to the scope of one's tool. This was demonstrated when a number of participants replied to a question about the approach they would adopt if their VLE were to be withdrawn by stating that they would revert to their previous methods. Thus, they seemed to overlook or ignore the possibility of finding and using other tools to recreate VLE experiences outside the VLE. This led the research team to conclude that the introduction of a VLE may indeed change teachers' approaches to design for learning, but that where they are not highly aware of or reflective about the nature of these changes, the innovations do not become embedded in their practice.

On reflection, it may be inapposite to look for a wholesale shift in practitioners' fundamental approach to designing for learning, for two principal reasons. First, change may occur through the step-wise adoption of new activities, which individually may not signify much but which, if sustained over time and accompanied by critical reflection on the part of the practitioner, might add up to a seismic shift in their pedagogy. Second, it may be a question of the wrong emphasis. Rather than shoe-horn observed designs into some 'desired' model of learning, we should identify and congratulate those pioneering practitioners who either intrepidly experiment with promising but untried technologies (as did participants in the LAMS evaluation) or use current tools in unconventional and creative ways (as some participants in the VLE project and LD tools project did). They are what Helen Beetham, reflecting the notion of 'agile development' in the Learning Design community (Agile Alliance n.d.; Oliver 2005), has called 'agile adopters', simultaneously well grounded in existing practice and alive to experimentation with the new technologies, and propagating these among their peers. In this way, carrying out exploratory, interpretative research with a non-random, or self-selected, sample can be turned to very real practical advantage.

Implications and conclusions

Our research into the practices and process of design for learning has painted a complex, composite picture that has as much to do with the dispositions and preferences of individual practitioners, their subject domains and the community pressures on them as with the availability and affordances of the tools used. This resonates with Oliver's characterization of curriculum design as 'a social practice that involves orientation to historical precedents, accessible resources [and] local values' (Oliver 2002: 13–14), rather than one that is governed by a 'rationalistic and linear' model (Oliver 2003: 23).

In considering the implications of their findings, all three projects thus faced a challenge common to much applied social research: namely to explain – or, at the very least, interpret – a given social reality without imposing models that attempt to 'reduce the business of explanation to drawing causal references' (Pawson and Tilley 1997: 69). Therefore, we did not assume that our work to would lead to a definitive understanding of the phenomena under scrutiny; rather, we expected to uncover a multifaceted working truth that reveals practical issues for decision-makers as well as avenues for further investigation by the research community. In these concluding reflections, therefore, we highlight the key outcomes of our projects in terms of their common threefold aims: furthering the understanding of effective practice, informing the packaging and sharing of learning designs, and eliciting requirements for future learning design systems.

Since practice is so heavily bound to context, all three projects were reticent about prescribing what does and does not constitute 'effective practice' in design for learning. The LAMS evaluation tackled this problem by synthesizing its findings into a set of conditions that appear to be conducive to a positive LAMS-mediated teaching and learning experience. These include willingness on the part of teachers to experiment, an in-depth knowledge of their students, creativity in identifying opportunities to broaden their approach and, on the part of the students, readiness to profit from those new opportunities.

Acknowledging that their findings did not support a 'one-size-fits-all' model of tool usage, but mindful of the requirement to provide recommendations of more general applicability, the LD tools project researchers put forward a framework derived by integrating Activity Theory (Leont'ev 1981) with a cognitive perspective on representation (Peterson 1996). This framework was intended to assist stake-holders in evaluating the potential for different tools within their own contexts and thereby derive their own recommendations. It included considerations such as the selection of tools according to their suitability both to the individual practitioner and the task, institutional encouragement for agile adopters, and the fostering of communities to disseminate effective practice.

The VLE project expressed its findings vis-à-vis effective practice in the form of a model for putting a VLE in place and a description of the aspects of designing for learning in VLEs. Nevertheless, although the participating teachers had been recommended by their institutions' e-learning leads for their exemplary practice, this practice remained difficult to understand, largely because of the incremental development of most course areas (involving decisions that can be difficult to rationalize in retrospect) and the dispersal and fragmentation of representations.

Highly manifest learning designs are not merely a researcher's desiderata, they are integral to the second of our considerations: the packaging and sharing of learning designs. Sharing and reuse can be a valid response to lack of time and resources on the part of teachers but only where they genuinely add value to the experience of learners and are acceptable to teachers themselves. For the 'sharing' teacher, this means having tools for creating a learning design that is simultaneously pedagogically effective in their own context and, with minimal additional effort on their part, can be represented in a form that readily permits others to decide on its suitability for their context. For the 'reusing' teacher, it means not only being able to find and adapt learning designs as efficiently as developing their own, it also raises the fundamental question of how to preserve the creative dimension of designing for learning: namely, that continuous, reflective, evolution of a design which arguably risks being overlooked in the increasing formalization of reuse through 'top-down' initiatives.

If, as Engeström (1999) among others argues, the creative act, rather than the *product* of that act, is the key to an individual's development, then there is a deep-rooted need to continue to offer formative opportunities for individual teachers. In rapidly evolving domains (such as medicine and IT) that require teachers to keep abreast of developments, the iterative design of learning activities can promote the advancement of teachers' own knowledge. Thus, although both the authoring and realization of learning activities can be construed as creative acts, it is essential to afford teachers the same constructivist opportunities we value for learners, by eschewing the division of labour into those who 'author' and those who 'realize' (indeed, we have already suggested that the two activities are not wholly separable), and promoting agile adoption.

Finally, in relation to requirements for future learning design systems, although the LAMS evaluation and LD tools project yielded a number of concrete recommendations, we choose here to present two, more durable, issues for consideration by the learning design community. The first is the extent to which a particular theory of learning can – or should – be embedded in a learning design tool. For example, although LAMS is lauded for supporting structured collaborative learning experiences, it lends itself equally to the design of 'instructivist' sequences for individual study, as we noted earlier, and such approaches may be valid in certain settings. Conversely, VLEs that may have started out as 'pedagogically neutral' (assuming such a stance is tenable!) repositories of content now include support for both reflective and social-constructive learning.

The second issue, epitomized in the 'Learning Design'/'design for learning' dichotomy, is the relationship between current observed practice and the IMS Learning Design specification as implemented in the emergent generation of learning design tools. To what extent should teachers 'bend' their practice to comply with the standards embodied in the technology? To what extent should they become conversant with that technology? How can technology accommodate the spontaneous irruptions that can send the most meticulously planned learning session into unexpected, and fruitful, directions? Are technology and pedagogy the opposite poles of a continuum or are they, as Wilbert Kraan argues, 'windows onto the same thing' (Kraan 2006)? The debate is set to be keen and productive, both within the pages of this book and, we hope, beyond.

References

Agile Alliance (n.d.) *Principles of Agile Software*. Online. Available www.agilemanifesto. org/principles.html (accessed 21 January 2007).

Engeström, Y. (1999) *Learning by Expanding: An Activity-Theoretical Approach to Developmental Research*. Online. Available http://lchc.ucsd.edu/mca/paper/engestrom/expanding/toc.htm (accessed 21 January 2007).

Greeno, J.G. (1994) 'Gibson's affordances', *Psychological Review*, 101 (2): 336–42.

JISC (2004) *Effective Practice with E-learning*, JISC: Bristol. Online. Available www.jisc.ac.uk/uploaded_documents/jisc%20effective%20practice3.pdf (accessed 22 August 2006).

Kraan, W. (2006) Contribution to the initial meeting of the JISC Design for Learning programme, University of Aston, May 2006.

LADIE (2005) *LADIE*, The E-learning Framework. Online. Available www.elframework.org/refmodels/ladie (accessed 22 August 2006).

LAMS Community web site (n.d.) *Welcome to the LAMS Community*. Online. Available www.lamscommunity.org (accessed 22 August 2006).

Leont'ev, A.N. (1981) 'The problem of activity in psychology', in J.V. Wertsch (ed.) *The Concept of Activity in Soviet Psychology*, Armonk, NY: M.E. Sharpe.

Masterman, L. (2006) *The Learning Design Tools Project: An Evaluation of Generic Tools Used in Design for Learning*. Online. Available www.jisc.ac.uk/uploaded_documents/LD%20Tools%20Report%20v1.1.pdf (accessed 22 August 2006).

Masterman, L. and Lee, S. (2005a) *Evaluation of the Practitioner Trial of LAMS: Final Report*. Online. Available www.jisc.ac.uk/uploaded_documents/LAMS%20Final%20Report.pdf (accessed 22 August 2006).

Masterman, L. and Lee, S. (2005b) *Reusing Learning Materials in English Literature and Language: Perspectives from Three Universities*, Egham, Surrey: The Higher Education Academy English Subject Centre. Online. Available www.english.heacademy.ac.uk/explore/projects/archive/technology/tech10.php (accessed 21 January 2007).

Oliver, M. (2002) *Creativity and the Curriculum Design Process: A Case Study*, York: Higher Education Academy. Online. Available www.heacademy.ac.uk/resources.asp?process=full_record&section=generic&id=153 (accessed 22 August 2006).

Oliver, M. (2003) 'Curriculum design as acquired social practice: a case study', paper presented at the 84th Annual Meeting of the American Educational Research Association, Chicago, April 2003.

Oliver, W. (2005) 'Why reference models?', paper presented at JISC–CETIS Conference 2005, Edinburgh, November 2005.

Pawson, R. and Tilley, N. (1997) *Realistic Evaluation*, London: Sage.

Peterson, D. (ed.) (1996) *Forms of Representation: An Interdisciplinary Theme for Cognitive Science*, Exeter: Intellect.

Säljö, R. (1996) 'Mental and physical artifacts in cognitive practices', in P. Reimann and N. Spada (eds) *Learning in Humans and Machines: Towards an Interdisciplinary Learning Science*, Oxford: Pergamon.

Vogel, M. and Oliver, M. (2006) *Design for Learning in Virtual Learning Environments: Insider Perspectives*. Online. Available www.jisc.ac.uk/uploaded_documents/D4L_VLE_report_final.pdf (accessed 22 August 2006).

Vygotsky, L.S. (1981a) 'The genesis of higher mental functions', in J.V. Wertsch (ed.) *The Concept of Activity in Soviet Psychology*, Armonk, NY: M.E. Sharpe.

Vygotsky, L.S. (1981b) 'The instrumental method in psychology', in J.V. Wertsch (ed.) *The Concept of Activity in Soviet Psychology*, Armonk, NY: M.E. Sharpe.

Chapter 5

Describing ICT-based learning designs that promote quality learning outcomes

Ron Oliver, Barry Harper, Sandra Wills,
Shirley Agostinho and John Hedberg

EDITORS' INTRODUCTION

This chapter uses a grounded approach to describe a framework by which various forms of learning design can be described. The framework was developed from the work of Jonassen (2000) and formed the basis of categorising the learning designs selected for inclusion in the Australian University Teaching Committee (AUTC) project: Information and Communication Technologies and Their Role in Flexible Learning. The chapter showcases examples of the various types of learning design in the framework, and demonstrates the forms of learning environment described by each.

Introduction

The widespread implementation and use of virtual learning environments (VLEs) and courseware management systems (CMSs) in higher education today provide many teachers with the opportunity to create engaging and effective learning settings. The ongoing activities to develop online content in the form of learning objects, delivered seamlessly through standardized digital repositories, can provide many digital resources for teachers looking to make meaningful use of learning technologies (e.g. Harper *et al.* 2005; Oliver *et al.* 2005). What appears to be still missing for teachers is appropriate guidance on the effective pedagogical practice needed to support such activities (Beetham 2004; Ilomäki and Lakkala 2004).

The plethora of technology-supports and digital tools and resources for learning has garnered strong interest among teachers in the use of technology as an integral and mainstream component of course delivery. However, while educational theory has for many years advanced the practice of more constructivist and authentic approaches to e-learning, many technology-supports and templates can encourage the use of more conventional, structured and linear approaches. For example, much of the work in describing standards for learning objects as building blocks for online learning presupposes very directed and structured presentation modes (Rehak and Mason 2003). In the meantime, teachers are still looking for theoretical and practical guidance in the design of effective e-learning strategies and activities (Littlejohn 2004).

This chapter describes outcomes from a recent AUTC-funded project: Information and Communication Technologies and Their Role in Flexible Learning (AUTC 2003). The project involved the development of a framework for distinguishing between learning designs and a means for providing a formal description of each design. The project identified a number of information and communication technology (ICT)-based learning designs that promoted high-quality learning outcomes and developed generic descriptions of each to facilitate their reuse in settings beyond their original context. The resulting set of learning designs has since been used in practice by a large number of higher education teachers to support quality learning outcomes.

Learning designs

In classrooms where teachers and students interact with each other, the learning setting tends to be governed and led by the teacher. In planning such lessons, a teacher plans learning activities for the students that can engage them and provide an experience from which learning would result. In technology-facilitated settings, the role of the teacher in learning activities is often less direct. Learners must make many decisions for themselves that otherwise might have been made by the teacher. E-learning settings typically provide students with notes, activities and directions to guide their learning. These notes, activities and directions are created by teachers but not necessarily the same teachers who are involved with the students.

As explained in Beetham and Sharpe's Introduction to this book, we use the term learning design to describe a representation of the learning experience to which students are exposed. For example, students might be required to read a chapter from a text and to glean certain information. They may be asked to use certain information to plan an approach to solving a given problem. They may be formed into groups and required to gather information and to produce a report. These tasks are part of a learning design, a deliberately planned set of experiences that are intended to help them to learn. A learning design typically involves descriptions of the learners and a space where they act with tools and devices to collect and interpret information through a process of interaction with others (e.g. Britain 2004). Learning designs involve descriptions of learning environments and spaces that are typically quite flexible and in many ways different to the instructional sequences that have previously characterized instructional design strategies.

While the literature abounds with descriptions of the forms of learning settings that support quality learning outcomes, there is considerably less information available that provides discrete and detailed descriptions of teaching and learning processes in forms that teachers can understand and apply. Britain (2004) describes this process of designing for learning as creating a learner workflow. The value of designing for learning lies in the fact that teachers can use the resulting learning designs to plan the learning experiences that learners need to achieve the planned learning outcomes. Well-designed workflows can cater for the needs of individual learners. They can provide motivating and stimulating environments to maintain learner interest and they can provide the support learners need to work beyond their comfort zones as they develop their skills, knowledge and understanding. Well-designed learner workflows also provide scope for students to choose the activities in which they will engage, recognizing the need for learners to assume some ownership of their learning experiences. At the same time, learner workflows, if well articulated and described, can be used over and over again by other teachers and students to achieve other learning outcomes.

With the high levels of interest and activity in the development and sharing of learning objects, there is growing interest in learning designs. The interest stems from the fact that learning objects by themselves can provide limited advantage to teachers. Learning objects, however, when utilized with sound learning designs to create meaningful learning experiences, can deliver far more beneficial outcomes.

Learning designs that support quality learning outcomes

There are a wide variety of forms that students' learning experiences can take in higher education settings. In Chapter 1, Mayes and de Freitas describe three perspectives that they argue embrace contemporary teaching and learning processes with respect to e-learning. The perspectives are described as associationist, cognitive and situative. When applied to the design of learning environments, each of the perspectives leads to learning experiences with particular forms of learning outcomes.

It was the intent in our project to explore ICT-based learning designs that could support quality learning outcomes. By this we mean learning outcomes that involve conceptual change and a deep understanding of the unit content. The project sought expert opinion to determine what constituted 'high-quality learning' and in conjunction with feedback from the project team, developed of a set of principles that described high-quality student learning in higher education (Boud and Prosser 2002). The principles used a learning perspective to characterize the essential elements of a learning design with the potential to foster high-quality learning in higher education. These are described as (paraphrased from Boud and Prosser 2002):

- *Learner engagement*: A consideration of learners' prior knowledge and their desires and building on their expectations.
- *Acknowledgement of the learning context*: A consideration of the implementation of the learning design and its position within the broader programme of study for the learner.
- *Learner challenge*: Seeking active participation of learners, encouraging learners to be self-critical and supportive of learners' ampliative skills.
- *Provision of practice*: Encouraging learners to articulate and demonstrate to themselves and their peers what they are learning.

These principles can also be found in the descriptions of curriculum design presented by Sharpe and Oliver in Chapter 3. In different learning contexts some of these principles may be more prominent than others; however, all four principles are important in any higher education context. The principles are holistic in that they incorporate both learning outcomes and learning processes and are based on the premise that learning arises from what students experience from an implementation of a learning design. Designers need to examine their learning designs from the perspective of their impact on learning, that is, placing themselves in the 'students' shoes' and thus examining their learning designs from the student perspective.

The conventional art of instructional design has previously been very well defined and many guidelines and models have been developed to guide instructional designers in the process of developing instructional sequences (e.g. Dick and Carey 1990; Gagné *et al*. 1992). Instructional design for learning settings that promote the quality learning outcomes described above involves a far more complex process and there appears to be a distinct shortage of models and explicit frameworks for instructional designers. Jonasssen (1994) argues that there cannot really be any firm models guiding the design of constructivist settings since knowledge construction is so context-specific. Lefoe (1998) argues that learning design theory today provides principles and general concepts by which learning environments can be planned. The use of learning designs in an instructional planning process, however, is less rigid and has fewer guidelines than those to which many teachers are accustomed. Our project sought to produce what Masterman and Vogel in Chapter 4 call 'manifest' designs as distinct from the more rough and ready sketches, the tacit rules of practice that teachers typically employ and that are not readily shared, which they call 'latent designs'.

Establishing a framework to describing learning designs

In our project, we needed to be able to articulate clearly the nature and scope of different forms of learning design in ways that would enable a design to be applied across a variety of settings and disciplines. We required some strategy by which the various learning designs could be described and variations and instances accommodated. We were guided in our efforts by the work of Jonassen (2000), which provides a useful framework based on his notion of activity theory. Activity theory provides a means to focus on the actions of a learner within an activity system that involves a group pursuing a learning goal in a deliberate fashion.

The Jonassen (2000) framework describes learning designs as a range of activity or problem settings comprising 11 problem-types in a continuum from activities that involve the application of rules, through those based on incidents and events, through to activities that involve strategic planning, and activities whose solutions are based on learners' performances.

When the problem-types of Jonassen (2000) were further explored, there appeared three discrete forms of learning design within the 11. These discrete forms each encompassed a number of the problem-types and appeared capable of being used to further categorize potential learning designs. The problems encompassed within Jonasssen's descriptions are typically either of a rule-based, an incident-based, or a strategy-based form. Our inquiry suggested a fourth type of learning design: role-based. The four types of learning designs that emerged from this form of analysis and development are shown in Table 5.1. The learning designs are discrete and follow what might be seen as a continuum describing the scope of their complexity and openness. Table 5.1 shows these forms and provides descriptions of each type of learning activity and the forms of learning outcome that are associated with each.

The nature of the various learning designs described in Table 5.1 can be further demonstrated and exemplified by considering the forms of tasks, supports and learning resources that each would require in a learning setting (Oliver and Herrington 2001). Table 5.2 uses this strategy to further exemplify and distinguish the four types of learning design suggested by this process.

Table 5.1 A framework for a learning design typology

Learning design focus	Description	Learning outcomes
Rule-based	The learning task requires learners to apply standard procedures and rules in the solution. For example, algorithmic approaches, the application of given procedures and rules if defined ways to effect a solution.	A capacity to meaningfully and reflectively apply procedures and processes.
Incident-based	The learning activity is based around learners' exposure and participation to events or incidents of an authentic and real nature. The learning is based around activities that require learners to reflect and take decisions based on the actions and events.	Understanding procedures, roles and an ability to apply the knowledge.
Strategy-based	Learning is based around tasks that require strategic planning and activity.	A capacity to apply knowledge in meaningful ways in real-life settings.
Role-based	The learning is achieved through learners' participation as players and participants in a setting that models a real-world application. Learners apply judgements and make decisions based on understanding of the setting in real-time scenarios.	An understanding of issues, processes and interactions of multi-variable situations.

Table 5.2 Characteristic elements of learning designs

Learning design focus	Learning tasks	Learning resources	Learning supports
Rule-based processes	Closed tasks, logical and bounded tasks in authentic settings, procedural sequence of manipulations, projects and inquiry-based forms.	Case-based materials, authentic resources, multiple sources, algorithmic descriptions and tutorials.	Collaborative learning, teacher as coach/guide, opportunities to articulate and reflect.
Incident-based processes	Story-based tasks with disambiguate variables, case analysis tasks.	Incident/event descriptions and scenarios, case materials, theoretical underpinnings.	Collaborative learning, opportunities to articulate and reflect, teacher as coach/guide.
Strategy-based processes	Complex and ill-defined tasks, decision making tasks, troubleshooting tasks, diagnosis solutions, strategic performance tasks.	Authentic resources, multiple perspectives, expert judgements, theoretical underpinnings sample tasks and solutions.	Teacher as coach, collaborative learning, peer assessments, opportunities to articulate and reflect.
Role-based interactions	Assumption of roles within real-life settings, assuming the role, playing the role in scenarios.	Procedural descriptions, role definitions, resources to define and guide role, scenarios, theoretical underpinnings.	Learners assume individual roles, teacher as moderator, opportunities to articulate and reflect.

Describing learning designs in generic forms

In order to provide a consistent means to describe the underpinning elements in each learning design, the project developed a temporal sequencing strategy based on the three critical elements of learning environments proposed by Oliver and Herrington (2001). These elements are the learning task, learning resources and learning supports. To enable a visual representation of the learning design as in Figure 5.1, learning tasks are shown as a rectangle, learning resources as a triangle and supports as a circle. The following sections describe generic categorizations of the discrete types of learning designs using the temporal representation describing the interactions of the tasks, resources and supports. The sections also include examples of particular learning settings designed around such learning designs that form part of the AUTC learning designs resource collection (AUTC 2003). Readers wishing to explore any of the designs further can access the examples described in the sections and a variety of accompanying materials from the web addresses provided.

Rule-based designs

Figure 5.1 shows a temporal sequence for the form of learning design we have designated rule-based. Rule-based designs are those that are primarily comprised of closed tasks whose completion requires the application of some form of rules, procedures or algorithms. In rule-based learning designs, the resources that learners use include the procedural and system descriptions needed for the application and the environment the necessary supports to enable learners to achieve success in their efforts. The learning is achieved through learners applying standard procedures and rules in developing a solution. For example, algorithmic approaches involve the application of given procedures and rules in defined ways to effect a solution. The tasks need to provide learners with opportunities to meaningfully and reflectively apply procedures and processes to specific closed, logical and bounded tasks. Figure 5.1 shows a possible form of this learning design using developed schema. It was intended in the project to determine if there was a generic form of representation that could be used to describe rule-based learning designs. As we explored a number of different rule-based learning designs in different settings and disciplines, it became evident that our system for describing the design yielded a variety of forms when applied to the different settings.

An example of a rule-based learning design is in the example *Communicating with the Tired Patient* (Liaw *et al.* 2002). This is a learning setting produced on a CD-ROM that aims to assist medical students with their clinical communication skills, and to help them develop an integrated biopsychosocial approach to identifying a patient's problems. Students are asked to play the role of the doctor in a simulated clinical interview. As the doctor, students listen to up to four audio options comprising questions they could potentially ask the patient. The student selects what he or she believes to be the most appropriate question given the current

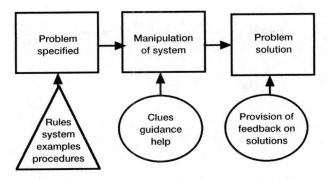

Figure 5.1 A temporal sequence describing a rule-based learning design

state of the interview and then views the patient's response via an audio visual display. Students are able to see the ramifications and implications of asking different questions by listening to and observing the patient's response. Students are challenged to reflect on specific sequences in their interview through expert 'comments and questions'. As students progress they are able to view a transcript of the interview at any time, which allows them to review the questions they have asked, the patient's response, the expert comments made and their own notes. Students can complete an introductory tutorial before they begin an interview and they are supported by a glossary and a library of microskill resources as they conduct their interview. A full description of the learning setting and strategies for its reuse in other settings is provided. Figure 5.2 shows a detailed form of the underpinning learning design.

Incident-based learning designs

In an incident-based learning design, the learning activity is based around learners' exposure to, and participation in, events or incidents of an authentic and real nature. The learning is based around activities that require learners to reflect and take decisions about the actions and events. The temporal sequence shows learning based around a description of the incident, elaboration of that incident through reflection, a group or individual process to find a solution or to come to a decision, declaration of a solution or decision, and provision of feedback on solution or decision. Incident-based learning designs can be supported through learner collaboration and through opportunities to articulate and reflect on the learning provided by a teacher acting as a mentor. The learning is based around activities that require learners to reflect and take decisions based on the incidents and events that are represented. The setting requires a range of resources to provide rich descriptions and information about the incident and event upon which the learning is based (Figure 5.3).

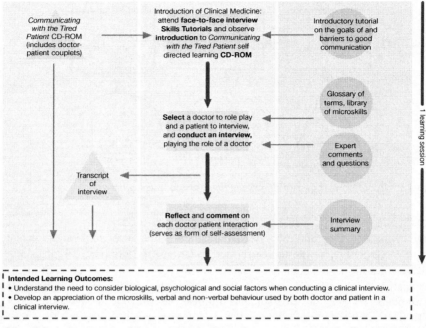

Figure 5.2 A description of the learning design in *Communicating with the Tired Patient*

An example of an incident-based learning design is *Real-life Cases in Multimedia* (Bennett 2002). The learning environment is centred around a collaborative project task in which students enrolled in a graduate-level educational technology subject develop a multimedia package for a real client. The exploration of the problem is supported by an analysis of two real-life cases, through individual writing, and small group and whole-class discussions. These real-life cases give students a 'behind-the-scenes' look at two large interactive multimedia CD-ROM projects,

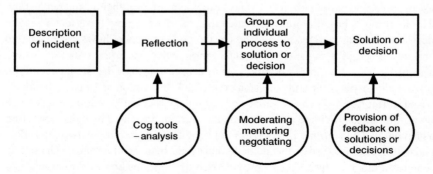

Figure 5.3 A temporal sequence describing an incident-based learning design

with access to interviews with the key designers and archival documents. Students work together in teams of three or four to develop their project designs and solutions. Each team member assumes a particular role and responsibilities typical of a real-world multimedia development team. The final phase of the learning design requires students to reflect on their experiences through individual and collaborative writing tasks. Appropriate social and technological supports are integrated into the learning environment, including access to class meetings and tutorials, computer laboratories, online discussion and file storage. A full description of the learning setting and strategies for its reuse in other settings is provided on the AUTC web site. Figure 5.4 shows a detailed form of the underpinning learning design.

Strategy-based learning designs

Strategy-based learning designs are characterized by such activities as complex and ill-defined tasks, decision-making tasks, some troubleshooting tasks, diagnosis

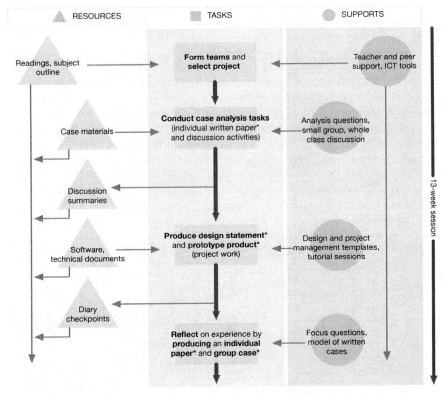

Figure 5.4 A description of the learning design in *Real-life Cases in Multimedia*

Note: * indicates a discrete assessment task.

solutions and strategic performance tasks. The temporal sequence shown in Figure 5.5 suggests a learning design where learners undertake a series of activities and at the same time interact with a variety of resources and learning supports. The process involves specification of the strategic problem, elaboration of that problem through reflection, a group or individual process to carry out the task, declaration of a solution or outcome from the tasks and reflection on the learning process.

In strategy-based learning designs, learning is based around tasks that require strategic planning and activity. The environment requires authentic resources that support multiple perspectives, provide such elaborations as expert judgements, and that also provide descriptions of theoretical underpinnings. Typically learners are also provided with sample tasks and solutions, cases, tactics, strategies and treatments. Support is provided through a teacher acting as a coach and facilitator, and often through collaborative learning tasks involving such strategies as peer assessments and the provision of meaningful opportunities and contexts for articulation and reflection.

An example of a strategy-based learning design is *Investigating Mathematical Assessment Strategies* (Herrington *et al.* 2002). The learning experience provided to students in this environment is one where students are given the opportunity to reflect on the appropriate use of assessment strategies in mathematics in much the same way that practising teachers might. Rather than learning a raft of different strategies one by one, and possibly not really knowing when to apply them, students are not given any direct instruction on the various strategies. Instead they are given realistic problems (there are five of them) presented in the form of two documents (such as memos and letters), not unlike being given such a task in real life. The students then, in groups, use a range of resources and personal perspectives provided on a CD-ROM to investigate the task. They then present their findings also in a realistic, if simulated, context, as if they were presenting at a staff meeting or information night for parents. In this way, students can understand that a good knowledge of assessment strategies can be useful within a variety of contexts, and they have a broad range of strategies, beyond the standard pencil and paper test, that they can draw on as teachers of mathematics. Figure 5.6 shows a detailed form of the underpinning learning design.

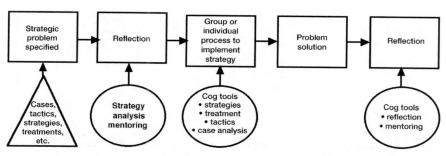

Figure 5.5 Temporal sequence describing a strategy-based learning design

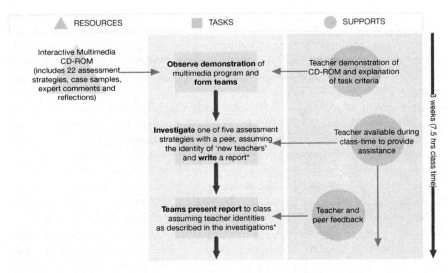

Figure 5.6 A description of the learning design in *Investigating Mathematical Assessment Strategies*

Role-based learning designs

In role-based learning, learners acquire skills, knowledge and understanding through the assumption of roles within real-life settings. The design typically involves some purposeful and directed preparation and role-playing in scenarios that have been developed to provide the forms of learning opportunities sought in the objectives. The temporal sequence shown in Figure 5.7 involves the declaration of learner role, online dialogue to clarify this role, presentation of a dilemma to resolve, online dialogue to resolve the dilemma within the perspective of a role, a possible negotiated resolution to the dilemma and reflection on the process.

In role-based settings, learning is achieved through learners' participation as players and participants in a setting, which models a real-world application.

Figure 5.7 Temporal sequence describing a role-based learning design

Learners apply judgements and make decisions based on understanding of the setting in real-time scenarios. They require an array of resources to support the learners' role including procedural descriptions, role definitions, resources to define and guide roles, scenarios, topical content and cases. Typically the role of the teacher is that of a moderator and mentor, who creates opportunities for the learners to articulate and reflect on their learning experiences.

An example of a role-based learning design is *Political Science Simulation* (Yasmeen and Fardon 2002). This learning setting has political science students engaging in a role-play simulation that spans a period of five weeks and has students assuming the role of members of the United Nations Security Council. The Security Council has been convened to discuss the critical issue of the sanctions imposed on Iraq. The learning design has been divided into the three critical phases normally associated with role-play activities: planning and preparation, interaction, and reflection and evaluation. The first phase sees students preparing for the activity by researching their particular role. For this they are provided with specific references for their role and general references regarding international diplomacy, both electronic and paper-based. The next phase involves both face-to-face and electronic communication in the form of 'meetings' of the United Nations Security Council and secret diplomacy via the web site. The final phase involves students reverting to themselves and reflecting on the process and experience, leading to a collaborative group report. Facilitation of the activity by tutors is critical, particularly during the interaction phase.

A comprehensive designer template, plus a number of checklists and associated documentation were provided to guide the design and implementation of such an online role-play model. These resources are included in the AUTC web site. Figure 5.8 shows a detailed form of the underpinning learning design.

Summary and conclusions

When we reflect on the processes and products from the project, a number of interesting issues appear to emerge. The first relates to the success of the temporal sequence framework we developed to adequately describe learning designs. This framework appears to provide a means to describe what we see as the critical elements in a learning design description. The framework provides an efficient means to represent teachers' plans for a learning experience by providing a representation for tasks, resources and supports together with the various connections between them and an indication of their various positions demonstrated in a temporal fashion. Among the team members it was found that when presented with a sequence, we could generally agree as to whether or not it provided an adequate description of a particular learning design. What was interesting was that given a particular learning approach, for example, an instance of a problem-based learning setting, the members of the team would usually provide quite different representations of this approach using the temporal sequence framework.

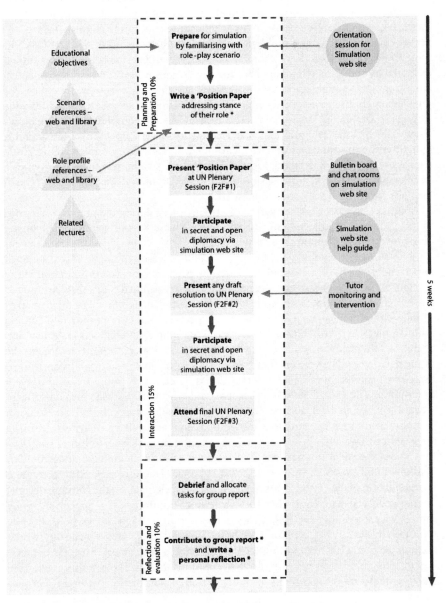

Figure 5.8 The learning design underpinning *Political Science Simulation*

It was apparent that the difficulty lay in identifying the critical elements in the learning approach being investigated. In a problem-based case, for example, there is a degree of interpretation involved in identifying the particular tasks that learners might be required to undertake. One teacher might describe the first task in the sequence as 'identifying a problem' whereas another might see the first task in a more microscopic form, for example, 'developing and understanding the context' followed by 'creating a boundary for the investigation'. It became clear to us that consistent and reliable use of this model would likely require a controlled vocabulary for the various elements and very detailed descriptions of the learning settings to enable the vocabulary to be applied. As we completed the project, we recognized that the temporal sequence framework would benefit from considerable more investigation and enquiry. The learning design toolkit (Conole and Fill 2005) appears to support these thoughts. Designed for a similar purpose, it provides a detailed set of elements for describing learning designs and appears to fill some of the gaps we recognized in our framework.

Another issue we found ourselves discussing often during the project concerned the size and scope of the learning designs that we were seeking to describe. In many classrooms and instructional settings, teachers tend to plan learning experiences for their students as single sessions. For example, a lesson might involve a series of experiences based on a plan, do and review process completed in an hour-long session. In our project, we were investigating some learning designs that represented a complete unit of study, with up to 100 hours of student activity. The relative sizes of these learning designs meant that in one instance the description could contain quite detailed elements while in the semester-long course, the elements in the learning design would necessarily have to be much broader. It was recognized among the group that it would be very useful to develop a schema that in some way constrained the size of the learning design so that the same elements could be used in each description. The Learning Activity Management System (LAMS) provides a very elegant solution to the problem of size though its modular approach (Dalziel 2003).

Another interesting outcome concerned the fact that the various learning approaches that were chosen for inclusion in the project were selected based on their perceived learning quality against such criteria as engagement, context, challenge and practice. In the temporal sequence framework used to provide a representation of the various learning designs, these elements of the learning designs are noticeably absent. More than this, there does not necessarily appear to be any logical way to include these elements in the learning design descriptions, despite their importance. It has been noted that the sequence provides a means by which the elements can be ordered but does not provide a framework for their content. Again, this appears to be an issue that could be further explored to enable the framework to more accurately provide a representation for different learning designs.

While the project has been completed, it has highlighted a number of pressing areas for further enquiry if we are going to be able to provide a means to formally describe learning designs in clear and concise and unambiguous ways. The project has highlighted the challenges in categorizing learning designs and describing learning designs and the need for further work, much of which remains in progress (e.g. Littlejohn 2004; Conole and Fill 2005). There still remains no agreed or commonly used formal processes for categorizing learning designs. While strategies are now emerging for describing learning designs, an overarching typology is still to be described. Important in this process will be the description of the various elements in learning designs, ways to capture and describe contexts and ways to ensure that the language used can be understood by all teachers. We are pleased to see the high levels of enthusiasm that many researchers still retain for these areas of enquiry and look forward to seeing the solutions that are developed.

References

AUTC (2003) *Australian University Teaching Committee Project: Information and Communication Technologies and Their Role in Flexible Learning*. Online. Available http:// learningdesigns.uow.edu.au (accessed 24 August 2006).

Beetham, H. (2004) *Review: Developing E-learning Models for the JISC Practitioner Communities*. Online. Available www.jisc.ac.uk/uploaded_documents/Review_emodels_ draft.doc (accessed 23 January 2006).

Bennett, S. (2002) *Description of a Technology-supported Constructivist Learning Environment that Uses Real-life Cases to Support Collaborative Project Work*. Online. Available http://learningdesigns.uow.edu.au/exemplars/info/LD1/index.html (accessed 23 January 2006).

Boud, D. and Prosser, M. (2002) 'Key principles for high quality student learning in higher education: a framework for evaluation', *Educational Media International*, 39 (3): 237–45.

Britain, S. (2004) *A Review of Learning Design: Concept, Specification and Tools*. Online. Available http://scholar.google.com/url?sa=U&q=www.jisc.ac.uk/uploaded_documents/ ACF1ABB.doc (accessed 10 August 2006).

Conole, G. and Fill, K. (2005) *A Learning Design Toolkit to Create Pedagogically Effective Learning Activities*. Online. Available www-jime.open.ac.uk/2005/08/ (accessed 23 January 2006).

Dalziel, J. (2003) 'Implementing learning design: the Learning Activity Management System', paper presented at the Australasian Society for Computers in Learning in Tertiary Education annual conference, Melbourne, December 2003.

Dick, W. and Carey, L. (1990) *The Systematic Design of Instruction*, Glenview: Harper Collins.

Gagné, R.M., Briggs, L.J. and Wagner, W.W. (1992) *Principles of Instructional Design*, New York: Holt, Reihhart & Winston Inc.

Harper, B., Agostinho, S., Bennett, S., Lukasiak, J. and Lockyer, L. (2005) 'Constructing high quality learning environments using learning designs and learning objects', in *Proceedings of the 5th IEEE International Conference on Advanced Learning Technologies*, Kaohsiung, Taiwan: IEEE Computer Society.

Herrington, A., Herrington, J., Sparrow, L. and Oliver, R. (2002) *Description of Investigating Assessment Strategies in Mathematics Classrooms*. Online. Available http://learning designs.uow.edu.au/exemplars/info/LD2/index.htm (accessed 3 April 2006).

Illomäki, L. and Lakkala, M. (eds) (2004) *Learning Objects in Classroom Settings. A Report of 13 Case Studies Conducted in Finland, France, Hungary, Ireland and United Kingdom*.

Online. Available www.helsinki.fi/science/networkedlearning/texts/celebratecasestudies. pdf (accessed 10 August 2006).

Jonassen, D. (1994) 'Thinking technology: toward a constructivist design model', *Educational Technology*, 34 (3): 34–7.

Jonassen, D. (2000) 'Toward a design theory of problem solving', *Educational Technology Research and Development*, 48 (4): 63–85.

Lefoe, G. (1998) 'Creating constructivist learning environments on the Web: the challenge in higher education', paper presented at the Australasian Society for Computers in Learning in Tertiary Education annual conference, University of Wollongong, December 1998.

Liaw, S., Kennedy, G., Marty, J., Judd, T., Keppell, M. and McNair, R. (2002) *Description of Communicating with the Tired Patient* (Version 2.0). Online. Available http://learning designs.uow.edu.au/exemplars/info/LD46/index.html (accessed 3 April 2006).

Littlejohn, A. (2004) *The Effectiveness of Resources, Tools and Support Services used by Practitioners in Designing and Delivering E-learning Activities*. Online. Available www.jisc.ac.uk/uploaded_documents/Final%20report%20(final).doc (accessed 10 August 2006).

Oliver, R. and Herrington, J. (2001) *Teaching and Learning Online: A Beginner's Guide to E-learning and E-teaching in Higher Education*, Mt Lawley, WA: Edith Cowan University.

Oliver, R., Wirski, R., Wait, L. and Blanksby, V. (2005) 'Learning designs and learning objects: where pedagogy meets technology', in C. Looi, D. Jonassen and M. Ikeda (eds) *Towards Sustainable and Scalable Educational Innovations Informed by the Learning Sciences*, Amsterdam: IOS Press.

Rehak, D. and Mason, R. (2003) 'Keeping the learning in learning objects', in A. Littlejohn (ed.) *Reusing Online Resources: A Sustainable Approach to E-learning*, London: Kogan Page.

Yasmeen, S. and Fardon, M. (2002) *Description of Political Science Simulation Exercise.* Online. Available http://learningdesigns.uow.edu.au/exemplars/info/LD25/index.html (accessed 3 April 2006).

Chapter 6

Describing learning activities
Tools and resources to guide practice

Gráinne Conole

EDITORS' INTRODUCTION

We have seen already that there are a multitude of learning theories available to guide the development of learning activities (Mayes and de Freitas, Chapter 1) and a rich variety of information and communication technology (ICT) tools that can be used to support the design and delivery of learning (Beetham, Chapter 2 and Masterman and Vogel, Chapter 4). This chapter argues that despite the range of theories and tools available, designs based on educational theory (such as those highlighted by Sharpe and Oliver in Chapter 3) or the innovative use of ICT tools (such as those described by Kukulska-Hulme and Traxler in Chapter 14), are still too few and far between. The author argues that the gap between the potential of technologies to support learning and the reality of how they are actually being used may be due to a lack of understanding about how technologies can be used to afford specific learning advantages. She presents a taxonomy that characterizes and describes the components of a learning activity, and suggests how it could be used to support practitioners to make informed choices in their designing for learning.

Contextualizing the problem

Technological developments are continuing at a phenomenal rate. Indeed, we may be entering a new phase in the use of technologies – particularly with the emergences of new forms of social software and what is being referred to as Web 2.0 (Conole and Dyke forthcoming). Furthermore technologies are now beginning to be used in a rich range of ways to support learning. We are seeing the emergence of technology-enabled spaces and adaptive technologies that offer new and exciting opportunities in terms of contextual, ambient, augmented, distributed and social networked learning. While much of the early focus of activity in Internet developments was on content (and ways of creating, storing, retrieving and managing information), more recently interest has shifted towards the social potential of technologies. This is reflected in the emergence of wikis, blogs, podcasting and other forms of social software (Conole and Oliver 2007; Weller 2007).

In essence, this suggests that there are three fundamental shifts: a shift from a focus on information to communication, a shift from a passive to more interactive engagement, and a shift from a focus on individual learners to more socially situative learning. Boundaries are blurring – chat is conventionally labelled as a communicative medium, however recent research (Conole *et al.* 2006) has shown how it is being used as 'information' as the students are accessing and reading the archived chat transcripts. Similarly, two recent surveys of students' experiences of e-learning (Conole *et al.* 2006; Creanor *et al.* 2006) highlight the complex and multifaceted ways in which students are appropriating and personalizing technologies. How can practitioners be supported to capitalize on the potential opportunities for creating innovative and engaging learning activities that maximize the potential of technologies and aligns with these three key shifts? This chapter will argue that describing these shifts is complex as they represent more tacit aspects of practice that are hard to describe whereas focusing on content or information is easier and now fairly well understood.

Early e-learning developments tended to focus on the development of content. A considerable body of research has accumulated on the development of standards for learning objects concepts (although the use of this term is hotly contested, Polsani 2003). One of the key issues is to what extent a 'learning object' embodies aspects of learning outcomes and activities – definitions range from the notion of 'learning objects' as simple, neutral 'digital assets' to 'learning objects' as whole course courses. As a result, recent thinking (Duncan 2003; Rehak and Mason 2003; Littlejohn *et al.* forthcoming) has shifted towards defining levels of granularity of resources. Littlejohn *et al.* (forthcoming) consider this in four levels of increasing complexity:

- digital assets – normally a single file (e.g. an image, video or audio clip), sometimes called a 'raw media asset';
- information objects – a structured aggregation of digital assets, designed purely to present information;
- learning activities – tasks involving interactions with information to attain a specific learning outcome;
- learning design – structured sequences of information and activities to promote learning.

A range of standards has now been developed to cover this spectrum of resources and their use in context; such as the IEEE Learning Object Metadata (LOM) and the IMS Learning Design specification. These standards are being used as a basis for the development of new technical architectures and are enabling the move towards a service-orientated approach to the development of software and true interoperability.

However, learning is a complex, dynamic process and there are limitations with focusing purely on content. In particular a focus on content tends to instantiate particular pedagogical approaches. Mayes and Fowler (1999) point out that one problem in focusing on learning objects is that teachers tend to plan e-learning around 'instructivist' learning models, which focus on single learners accessing content. Learning Design (as defined in the Introduction to this volume) specifies the teaching and learning process, along with the conditions under which it occurs and the activities performed by the teachers and learners in order to achieve the required learning objectives. It is based on the concept of a 'unit of learning' (Britain 2004) and includes learning objectives, roles, activities (*learning activities* or *support activities*), activity-structures, environment (including *learning objects and services such as chat rooms, quiz tools, etc.*), resources and method.

Describing practice

There has been considerable interest in recent years in the development of educational vocabularies to describe practice and curriculum design that goes beyond the description of resources and focuses more at the level of learning activities (see the discussion of metadata and vocabularies in McAndrew and Goodyear, Chapter 7). A comprehensive review of educational vocabularies is provided by Currier *et al.* (2006), which includes an inventory of existing pedagogical vocabularies, including flat lists, taxonomies, thesauri, ontologies and classification schemes. The report highlights that vocabularies are being seen as increasingly important in terms of providing a bridge between practice and more abstract technical services and reference models.

Interest in this area has arisen in part because of the increasing impact of e-learning on educational processes and in part from the opportunity to create, store and share educational practice, afforded through the emergence of new technologies and in particular online portals and digital repositories. For example, the Joint Information Systems Committee (JISC) has established the Jorum national repository for resources (JISC 2006). Such sharable databases require metadata in order to describe and access their content, which immediately gives rise to issues about how such practice can be adequately described.

However, there is a tension between adoption of an atomistic, content-driven description of content and a more holistic, contextual description. Currier *et al.* (2006) describe one approach that could potentially address this tension. They discuss the rise of 'folksonomies' (defined as 'a new methodology for developing shared vocabularies') within the suite of vocabularies being developed to describe practice. They go on the state:

> Folksonomy systems allow community members, or users of a shared resource, archive, wiki, repository *etc.*, to assign their own indexing terms to resources ('tagging': a process previously known as natural language keyword indexing) and the system organises its interface by clustering the terms and/or the resources, although hierarchies of concepts are not always generated. Still in its infancy, this approach has both its proponents and its detractors.
>
> (Currier *et al.* 2006: 13)

At the heart of the issue is the fact that if learning activities are to be reusable, then they have to be described in commonly understood and standardized vocabularies that will allow users to source and share resources through searching or browsing. Recent and evolving taxonomies form the basis for standardized vocabularies. Also important is the parallel development of international standards for learning technologies that has grown in significance in recent years, in part in recognition of the importance of and need for interoperability. In line with this, current thinking in software development has shifted from the creation of 'monolithic all-in-one' information technology (IT) systems to more of a 'pick and mix' approach, which is in part a consequence and recognition of the constantly changing and volatile nature of this area.

Defining learning activities

A taxonomy has been developed that defines the components involved in a learning activity (Conole and Fill 2005; Bailey *et al*. 2006). The taxonomy attempts to consider all aspects and factors involved in developing a learning activity, from the pedagogical context in which the activity occurs through to the nature and types of tasks undertaken by the learner. At the heart of the taxonomy is the assertion that learning activities are achieved through completion of a series of *tasks* in order to achieve intended *learning outcomes* (see Beetham, Chapter 2). We have defined the components that constitute a learning activity as:

- The *context* within which the activity occurs; this includes the subject, level of difficulty, the intended learning outcomes and the environment within which the activity takes place. Learning outcomes are mapped to Bloom's taxonomy of learning outcomes and grouped into three types: cognitive, affective and psychomotor and are what the learners should know, or be able to do, after completing a learning activity; for example they might be required to be able to: understand, demonstrate, design, produce or appraise (Bloom 1956).
- The *pedagogy* (learning and teaching approaches) adopted. These are grouped according to Mayes and de Frietas' three categories introduced in Chapter 1 – associative, cognitive and situative.
- The *tasks* undertaken. This specifies the type of task, the (teaching) techniques used to support the task, any associated tools and resources, the interaction and roles of those involved and the assessments associated with the learning activity.

The taxonomy is presented in Appendix 7. Perhaps the most useful aspect of the taxonomy is the detailed description of the nature of tasks that students will undertake as part of the learning activity to achieve the intended learning outcomes. The taxonomy is similar to that developed by Laurillard (1993) and classifies task types into six areas:

- assimilative tasks (essentially passive in nature such as reading, viewing or listening);

- information handling (such as getting students to gather and classify resources from the Web or manipulate data in a spreadsheet);
- adaptive (where students are engaged in using modelling or simulation software);
- communicative (in terms of engaging in a range of dialogic activities, such as pair dialogue group-based discussions);
- productive (where the students actively construct an artefact such as a written essay, production of a new chemical compound or creation of a sculpture);
- experiential (such as practising skills in a particular context or undertaking an investigation).

These tasks can be supported by a range of techniques that are essentially the way in which the task type is undertaken; i.e. the structure or scaffolding of the task. These might include using a scavenger hunt metaphor to enable students to gather resources or the setting up of a formal structured debate with students arguing for and against a particular issue as a means of fostering communication or using mind-mapping software to get a group of students to brainstorm a concept. Depending on the type of task and the technique used to instantiate it, there will be a number of roles and interactions associated with those involved. For example an online group discussion might include one student acting as a presenter, one as a facilitator and the rest as group participants. Activities might be focused at the level of the individual learner, pairs of students, group based or whole-class based. Depending on the nature of the task being undertaken there may be a range of tools and resources that the students use in order to complete the task. Finally tasks may contain an assessment component that might be diagnostic, formative or summative in nature.

Uses and limitations

The taxonomy outlined above provides a useful checklist for identifying the components involved in creating a learning activity and can be helpful in terms of guiding practitioners through their decision making. To create learning activities practitioners have to make complex decisions about which tools and theories to use.

The taxonomy has been used as the basis for an online toolkit that guides practitioners through the process of developing pedagogically informed learning activities (Conole and Fill 2005; Bailey *et al.* 2006). The toolkit provides the user with layered information on each of the components involved in creating a learning activity. For example it provides details of different pedagogical approaches and links to examples of how different approaches are being used. It also gives help on the different kinds of tasks that can be used to achieve particular learning outcomes along with suggestions of ways in which these tasks can be structured.

However, one could argue that this is still very much a component-based approach; as yet the relationships between the components are not well understood and hence this still does not lead to providing a template for adopting a holistic approach to designing for learning where the sum of the components is greater than the parts. The next section takes a broader look at other approaches practitioners use to create effective learning activities, highlighting the advantages that each of these provide.

Alternative approaches

Although the taxonomy described above provides a useful 'checklist' for practitioners to create learning activities, in reality practitioners use a much wider range of mediating artefacts to support and guide decision making in creating learning activities (Conole forthcoming). The application of the use of mediating artefacts and their role in supporting the creation and use of learning activities defined in this paper resonates with broader contemporary thinking concerned with the relationship between tools, discourse and individuals. Of particular relevance to the work described here is activity theory and associated theoretical perspectives (Engeström et al. 1999). Vygosky's (1978) seminal and deceptively simple work on the relationship between subjects, objects and mediating tools has underpinned much of current socio-cultural thinking in the nature and role of semiotic tools. Different tools and resources can provide support and guidance on the context of a learning activity, the choice of pedagogy, the creation of associated learner tasks or any combination of these. They range from contextually rich illustrative examples of good practice (case studies, guidelines, narratives, etc.) to more abstract forms of representation that distil out the 'essences' of good practice (models or patterns).

Mediating artefacts help practitioners to make informed decisions and choices in order to undertake specific teaching and learning activities (Beetham 2002). A recent review classified the different types of tools, resources and services that are currently being used to support the design process (see Sharpe and Oliver, Chapter 9). This found that resources can be viewed in terms of 'representation of knowledge', 'people' (a member of support staff, such as a librarian, audio visual technician or educational developer) or the 'services' they offer. The taxonomy groups tools according to Laurillard's (1993) schema (adaptive, narrative, productive, communicative and interactive) and describes the nature of the media and the types of activities that are supported and categorizes tools according to their main use, namely: manipulation, presentation, analysis, searching, managing, communicating, visualising, supporting, evaluating and adaptation.

It is evident that there are a range of different types of mediating artefacts that can provide guidance and support, such as illustrative examples of good practice (case studies, guidelines, narratives, etc.) or more abstract forms of representation that distil out the 'essences' of good practice (models, use cases or patterns) (see also Beetham 2002; Sharpe et al. 2004). Each of these will now be described, in particular focusing on how different mediating artefacts provide different types of support to guide practitioner decision making.

Narratives and case studies

Narratives and case studies tend to be rich and contextually located, which is valuable in that they describe the details of a particular pedagogical intervention. The drawback is that precisely because they are so contextually located they may be difficult to adapt or repurpose. Practitioners also use a range of dialogic approaches to informing their practice, which enables flexibility as these provide an opportunity to clarify and discuss ideas with colleagues. Perhaps the most important of these are those based on peer dialogue – such as asking advice from a fellow teacher about how they have gone about setting up a teaching session. Conferences, workshops, staff development events, online networks and mailing lists provide more extended forms of peer dialogue and networked expertise.

Lesson plans

Lesson plans provide a means of formalizing learning activities and a framework for teachers to reflect in a deeper and more creative way about how they design and structure activities for different students and help achieve constructive alignment between theory and practice (Littlejohn 2003; Conole and Fill 2005). They are particularly useful in helping tutors to plan *blended learning* (i.e. the integration of technology supported methods with face-to-face teaching), since they can be used to reflect explicitly upon different educational approaches. An example of 'tips and tricks' include Salmon's suggested e-activities to promote effective online communication (Salmon 2002).

Templates and wizards

Most commercial software now comes with some form of in-built help system. In addition many also provide templates or how-to wizards to guide the user through a particular set of activities. As a consequence practice has shifted from a culture of reading the manual of instructions to a 'just-in-time' culture based on immediate need. Another type of guidance tool is exemplified by a tool for guiding practitioners through the process of learning design called Learning Activity Management System (LAMS) as described by Dalziel (2003 and Chapter 15, this volume). Tools are organized so that users can pick and mix different types of learning activities.

Toolkits

Another category of support tool is toolkits that can provide a theoretical overview of an area and hence be used as a point of reference for decision making. A toolkit provides a structured resource that can be used to plan, scope and cost an activity (examples include the development of an evaluation plan, choosing and integrating different types of media into teaching, or managing information). By providing increasingly detailed layers of information, the user can follow up relevant issues when and if such detail is required. In addition, by providing a simple, logically organized structure, toolkits help to reduce the time required to plan work of this type. As described earlier, the DialogPlus is an example of a learning activity design toolkit that aims to guide practitioners through the process of developing pedagogically effective learning activities and appropriate use of relevant tools and resources (Conole and Fill 2005).

Models and patterns

Models and patterns both provide more abstract forms of representation. Simplistically, a model is an abstract representation that helps us understand something we cannot see or experience directly. Patterns, as examined by McAndrew and Goodyear in Chapter 7, are more flexible descriptions of problems that practitioners will not directly reuse, but that provide guidance and illustration of an approach to the problem.

Kolb's learning cycle is probably the best-known experiential model (Kolb 1984). Kolb presents an action-based or 'learning by doing' approach through a four-stage cycle (experience, reflection, abstraction and experimentation). Recently, Cowan has extended Kolb's learning cycle by considering explicitly how to plan interactive activities to support each of the four stages (Cowan 1998).

A specific e-learning model that describes the stages of increasing competence in participating in an online community is Salmon's five-stage framework (2004) for supporting effective e-moderating in discussion forums, which emphasizes the dialogic aspects of socially situated theoretical perspectives. Her stages are: access and motivation; online socialization; information exchange; knowledge construction; and development. This model has been incredibly popular and has been taken up and applied extensively. However there has also been some criticism of the use of models (Lisewski and Joyce 2003). Because they are abstractions, practitioners may misunderstand how to apply the model effectively, by adopting a surface application of the model to their practice.

The benefits of mediating artefacts

The tools and resources that practitioners use to inform their practice have a number of benefits. First, they can be used as a means of sharing good practice between practitioners and enable reuse of learning activities, thereby creating economies of scale (Littlejohn 2003). Second, examples of effective practice may be communicated to other teachers. This could aid practitioners in making informed decisions between comparable activities and approaches (Beetham 2004). Third, they can be used as a framework for planning for accessibility, since resources can be replaced by other materials that closely match learners' needs. Fourth, they provide an effective means of communicating design requirements to developers, for example by providing outline lesson plans or schemas that illustrate to the developers the key stages involved in the process and the intended outcomes.

Despite a well-established practice of teachers adopting and adapting pre-designed resources such as case studies, lesson plans, etc., there is still little evidence of generic resources being developed and shared without specific subject content (Beetham 2004). This is partly because it is difficult to abstract an activity that can be reused across a range of subject disciplines (Britain 2004).

Conclusion

This chapter has attempted to describe the range of mediating artefacts practitioners are using to guide practice in creating learning activities. It has referred to some of the educational vocabularies developed that attempt to define practice, focusing beyond the level of content resource to the nature of learning activities. It has presented a taxonomy that has been developed, which provides a rich description of the components of learning activities and can be used to guide practice. It then contextualized this in terms of the wide range of mediating artefacts used by practitioners to inform their practice. The chapter demonstrates that the definition and creation of learning activities is complex and multifaceted and also that further research is needed into understanding how we can design more effectively, in order to create engaging and innovative learning activities that maximize the potential of new and emergent technologies.

References

Bailey, C., Fill, K., Zalfan, M.T., Davis, H.C., Conole, G. and Olivier, B. (2006) 'Panning for gold: designing pedagogically-inspired learning nuggets', *Educational Technology and Society*, 9 (1): 113–22.

Beetham, H. (2002) 'Developing learning technology networks through shared representations of practice', in C. Rust (ed.) *Improving Student Learning Using Learning Technologies*, Oxford: OCSLD.

Beetham, H. (2004) 'Review: developing e-learning models for the JISC practitioner communities: a report for the JISC e-pedagogy programme', Bristol: JISC. Online. Available www.elearning.ac.uk/resources/modelsreview (accessed 20 September 2006).

Bloom, B.S. (1956). *Taxonomy of Educational Objectives, Handbook I: The Cognitive Domain*, New York: David McKay Co Inc.

Britain, S. (2004) 'A review of learning design: concept, specifications and tools. A report for the JISC E-learning Pedagogy programme', Bristol: JISC.

Conole, G. (forthcoming) 'Mediating artefacts to guide choice in creating and undertaking learning activities', in submission.

Conole, G. and Dyke, M. (forthcoming) 'Complexity and interconnection: steering e-learning developments from commodification towards "co-modification",' in H. Oatley-Spencer (ed.) *Education in China: Reform and Diversity – eLearning in China: eChina Perspectives on Policy, Pedagogy and Innovation*, Aberdeen, Hong Kong: Hong Kong University Press.

Conole, G. and Fill, K. (2005) 'A learning design toolkit to create pedagogically effective learning activities', *Journal of Interactive Multimedia Education*, 8. Available www.jime.open.ac.uk/2005/08/ (accessed 28 August 2006).

Conole, G. and Oliver, M. (eds) (2007) *Contemporary Perspectives in E-learning Research: Themes, Tensions and Impact on Practice*, Oxford: RoutledgeFalmer.

Conole, G., de Laat, M., Darby, J. and Dillon, T. (2006) *An In-depth Case Study of Students' Experiences of E-learning – How is Learning Changing? Final Report of the JISC-funded LXP Learning Experiences Study project*, Milton Keynes: Open University.

Cowan, J. (1998) *On Becoming an Innovative University Teacher*, Buckingham: Open University Press.

Creanor, L., Trinder, K., Gowan, D. and Howells, C. (2006) *LEX – The Learning Experience Project, Final Report of the JISC-funded LEX Project*, Glasgow: Glasgow Caledonian University.

Currier, S., Campbell, L. and Beetham, H. (2006) 'JISC pedagogical vocabularies project report 1: pedagogical vocabularies review', Bristol: JISC. Online. Available www.jisc.ac.uk/elp_vocabularies.html (accessed 20 March 2006).

Dalziel, J.R. (2003) 'Implementing learning design: the Learning Activity Management System (LAMS)', in *Interact, Integrate, Impact*, Proceedings of the ASCILITE conference, pp. 593–6. Online. Available www.ascilite.org.au/conferences/adelaide03/docs/pdf/593.pdf (accessed 28 August 2006).

Duncan, C. (2003) 'Granularization', in A. Littlejohn (ed.) *Reusing Online Resources – A Sustainable Approach to e-Learning*, London: KoganPage, pp. 12–19.

Engeström, Y., Miettinen, R. and Punamäki , R.-J. (eds) (1999) *Perspectives on Activity Theory. Learning in Doing: Social, Cognitive and Computational Perspectives*, Cambridge: Cambridge University Press.

JISC (2006) The JORUM project. Online. Available www.jorum.ac.uk (accessed 24 August 2006).

Kolb, D. (1984) *Experiential Learning; Experience as the Source of Learning and Development*, Englewood Cliffs, NJ: Prentice Hall.

Laurillard, D. (1993) *Rethinking University Teaching: A Framework for the Effective Use of Educational Technology*, London: Routledge.

Lisewski, B. and Joyce, P. (2003) 'Examining the five-stage e-moderating model: design and emergent practice in the learning technology profession', *ALT-J, Research in Learning Technology*, 11 (2): 55–66.

Littlejohn, A. (2003) *Reusing Online Resources: A Sustainable Approach to E-learning*, London: Kogan Page.

Littlejohn, A., Falconer, I. and McGill, L. (forthcoming) 'Characterising effective eLearning resources', *Computers in Education*.

Mayes, J.T. and Fowler, C.J.H. (1999) 'Learning technology and usability: a framework for understanding courseware', *Interacting with Computers*, 11: 485–97.

Polsani, P. (2003) 'Use and abuse of reusable learning objects', *Journal of Digital Information*, 3 (4). Online. Available http://jodi.ecs.soton.ac.uk/Articles/v03/i04/Polsani/ (accessed 28 August 2006).

Rehak, D. and Mason, R. (2003) 'Keeping the learning in learning objects', in A. Littlejohn (ed.) *Reusing Online Resources – A Sustainable Approach to E-learning*, London: Kogan Page, pp. 20–34.

Salmon, G. (2002) *E-tivities: The Key to Online Teaching, Training and Learning*, London: Routledge.

Salmon, G. (2004) *E-moderating: The Key to Teaching and Learning Online*, 2nd edn, London: Routledge.

Sharpe, R., Beetham, H. and Ravenscroft, A. (2004) 'Active artefacts: representing our knowledge of learning and teaching', *Educational Developments*, 5 (2): 16–21.

Vygotsky, L.S. (1978) *Mind in Society: The Development of Higher Psychological Processes*, Cambridge, MA: Harvard University Press.

Weller, M.J. (2007) *Virtual Learning Environments – Using, Choosing and Developing your VLE*, Oxford: RoutledgeFalmer.

Chapter 7

Representing practitioner experiences through learning design and patterns

Patrick McAndrew and Peter Goodyear

EDITORS' INTRODUCTION

This chapter considers alternative ways in which learning activities can be represented in order to be shared. In particular it looks at a 'learning design' approach, where the aim is to build a formal description that can be handled by a computer and played to an end user. The strengths of this approach are considered in relation to the tools that are being developed to support the IMS Learning Design specification, and the portability of the resulting designs. The chapter goes on to consider an alternative approach that may have lower barriers to take-up by practitioners. 'Patterns' provide flexible descriptions that engage and challenge their users, and can be mapped to different contexts of use. A pilot patterns-based approach is described, whereby existing materials are reworked as online open content with patterns extracted and stored to assist the process of design in the future.

Learning Design

Learning Design is a specification that allows the representation of units of learning and as such is a candidate for the representation of practitioner experiences. Bill Olivier, one of the architects of the specification, has stated that 'the ability to share and modify LDs will enable us to build up better practice for eLearning – and that is the main aim of LD' (Griffiths 2004). In reviewing the state of Learning Design, Britain (2004: 2) drew the distinction between '"learning design" (small "l", small "d") when we are talking about the general concept and "Learning Design" (Capital "L" and "D") when referring to the concept as implemented in the IMS specification'. This is an important distinction, as discussion about learning design has encouraged a greater focus on activities and collaboration, which were the features that inspired the developers of Educational Modelling Language (EML) and the IMS Learning Design specification. However, use of the specification itself has been inhibited by the lack of tools and limitations in the existing specification. For example Dalziel (2003) and Britain (Chapter 8) here have commented on the absence of tools to support collaborative tasks and to allow for group creation and monitoring.

Britain highlights in his first recommendation 'that the concept of learning design can be usefully distinguished from the implementational level' and that 'work needs to be conducted to examine the range of approaches to "designing for learning" in use by teachers and lecturers, and the software tools that are or could be used to support these activities' (Britain 2004: 25). Masterman and Vogel in this volume (Chapter 4) discuss some of the research that has since been done to explore current practice in 'designing for learning'.

Given that Learning Design is a developing specification and that there is a continuing lack of proven tools, it remains difficult to commit to the use of the complete specification. Tools available from development projects have been focused on proving that the specification is viable. Second-generation tools are expected that will offer greater usability and robustness but they have been relatively slow to arrive. However, those who do invest in describing their own learning activities in the framework of Learning Design can expect to have improving support for the process of transferring these designs to learners in runable form. Learning Design remains a good candidate for formally capturing activity descriptions and making them available for use in other circumstances. Even so, attempts to engage practitioners in the learning design approach have met with only partial success. This is a reflection on learning design being a developing area, but also could be an indication of more fundamental difficulties with the transfer of vocabularies and methods from an expert group to wider use.

Specific barriers to the adoption of Learning Design include the following:

1   *The lack of a way to describe learning tools.* There are very few generic descriptions of the services needed to run learning designs. For designs to be transferable a wide range of generic services need to be described, and then matched to appropriate local services at the point of delivery, but only a very limited number of services are included in the specification of Learning Design. This is proving problematic for projects seeking to transfer learning designs, such as the Sakai project (http://sakaiproject.org/), where work on describing such services has concentrated on developer support (e.g. Open Service Interface Definitions – OSIDs) and has yet to address how the different services should be represented at the design level. Working from the requirements end, the Learning Activity Management System (LAMS) (Dalziel 2003) has demonstrated that providing a set of configurable tools to support a range of pedagogically sound activities is very engaging to the teacher community, and, with the release of the LAMS Tools contract, offers a way to change the toolset inside the system. However, the representation and ways of working with tools has proved hard to represent in a way that is compatible with the Learning Design specification.

2   *Difficulty in creating the designs.* The process of writing down a design – as described in the IMS Learning Design Best Practice Guide – is time-consuming and technically involved. The process includes building use cases, representing activities through Unified Modelling Language (UML) diagrams and then

codifying the design in Extensible Markup Language (XML). Only the last stage of this process is supported by the current range of software tools, and the result can be a rigid design that is transferable for reuse but does not engage the teacher or require any understanding of how the activity works before it can be taken and reused. This could mean that it is not reused in the most appropriate way.

3   *The tension of working with a complex specification.* The IMS Learning Design specification is powerful in that it includes support for programmed logic and flexibility in describing the sequence. But it can be initially frustrating in the limited number of services that are explicitly supported, the verbose structures that need to be described in XML, and the lack of explicit support for either hierarchical or generic levels of design.

These issues may be addressed by using a less rigid approach instead of the Learning Design formulation. Possible structures include templates, lesson plans or simplified learning designs. One candidate is to take a patterns-based approach, drawing on experience from other fields that have aimed to share designs.

Patterns

Learning patterns (Goodyear *et al.* 2004) is an approach that looks to architectural design patterns (Alexander 1979) as a way to capture knowledge from designers and share it with practitioners. In particular it aims to consider patterns as a source for advice to reproduce the general forms of architecture without the expectation that any cases are exactly the same. Thus a pattern

> describes a problem which occurs over and over again in our environment, and then describes the core of the solution to that problem, in such a way that you can use this solution a million times over, without ever doing it the same way twice.
>
> (Alexander *et al.* 1977: x)

Applied to learning, the design patterns approach seeks to identify what needs to be provided as useful background, guidance and illustration in describing ways to assist learning. A pattern is seen as something that will not be reused directly but can help informed teachers build up their own range of tasks, tools or materials by drawing on a collective body of experience. This is quite different from the Learning Design paradigm, in which the design must be specified tightly enough to be implemented within a player: the pattern is *not* intended to supply a complete solution but rather to give enough guidance to support human intervention and variation in each reuse. This approach may be integrated with more specific solutions such as coded Learning Designs or LAMS sequences; however the focus is on producing abstracted descriptions that engage the designer rather than packaged answers.

The format for a pattern, adapted from Goodyear *et al.* (2004), is:

1   A *picture* (showing an archetypal *example* of the pattern).
2   An *introductory paragraph* setting the *context* for the pattern (explaining how it helps to complete some larger patterns).
3   Problem *headline*, to give the essence of the problem in one or two sentences.
4   The *body* of the problem (its empirical background, evidence for its validity, examples of different ways the pattern can be manifested).
5   The *solution*. Stated as an instruction, so that you know what to do to build the pattern.
6   A *diagrammatic representation* of the solution.
7   A *paragraph* linking the pattern to the smaller patterns that are needed to complete and embellish it.

Such patterns are then integrated into a pattern language by providing related components – the example given by Goodyear *et al.* is a *discussion group* pattern that draws on patterns for *discussion role, facilitator* and *discursive task*. This format seeks to encompass a range of useful aspects that needs to be recorded to enable the reader to understand the reason for the pattern and the solution that is being addressed. The way in which a pattern is stored is not itself rigid, and other projects have used variations on the format, with alternative labels. However, the key is the ability to identify the three aspects of context, problem and solutions. It is interesting to compare this format with work done on how different representations of practice are used by practitioners (Sharpe and Oliver, Chapter 9).

The strength of the patterns approach is shown in communities that adopt them, such as the original Architecture community and more recently also communities of software developers. In these communities, design patterns are usually drafted, shared, critiqued and refined through an extended process of collaboration. Thus patterns have the potential to contribute to the sharing of techniques between developers of learning activities.

In contrast to Learning Design, patterns offer informality and are open to different interpretations and implementations at the detail level. This can raise difficulties over shared vocabulary and a relative lack of descriptive power, as has occurred with learning-related metadata (see following discussion); on the other hand it can also be seen as allowing contributions with a lower overhead and encouraging users to engage with and challenge the contents of patterns rather than adopt them unchanged. A further stage is to develop a collection of learning patterns as part of a pattern language. There are emerging collaborative efforts to achieve this: for example the E-LEN project (www2.tisip.no/E-LEN/) has produced sample templates and encouraged contributions.

Metadata and vocabularies

A barrier to the development of shared descriptions, whether in Learning Design or patterns, has been how to provide a way to summarize and search each design.

Metadata is one approach to solving this. Metadata is informally defined as the 'information about information', but this is a flawed definition: the key to understanding some of the problems with metadata is to see that it is a home for information that is about an object but not essential to the direct use of the object. For example, to read this chapter, you do not need to know the software that created it, the date it was written, or even the keywords used to catalogue it, yet these can all be considered as potentially useful items to capture. The problem is illustrated by the use of the word 'potentially'; the temptation then arises to record everything that might possibly be useful, resulting in much information that actually will never be used. To those involved in the development process there is little motivation to provide this information in a way that is accurate and reliable.

The development of metadata for learning objects, in particular IMS Metadata and its development into the IEEE Learning Object Metadata (LOM) in 2002 (see http://ltsc.ieee.org/wg12/) revealed that agreement about the different aspects of learning to record in the metadata was not enough; the vocabulary to be used for actually describing those elements was also vital. In early development of IMS Metadata specification, it was decided that appropriate vocabularies should be suggested while leaving the final choice to users. However, the suggested vocabularies have proved not to be sufficient (for example, some were based very specifically on the US model of education, others had been excessively simplified), and use of locally relevant vocabularies, such as course code systems internal to a university, have meant that the resulting metadata records are not transferable. The current view represented in work on vocabulary description exchange (see www.imsglobal.org/vdex/) is that it is important to allow local vocabulary development, but to a transferable format and available from a public site for others to use. At the same time there has been collaborative work on agreeing the use of

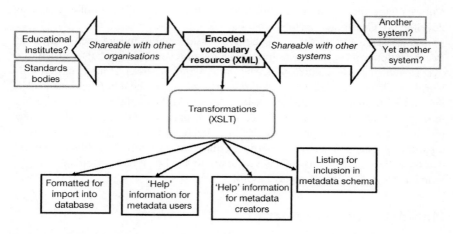

Figure 7.1 Mechanisms for exploiting vocabularies encoded using XML thesauri

Source: adapted from Brasher and McAndrew (2003)

vocabularies within sufficiently cohesive communities, for example the SeSDL Educational Taxonomy (Currier and Campbell 2000).

A proposed methodology for exploiting vocabularies for metadata is outlined in Figure 7.1, based on work led by Andrew Brasher (Brasher and McAndrew 2003). In this figure the suggested approach is to represent the vocabularies using shareable thesauri containing not only the terms but additional explanation, hierarchies and relationships. This approach would be applied within a community by identifying the particular terminology that is in use and any specialist meanings that are attached to them. In this way, we can attempt to be clear about the meaning for its original audience and also prepare for a more transferable version for other audiences. This provides some of the same flexibility, within a structured format, as the patterns approach.

Implementing a patterns approach for open content

The role of patterns is illustrated in Figure 7.2. This shows a hierarchy of representations, ranging from models of learning that can be drawn from theory, literature or existing examples (see for example Mayes and de Freitas, Chapter 1) through to patterns that can abstract a number of generic designs. At a more local level are instantiations based on how these designs are interpreted and matched to relevant learning materials and tools, and finally runable versions in a suitable environment, e.g. LAMS, the Moodle virtual learning environment (VLE), or in a player for IMS Learning Design.

Patterns are intended to inspire new instantiations; however the model assumes that good patterns can be identified as part of the development process. The concept of what is 'good' can itself cause problems. If there is an available collection of designs or patterns then we would like to know that they are worth the effort to reuse. We would like to use the good patterns and avoid the bad ones (there is a view that it is valuable to record the bad as 'antipatterns' to serve as warnings to others (Brown et al. 1998)). However, measuring the effectiveness of an educational technology and approach is notoriously difficult (Joy and Garcia 2000). Alexander, in his work on patterns (Alexander 1979: 19), gives an alternative by devising a 'quality without a name'. He states: 'This quality is objective and precise, but it cannot be named.' Alexander uses this concept to justify his listing of architectural patterns that will bring benefits, are somehow appealing and seem right, even if they have not been measured as better than others. This clearly raises a further question as to whether patterns are too subjective, but frees us from using only patterns that have passed through some kind of formal check.

In this view, patterns are proposals that are made with individual judgement that they possess sufficient quality but are then open to refinement and validation by the community to be proved in use. This approach fits well with the focus on community suggested by Sharpe and Oliver (Chapter 9). The source for patterns is, in general,

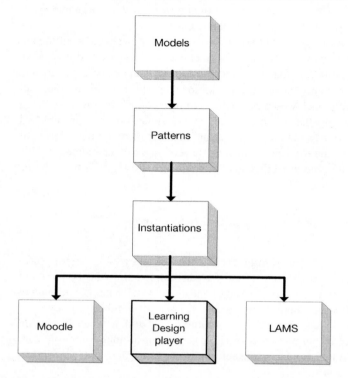

Figure 7.2 Patterns as part of the development process

the experience of those working on solutions to problems and in particular working with existing implementations. Any existing implementation will be set in a specific context and the format of a pattern encourages that to be described, but the overall premise is that the pattern can help inform reuse in a new context.

There has been some discussion of ways to automate extraction of patterns (Brouns *et al.* 2005), but these assume consistent structure for the material, such as already being encoded as IMS Learning Designs. In the Open University's OpenLearn project (www.open.ac.uk/openlearn) patterns are being piloted as a way to capture designs as part of a human process of academic transformation. OpenLearn aims to provide free access to a range of educational materials, both for learners using the content within a learning environment, and for educators re-using and remixing the content in new contexts. Content is currently provided as XML structured files and as courses in the Moodle VLE (http://moodle.org). Eventually IMS Learning Design may also be used. The initial content set is derived from proven Open University materials designed to work within its taught courses, i.e. quality assured content intended to enable cohorts of students supported by tutors to meet particular learning objectives. The new context for this material is as online open content, where there is much less control over timing and support, and activities must be viable in isolation from the associated course structures.

'Academic transformation' is the term used for the adjustments that need to be made to the content to make it available in this new context. A three-level view of the transformation sees the content as (1) maintaining its original integrity with unchanged intent, but being adjusted for the new platform; (2) keeping its essence but significantly changing some aspects, or (3) using the original as inspiration to be remixed into a new work. The initial focus is on material that will maintain its integrity. However, care is needed to identify what should be retained to keep academic integrity, what must be changed as it is too tied to the original context, and what might be open to change to take advantage of new tools and ways of learning in the new context.

Patterns have been introduced into this process as a tool to help academic transformers represent their interpretation of the original intent, and show how they intend to change the materials into the new context. A Pattern Analysis Template (PAT) based on the pattern structure has been used to capture the view of those involved in the process (see Figure 7.3). Once complete the template provides a candidate pattern and will be available as an additional resource to educators seeking to reuse the material. The hope is that the patterns will build towards a pattern language, potentially giving educators an alternative way of understanding the intention behind pedagogical source materials, alongside the instantiation intended for the learner. Patterns will help record how resources can be used and how the designer expects them to work. In the case of the material being used for OpenLearn the original content does not have a corresponding pattern set and so the templates are gathering and sharing views on how both the original and transformed content operate.

This approach is in its early stages and so only initial findings can be reported here. While the evidence is that designers find it helpful to review the pattern analysis before directly working on the content, feedback indicates that this can also be an uncomfortable experience, leading to alternative and sometimes conflicting views on the same material. These views may each be valid, and illustrate the different levels of perspective that are expected in a pattern language (in contrast to the approach that looks for a single 'runable' instantiation). A tension has also been observed between extracting patterns that focus on the learning experience, and extracting those that focus on the provider's viewpoint and the requirements of the transformation. Both of these viewpoints are valuable and indicate there may be a case for making alternative perspectives explicit in the way that patterns are recorded.

The pattern format encourages a large amount of information to be entered into a relatively small space, and as with the metadata problem described previously, it is difficult to encourage a consistent approach that provides the relevant information. The academic transformers had example completed patterns to help them in completing new templates. Analysis of the linguistic structure of the examples and the new templates has indicated that structure and language used in the example may have a significant influence on how the new templates are completed. Revised

Pattern Analysis Template

Completed by:
Date:
Comments:

Name: (short name to convey ideas to others)
Context: (what is needed to make this work, and any assumptions)
Problem: (background or statement of problem solved)
Solution: (key points any critical factors)
Diagram or illustration: (sketch out the solution or describe stages in words)
Related patterns: (similar sections, builds on another pattern)
Instantiation: (e.g. course name, section, chunk identifier, link)

Figure 7.3 The PAT used by OpenLearn

example templates need to be devised, with clear language to act as models and style guides for designers on how to word their own contributions.

Conclusion

Both patterns and learning design encourage the representation of activities alongside content, and this is important to encourage appropriate designs for learning with technologies. Perhaps the main distinction between the two approaches is that they aim in the one case to represent a design for a computer to understand and process, and in the other for a human being to understand and work with. Both of these aspects are important and deserve to be supported in an holistic approach to developing educational materials. In the Learning Design approach, if a unit of learning is described so that a computer can work out the roles that are involved, set up the unit's structure, and sequence the learners' access to the material, then we can be fairly sure that the description is complete and detailed enough. A pattern-based description will inevitably have lost some of the detail and may have failed to capture information necessary to reproduce the situation we want to describe. However, the key pedagogical points can now be made simply and argued for in a direct way, so that the human reader of the pattern can apply their own expertise. Rather than simply reproducing previous ideas, they can develop new ways of achieving the same goals that are suited to their own context. This matches well with Alexander's own vision for the use of patterns in architecture: 'A pattern language gives each person who uses it, the power to create an infinite variety of new and unique buildings, just as his ordinary language gives him the power to create an infinite variety of sentences' (Alexander 1979: 167).

There are tensions between human-understandable and computer-understandable forms of representation, and a way forward is to combine these different representations to take advantage of their different strengths. A proposed model is to use patterns for human–human communication and either Learning Design or, more awkwardly, multiple VLE specific instantiations to provide the computer-interpretable form. Although there is limited practice in using patterns, initial work within the OpenLearn project shows one approach that appears to focus attention on academic issues in working to reuse materials. The value of the approach would be greatly increased if a viable pattern set and pattern language emerged. This will be taken forward as the OpenLearn content is reviewed and reused but is also being addressed in other collaborative initiatives such as the pedagogical patterns project (Sharp *et al.* 2003) and the E-LEN project discussed in Goodyear *et al.* (2004).

Acknowledgements

This chapter draws on work funded by the Joint Information Systems Committee (JISC) as part of the research study on the effectiveness of resources, tools and support services used by practitioners in designing and delivering e-learning activities. OpenLearn is supported by the William and Flora Hewlett Foundation in conjunction with the Open University. Patrick McAndrew is grateful for discussion with members of OpenLearn, in particular Giselle Ferreira, Andy Lane, Jerard Bretts, Stephen Bradley and Steve Godwin. The linguistic analysis of example patterns was carried out by John McAndrew of Macquarie University.

References

Alexander, C. (1979) *The Timeless Way of Building*, New York: Oxford University Press.

Alexander, C., Ishikawa, S., Silverstein, M., Jacobson, M., Fiksdahl-King, I. and Angel, S. (1977) *A Pattern Language: Towns, Buildings, Construction*, New York: Oxford University Press.

Brasher, A.J. and McAndrew, P. (2003) 'Metadata vocabularies for describing learning objects: implementation and exploitation issues', *Learning Technology Newsletter of IEEE LTTF: Special Issue*. Online. Available http://lttf.ieee.org/learn_tech/issues/january2003/index.html#9 (accessed 29 September 2006).

Britain, S. (2004) *A Review of Learning Design: Concept, Specifications and Tools*, JISC Project Report. Online. Available www.jisc.ac.uk/uploaded_documents/ACF83C.doc (accessed 29 September 2006).

Brouns, F., Koper, R., Manderveld, J., van Bruggen, J., Sloep, P. *et al.* (2005) 'A first exploration of an inductive analysis approach for detecting learning design patterns', *Journal of Interactive Media in Education*. Online. Available http://jime.open.ac.uk/2005/03 (accessed 29 September 2006).

Brown, W.J., Malveau, R.C. and Mowbray, T.J. (1998) *AntiPatterns: Refactoring Software, Architectures, and Projects in Crisis*, New York: John Wiley & Sons.

Currier, S. and Campbell, L. (2000) *The SeSDL Taxonomy*. Online. Available www.sesdl.scotcit.ac.uk/ (accessed 29 September 2006).

Dalziel, J. (2003) 'Implementing learning design: the Learning Activity Management System (LAMS)', paper presented at *ASCILITE 2003*, Adelaide, December 2003. Online. Available www.melcoe.mq.edu.au/documents/ASCILITE2003%20Dalziel%20Final.pdf (accessed 29 September 2006).

Goodyear, P., Avgeriou, P., Baggetun, R., Bartoluzzi, S., Retalis, S. *et al.* (2004) 'Towards a pattern language for networked learning', in S. Banks, P. Goodyear, V. Hodgson, C. Jones, V. Lally *et al.* (eds) *Networked Learning 2004*, Lancaster: Lancaster University, pp. 449–55. Online. Available www.networkedlearningconference.org.uk/past/nlc2004/proceedings/individual_papers/goodyear_et_al.htm (accessed 29 September 2006).

Griffiths, D. (2004) 'Bill Olivier and panel discuss the state of Learning Design', UNFOLD moderated online chat 16 July 2004. Online. Available http://moodle.learningnetworks.org/file.php/34/transcripts/transcript16jun04.htm (accessed 29 September 2006).

Joy, E.H. and Garcia, F.E. (2000) 'Measuring learning effectiveness: a new look at no-significant-difference findings', *Journal of Asynchronous Learning Networks*, 4 (1): 33–9. Online. Available www.sloan-c.org/publications/jaln/v4n1/pdf/v4n1_joygarcia.pdf (accessed 29 September 2006).

Sharp, H., Manns, M.L. and Eckstein, J. (2003) 'Evolving pedagogical patterns: the work of the pedagogical patterns project', *Computer Science Education*, 13 (4): 315–30.

Chapter 8

Learning design systems
Current and future developments

Sandy Britain

EDITORS' INTRODUCTION

In this chapter, learning design is considered from a technical perspective – how the concept differs from earlier paradigms such as instructional design, and how learning activities might be represented in the systems that produce and 'run' or instantiate them. The IMS Learning Design specification is given special attention, due to its promise of interoperability and potentially universal sharing of designs. The authors go on to discuss the learning design tools currently available to practitioners and propose a framework for evaluating how well they support the human design processes of planning, implementing, orchestrating and sharing pedagogical ideas. This chapter provides an essential link between discussions of design practice (see e.g. Masterman and Vogel, Chapter 4) and the opportunities presented by new technical systems and specifications.

Introduction

The principal aim of this chapter is to report on the range of currently available software tools related to learning design. This is not a simple task since, over the past few years, a wide range of software tools that could be said to support some aspect of learning design has appeared. Moreover these tools demonstrate a wide variety of approaches and perspectives regarding the nature of learning design. Consequently it is impractical to attempt to present here a comprehensive review and evaluation of all the tools in this space. It seems more useful to classify the broad categories of software that have emerged, highlighting a few key examples of each. We then propose a scheme for evaluating learning design software in order to gain a robust picture of the merits and drawbacks of the various packages around. This methodology, which has been used to address similar problems in the past (e.g. Britain 2004; Britain and Liber 2004), enables us to identify gaps and challenges for future development.

One of the most significant contributions to work in this area has been the recent development of the IMS Learning Design specification (IMS 2005). This ambitious project, initiated by a team of educational researchers from the Open University of the Netherlands (OUNL), has produced a formal language that can model the activities that take place in teaching and learning. This can be represented in Extensible Markup Language (XML) and run in any conformant player environment. The IMS Learning Design specification and the process for modelling learning designs embedded within it share many of the same underlying motivations as other approaches to designing for learning, such as a focus on learning activities and a desire to capture a range of pedagogical models. The IMS Learning Design specification is, of course, only one of many possible ways to model and build software to support learning design, as noted by Dalziel (2005). However, the promise of interoperability and reuse of learning designs, and the wide range of recent developments in this area, both demand that it is given particular attention here.

The concept of learning design and models of (e-)learning

In the Introduction to this volume Beetham and Sharpe characterize 'design for learning' as 'designing, planning, orchestrating and supporting learning activities as part of a learning session or programme'. Despite its relatively recent appearance in connection with e-learning, the concept of learning as design is far from being a new idea. In a traditional face-to-face context, many teachers will consciously and reflectively engage in the process of design in this general sense of everyday lesson planning, while other teachers may never have given it much thought, but nonetheless make subconscious design decisions every time they prepare a teaching session.

From the teacher's perspective there are two main advantages associated with consciously thinking about the process of designing learning activities. The first is that it provides a framework for teachers to reflect in a deeper and more creative way about how they design and structure activities for different learners or groups of learners, and the second is that designs that prove to be effective may then be communicated and shared between teachers or archived for reuse on future occasions. While the benefits of engaging in the process of learning design exist regardless of the mode of delivery (electronic or face to face), they are particularly relevant to e-learning, which, unlike traditional face-to-face learning, has tended to focus on content and services at the expense of learning (inter)actions.

The scope of the term 'learning design' is not always clear. In some cases it is used as a synonym for 'instructional design', which is used (especially in North America) to refer to pedagogic design of all sorts. Instructional design in e-learning, however, has focused predominantly on *learning objects* as the core entity within a course, and has often adopted a programmed learning approach. Virtual learning environments (VLEs) have been designed to cater for this rather simplistic content-delivery model at the expense of a variety of pedagogical models that are built around collaborative activity on the part of learners. The use of 'learning design' as an alternative concept is associated with a feeling among many educators that the learning objects approach places too much emphasis on content delivery rather than looking more carefully at what learners do.

The first key idea in learning design, then, is that provision of content for 'read and test' activities is not sufficient for all purposes, and that to learn effectively people need to be involved in a wider range of *learning activities*. While learning is an active process of knowledge construction that humans perform quite naturally, not all learners are equally capable of effective and efficient learning on their own. Indeed, most if not all, benefit from some level of guidance and support. Successful teaching involves a variety of strategies and techniques for engaging, motivating and energizing students over and above merely presenting them with well-designed learning materials. The trend within e-learning to date has been to focus on quite a narrow set of learning activities that can be easily managed within the current generation of browser-based VLEs: the so-called 'content and quiz' model. Part of the aim of learning design is to help broaden the set of activities that are used to support learning in an e-learning context.

The second aspect of the learning design concept is that it involves giving thought to the sequential order and timing of the various activities and the presentation of the resources needed to support them. This orchestration may take the form of a simple sequential flow following a narrative description of the learning activities, or a logical but un-ordered clustering of activities and resources as is often the case in VLEs. There may sometimes be a call for a learning design that involves branching of workflow into parallel activities undertaken by sub-groups before coming back together. Or a design may be constructed that allows different routes to be taken based on achievement at a testing stage within a sequence. Thus a second key aspect of tools to support the concept of learning design will be the notion of workflow or structuring of activities.

A third, and related, idea is that abstract design patterns (such as a specific sequence of activities or workflow) can instantiate concrete realizations of a desired pedagogical model or approach (Van Es and Koper 2006). Thus workflows produced as part of the learning design process could be used to translate pedagogical theory into practical design patterns or templates that can be applied to multiple contexts.

Finally, it would be useful to be able to record 'learning designs' for sharing and reuse in the future, and this one of the key problems that the IMS Learning Design specification is intended to solve. It is not, however, a simple matter to represent learning designs in a way that is both powerful and flexible and also easy to understand and manipulate. The 'design', 'pattern' or 'recipe' needs to be described at a sufficient level of abstraction that it can be generalized beyond the single teaching and learning context for which it is created, but not at such an abstract level that the pedagogical value and richness is lost. This is one of the key challenges to be addressed in creating learning design tools.

The IMS Learning Design specification

In this section we outline the main features of the IMS Learning Design specification. For more comprehensive treatment of the subject of the IMS Learning Design specification see Koper and Tattersall (2005).

The origins of the IMS Learning Design specification lie in work undertaken in the development of Educational Modelling Language (EML) by Rob Koper and a team of researchers at the OUNL. EML is a notational system that provides a way of describing teaching and learning interactions at a level of abstraction above the specific instance of the context in which it was created. The resulting model can be seen as a design pattern for that teaching and learning instance. At the heart of EML is the concept of a Unit of Learning (UOL). A UOL represents any set of learning activities and resources required to fulfil identified learning objectives. In practice this may be a course, a module, a lesson or single activity such as a discussion. EML models the components of a UOL as *people in roles* performing *activities* in an *environment composed of resources and services*. According to Koper (2001), this general statement about the core entities and relationships involved in learning design expresses a key axiom that is common to all major educational approaches. As a result EML is theoretically capable of representing any pedagogical model (Van Es and Koper 2006). It should be clearly understood that this is a model of pedagogic processes, and not a model of learning. The IMS Learning Design specification has adopted many of the core features of EML including the idea of a UOL. For any given UOL some or all of the following elements need to be described in an IMS Learning Design:

- *Learning objectives*. One or more learning objectives.
- *Roles*. There are two categories of roles used to represent people: learner or staff. Specific individuals are not a generalizable component, but roles are, so the role is specified in the design rather than a person. A number of different roles can be defined in a UOL, together with the tasks which the people who fulfil them should carry out.
- *Activities*. These can be of two types, either *learning activities* or *support activities*. Activities can be aggregated using activity structures. Activity structures can also reference other activity structures and external units of learning.
- *Environment*. The environment element contains two basic types: *learning objects* and *services*. Learning objects would typically be a URL (universal resource locator) to external content, tools or tests with optional metadata, while services refers to a service or tool provided within the environment that is available at run-time but cannot be specified at design-time. Examples of services may be discussion forums, chat rooms, monitoring tools and other features typically provided by VLEs.

Some of the generalizable design components and the learning objectives described above need to be bound to specific instances at either at design, instantiation or run-time depending on the context. This binding is achieved using elements called *resources*. These can be of five different types: web content, imsld content, person, service facility or dossier.

Finally the learning design needs to specify how the learning and support activities performed by different roles using the various learning objects and services are organized into a coherent workflow. This facility is provided by the *method* element. The method consists of a *play* (or concurrent *plays*), which contains a sequence of *acts*. Each *act* contains one or more *role-parts*. Each *role-part* associates one *role* with one *activity* or *activity structure*.

As can be seen from the above, the Learning Design specification uses the metaphor of a theatrical play to describe the workflow involved in a learning and teaching scenario. The workflow is fundamentally sequential as the acts are sequential, but there may be more complex behaviour than a single sequence through the provision of concurrent role-parts, which means that branching and simultaneous activity by sub-groups is possible.

There are three levels of Learning Design specification document increasing in complexity. Level A, the first level, includes all the elements outlined in the previous section. Levels B and C add elements for allowing more powerful run-time behaviour such as personalization and adaptive sequencing, but also add considerably greater complexity.

Relationship of the IMS Learning Design specification to the concept of Learning Design

It is evident from the outline provided above that the IMS Learning Design specification is consistent in many ways with the general idea of learning design articulated above. It is centred on the idea of learners performing activities; it is intended to provide a means for describing the orchestration of activities into a learning workflow; it can capture a wide variety of pedagogical models; and it provides a vehicle for the sharing and reuse of learning design patterns.

The IMS Learning Design specification specification can be viewed in three different ways, as:

1   *An interoperability specification*, whose purpose is to move information around between applications in XML documents.
2   *An educational modelling language*. This could be used by people whose main aim was to model pedagogy, rather than to implement e-learning.
3   *A methodology and associated tools*. The Best Practice Guide in the specification describes a process for working with the specification in large-scale distance education. Other methodologies are also possible, but because this is the one included in the specification it has a certain authority.

When discussing the IMS Learning Design specification, therefore, it is important to be clear which of these aspects we are referring to (or all three). However, the IMS Learning Design specification is a complex specification and the best practice implementation guide is a difficult document to read and understand. Consequently there is currently some degree of confusion about how the specification relates to the overall concept of learning design described above.

Table 8.1 Key activities in learning design and their equivalents within the IMS Learning Design specification

Learning design processes	IMS Learning Design specification processes
Define learning objectives	Specify learning objectives
Develop narrative description of learning and teaching scenario	Recommended stage in the IMS Learning Design specification Best Practice Guide
Create learning activity workflow from narrative description	Create a method using play, acts and role-parts
Create or adapt learning content resources	Identify learning resources and create a content package (not defined within the IMS Learning Design specification)
Assign resources, tools and people to activities	Specify roles, resources environment and services
Running/performing the learning activity (real-time)	Initiate a 'run' using a Learning Design aware player
Learner support and on-the-fly adaptation	Not defined within the IMS Learning Design specification – although on-the-fly adaptation is
Reflecting (including sharing outputs for peer reflection)	Not defined

Table 8.1 summarizes a number of the elements we have suggested might be involved in designing a UOL and identifies corresponding elements within the IMS Learning Design specification design process. It also serves to illustrate quite a close correspondence between the activities that an educational practitioner might perform as part of the learning design process and the activities involved in developing and running a Learning Design with the IMS Learning Design specification. However, as we have seen there are also some important differences. It is a valuable exercise, then, to consider how well learning design tools support the human design processes involved in preparing learning activities and sequences.

An evaluation framework for learning design software tools

In order to differentiate and categorize the variety of tools in this area we have developed a framework of evaluation questions (see Appendix 8). These questions are designed to provide insight into not only the features and capabilities of each software tool but also its intended purpose and its target user group. In the next section we present an analysis of current learning design software based on these questions. We go on to identify gaps in the capabilities of current tools and challenges for software designers in the future.

Software tools to support aspects of learning design can be broadly described within three main categories: authoring environments; run-time environments; and integrated environments. Run-time environments are only relevant to the present discussion in the context of running the IMS Learning Design specification output. At the time of writing the main engine that can interpret an IMS Learning Design specification is the Coppercore LD Engine. Only a small number of players have been built on the engine (which itself provides only a basic user interface) such as the Reload preview player (Reload 2006) and SLeD (Barret-Baxendale *et al*. 2005). The behavioural properties of the interpreter can affect the way UOL runs (Olivier and Tattersall 2005), and other players could be built on the Coppercore Engine, or using a different engine. These could give a quite distinct user experiences even when following the same learning flow, perhaps specialized for the purposes of different groups of learners and teachers from various academic or professional contexts. Indeed this relative poverty to date of the IMS Learning Design specification players compared with authoring applications may have given a falsely limited picture of the capabilities of the specification. The true potential can only be fully assessed when a range of player applications is available. In this respect it is very encouraging that an integrated player has been developed for the .LRN VLE, and that the Moodle development roadmap foresees full adoption of the IMS Learning Design specification.

Authoring environments

The foremost priority for any software supporting learning design is to allow users to create a representation of their design. At the simplest level this might involve the use of a word processor or other general purpose authoring tool. Masterman and Vogel in Chapter 4 describe the use of Microsoft PowerPoint. One limitation of general tools like these is they provide no explicit pedagogical support, such as templates for structuring units of learning, activities and workflow. A second problem is that the designs that are produced are not expressed in any common format that would enable others to reuse them easily, although as Masterman and Vogel observe, for many teachers reuse is not a highly motivating factor at the present time. A more immediate problem in an e-learning context is that a design created in this way cannot be imported directly into a run-time environment such as a VLE for immediate use by learners. Furthermore the author cannot preview the design and its behaviour during the design process. For the purpose of this review we focus on authoring tools that provide this kind of functionality. There is a variety of tools for authoring educational content – reviewed fully in Britain (2005) – which support some aspects of learning design. Not surprisingly most of these are focused on content rather than activity design. One notable exception is eXe – an educational XML editor (eXe 2006), which provides templates for building educational activities known as I-Devices. It is designed to be easy to use for teachers and produces structured content and activities in SCORM (Sharable Courseware Object Reference Model) format. Other comparable tools are LessonBuilder and Lectora.

Until recently there were few tools that supported the IMS Learning Design specification. However a community of developers has sprung up around Learning Design, coordinated by the European-funded UNFOLD project and produced a number of tools (see UNFOLD 2004, for a list of then current tools). Learning Design authoring tools include the Reload LD editor that is built on the Eclipse framework. The Reload interface consists of property sheets for completing required elements of the specification such as method, roles, environment, activities and so on. While the designers have strived to simplify the process by providing default values for elements where possible, it remains a daunting task requiring a good knowledge of the specification to use. This is thus a tool more suitable for use by developers and technically capable learning designers than most teachers. Several other Learning Design editors would come into this category, e.g. Copperauthor, COSMOS, Al.Fanet editor (reviewed in Griffiths *et al.* 2005). A Learning Design authoring tool that implements a different approach is the MOT+ editor (Paquette *et al.* 2005). This adapts an existing graphical application for creating learning workflows and adds the ability to export this as a Level A IMS Learning Design specification. This is still more suitable for specialist learning designers than teachers. An interesting development to make Learning Design editors more user-friendly is the DialogPlus project (Bailey *et al.* 2005). A summary of the characteristics of a selection of these tools is contained in Table 8.2.

We can see from the comparison in Table 8.2 that those tools that are modelled closely on the IMS Learning Design specification and are intended to allow sophisticated editing of IMS Learning Designs are intended for use by specialist learning designers with a sound knowledge of the specification, while those tools intended to be easy to use by teachers have a less close 'fit' with the IMS Learning Design specification model and thus the machine interoperability and potential for reuse of designs is diminished. This parallels observations by Griffiths *et al.* (2005) among others in surveying the field; more work is needed to create learning design authoring tools that are both easy to use, allowing teachers to concentrate on pedagogy and that can output a validated the IMS Learning Design specification schema. In the future we hope to see tools such as eXe and DialogPlus be able to export the IMS Learning Design specification output after the fact. This may be a long-term goal given the complexity of the specification.

Integrated environments

More immediate advantages can be gained by developing learning design tools within an integrated environment. As Dalziel (2005) notes, the tighter coupling between design-time and run-time components that is possible in an integrated system greatly eases the complexity inherent in having to specify behaviours at design-time for unknown run-time tools – as is the case with the IMS Learning Design specification. A typical example would be designing an activity involving setting-up and creating an initial post in a discussion forum when the actual discussion tool that will be instantiated is unknown; hence the need for a Learning

Table 8.2 A comparison of selected authoring environments

	eXe	Reload LD editor	MOT+	DialogPlus
Purpose and scope	An authoring tool for educational content	A LD editor for creating and validating IMS Learning Designs	A graphical learning design editor with its own graphical language and support for the IMS Learning Design specification	Help teachers create and share successful learning activities
Who is it for?	Teachers (non-technical)	Developers and learning designers (technical)	Learning designers (technical)	Teachers (non-technical)
Activity management and workflow	Hierarchical structuring. Workflow implicit in SCORM output. I-Devices represent activities	Uses the IMS Learning Design specification elements. Stays close to specification	Graphical components and links to express relations. The IMS Learning Design specification components supported	Learning activities and sequences are created on a model of 'learning nuggets'. Sequential workflow is not enforced
Sharing and reuse (Support for the IMS Learning Design specification)	XHTML output in SCORM format. No current support for the IMS Learning Design specification	The IMS Learning Design specification A, B, C	The IMS Learning Design specification Level A support. Levels B and C under development	Shareable design templates that are human readable. With some manipulation the IMS Learning Design specification Level A export is possible
Pedagogical support	I-Devices provide pedagogical structuring and hints	Modelled on the IMS Learning Design specification. The IMS Learning Design specification Best Practice Guide. No additional support	Supports MISA ID Methodology. Described in users guide	Teachers explicitly select desired pedagogical approach
User interface	It provides a tree-node structuring panel and content editing panes. Desktop tool with preview function for offline editing	Tree editor with tabbed property sheets. Desktop tool for offline editing. XML output can be validated using tool and tested in Reload player	Graphical user interface with component objects and relational links	The editor is under development based on enhancement of Reload. Further details not supplied

Design engine to underpin the IMS Learning Design specification players. A much greater variety and richness of activity tools or services is attainable in an integrated environment, but the downside is that the potential for reusability of the design outside the environment within which it was created is hampered. This could be problematic if the tool in question were a costly proprietary system. Fortunately, most of the innovative tools in this area are distributed with Open Source licences.

One system that typifies an integrated environment is the Learning Activity Management System (LAMS). Much has been written about LAMS in recent years as it was the first integrated environment inspired by Learning Design to appear. It has an intuitive drag and drop graphic user interface that allows teachers to swiftly create an activity sequence using the rich activity tools provided with LAMS (see Dalziel, Chapter 15). The sequence can be monitored by the teacher during learner's engagement with it, providing the opportunity for teacher intervention if required. LAMS has been trialled extensively in a number of situations (see Masterman and Vogel, Chapter 4) but has yet to see widespread uptake in institutions and is the subject of ongoing research work.

By contrast Moodle, an integrated environment that typifies the more usual online VLE system, has seen a massive surge in uptake over the past few years. VLEs are still the most commonly used software for supporting online or blended teaching and learning interactions within education institutions, and these represent a large percentage of tools used to create online learning designs. The advantage of using the VLE directly is that it provides a familiar course structuring environment and the tutor does not have to learn additional tools. Among the disadvantages are that performing authoring tasks in a web-based environment can be clumsy if bandwidth is restricted; there is also a risk that the resulting course structure is not interoperable. Part of the attraction of Moodle, .LRN, Claroline, etc., is that they are Open Source and can be adapted to meet the specific needs of the institution. But if there is no interoperable data format for learning designs then lock in is still a major problem, both for the institution that decides it wants to standardize on a specific VLE, or for an individual who moves to an institution that runs a different VLE. There has been some work to date on developing integrated environments that make use of the IMS Learning Design specification (e.g. Al.Fanet) though this work is still in its infancy. Also there has been considerable interest within the Moodle community in looking at ways to create an IMS Learning Design specification Level A design from an existing Moodle course structure (Berggren *et al.* 2005).

Issues and challenges for learning design systems in the future

In this chapter we have looked at a variety of tools to support the process of designing for learning. Some have been developed in connection with the IMS Learning Design specification specification while others have arisen from the desire to support teachers in assembling courses, activities and learning materials. At the present time there is little cross-over between these communities, and while easier-to-use-tools that generate the IMS Learning Design specification are certainly possible, it remains to be seen whether they get built. This is a clear challenge for those interested in both ease of use and reuse. Both the Open Source projects eXe and DialogPlus are important steps in this direction. MOT+ and LAMS demonstrate how a graphical user interface can make tools more intuitive and easier to use.

One of the big questions that this chapter has raised is that of reuse of learning designs. A key aim of the IMS Learning Design specification is to make reuse possible, and yet as Masterman and Vogel point out in Chapter 4, few teachers are prepared to invest time and effort to create content or learning designs that are reusable. So key issues for the IMS Learning Design specification are:

1   Is the IMS Learning Design specification an effective solution for promoting reuse and economies of scale in large-scale distance education, where it was originally planned to be used?

2   Can the IMS Learning Design specification be used to generate reusable learning designs in other contexts? Clearly there is potential here but the methodology and tooling need to be carefully thought through.

Finally, in learning design, 'activities' are a core component. In the IMS Learning Design specification many activities are dependent on a variety of 'services'. As yet the IMS Learning Design specification only supports two services: email and conferencing. There is clearly a need for more run-time services to be supported by the specification (Olivier and Tattersall 2005) and yet the more services that are included, the more the design is tightly coupled to implementation details of the run-time environment, thus hindering abstraction and reuse. For this reason we can expect integrated environments such as LAMS and its successors to continue to play an important role in the future of learning design. One very important innovation is the development of run-time components that can be referenced using web services. A service-oriented architecture where service-based messaging could provide the desired de-coupling between design and run-time implementation may make it easier to handle the availability and set up of services, probably with a small supplementary specification.

While developments in learning design software are still immature, the growing interest in this area suggests that they will not remain so for very long.

Acknowledgements

The authors would like to thank Bill Olivier and Oleg Liber for their invaluable feedback on drafts of this chapter.

References

Bailey, C., Fill, K., Zalfan, M., Davis, H. and Conole, G. (2005) 'Panning for gold: designing pedagogically-inspired learning nuggets', *Educational Technology & Society*, 9 (1): 49–59.

Barrett-Baxendale, M., Hazlewood, P., Oddie, A., Anderson M. and Franklin, T. (2005) *SLeD Integration Demonstrator: Final Report*. Online. Available www.hope.ac.uk/slide/ (accessed 30 September 2006).

Berggren, A., Burgos, D., Fontana, J.M., Hinkelman, D., Hung, V. *et al.* (2005) 'Practical and Pedagogical issues for teacher adoption of IMS Learning Design standards in Moodle LMS', *Journal of Interactive Media in Education*, 2. Online. Available www-jime. open.ac.uk/2005/02/berggren-2005–02.pdf (accessed 30 September 2006).

Britain, S. (2004) *A Review of Learning Design: Concept, Specifications and Tools. A Report for the JISC E-learning and Pedagogy Programme*. Online. Available www.jisc. ac.uk/uploaded_documents/ACF83C.doc (accessed 4 September 2006).

Britain, S. (2005) *A Review and Analysis of Content Authoring Software in Relation to eXe. A Report Commissioned by the Tertiary Education Commission of New Zealand*. Online. Available http://eduforge.org/docman/?group_id=20 (accessed 4 September 2006).

Britain, S. and Liber, O. (2004) *A Framework for the Pedagogical Evaluation of E-learning Environments (Revised)*. Online. Available www.jisc.ac.uk/uploaded_documents/VLE% 20Full%20Report%2006.doc (accessed 30 September 2006).

Dalziel, J. (2005) *From Re-usable E-learning Content to Re-usable Learning Designs: Lessons from LAMS*. Online. Available www.lamsfoundation.org/CD/html/resources/ whitepapers/Dalziel.LAMS.doc. (accessed 30 September 2006).

eXe (2006) *E-learning XHTML Editor*. Online. Available http://exelearning.org/ (accessed 30 September 2006).

Griffiths, D., Blat, J., Garcia, R., Vogten, H. and Kwong, K.-L. (2005) 'Learning Design tools', in R. Koper and C. Tattersall (eds) *Learning Design – A Handbook on Modelling and Delivering Networked Education and Training*, Berlin-Heidelberg: Springer, pp. 109–35.

Koper, E.R.J. (2001) *Modelling Units of Study from a Pedagogical Perspective: The Pedagogical Meta Model Behind EML*. Online. Available http://eml.ou.nl/introduction/ docs/ped-metamodel.pdf (accessed 30 September 2006).

Koper, R. and Tattersall, C. (2005) *Learning Design – A Handbook on Modelling and Delivering Networked Education and Training*, Berlin-Hedelberg: Springer.

IMS (2005) *Learning Design Specification. Version 1.0 Final Specification*, IMS Global. Online. Available www.imsglobal.org/specifications.html (accessed 30 September 2006).

Olivier, B. and Tattersall, C. (2005) 'The Learning Design specification', in R. Koper and C.Tattersall (eds) *Learning Design – A Handbook on Modelling and Delivering Networked Education and Training*, Berlin-Heidelberg: Springer, pp. 21–40.

Paquette, G., De la Teja, I., Léonard, M., Lundgren-Cayrol, K. and Marino, O. (2005) 'Using an instructional engineering method and a modeling tool to design IMS-LD units of learning', in R. Koper and C. Tattersall (eds) *Learning Design: A Handbook on Modelling and Delivering Networked Education and Training*, Berlin-Heidelberg: Springer, pp. 161–83.

Reload (2006) *Reusable eLearning Object Authoring and Delivery*. Online. Available www.reload.ac.uk/ (accessed 30 September 2006).

UNFOLD (2004) *Learning Design Tools Currently Available or Under Development*. Online. Available www.unfold-project.net/general_resources_folder/tools/currenttools (accessed 30 September 2006).

Van Es, R. and Koper, R. (2006) 'Testing the pedagogical expressiveness of IMS', *Educational Technology and Society*, 9 (1): 229–49.

Part II

The practice of design

EDITORS' INTRODUCTION

In the Introduction, we asserted that different practices of design for learning can be found in different discipline areas. In Chapter 9, Sharpe and Oliver demonstrate that design is a highly contextualized activity that, if it is to be effective, must draw on established traditions in communities of practice such as subject-area teachers. The following chapters illustrate some of these different traditions. Not only does the meaning of 'design' take on different resonances in the fields represented here, but also these fields have made very different contributions to our overall understanding of the design process. Appropriately, the following chapters offer some challenges to the general definitions of 'design' and 'design for learning' given in our Introduction.

Throughout this second part of the book, the application of digital technologies is explored as both a challenge to existing approaches to design for learning, and a promise that new kinds of scholarly practice may be possible in the future. The chapters in this part of the book discuss approaches that have evolved from systems design (Chapter 10), the arts (Chapter 11) and social sciences (Chapter 13), and from vocational learning (Chapter 12). The remaining chapters look at how the new opportunities offered by mobile and wireless technologies (Chapter 14) and the Learning Activity Management System (LAMS) design tool (Chapter 15) can change what is considered effective in pedagogic design. Finally, Chapter 16 explores new horizons in learning design, based on findings from a series of case studies in successful e-learning innovation.

Chapter 9

Supporting practitioners' design for learning

Principles of effective resources and interventions

Rhona Sharpe and Martin Oliver

EDITORS' INTRODUCTION

This chapter considers support for practitioners as they incorporate technology into their teaching: how they use learning designs and other representations of practice, and how those representations promote professional learning. The authors discuss what characterizes effective interventions in practice, in order to develop a set of principles that can be used by staff and educational developers when planning work with practitioners. A final discussion of context and community brings together the process of staff development and the use of specific representations to support design for learning.

Introduction

There continues to be an enormous interest in developing e-learning and much of the work of staff and educational developers is now focused on improving the student experience of e-learning through working with practitioners. Historically, training for e-learning had focused on developing technical mastery (Littlejohn and Peacock 2003). However, in the UK, the work of initiatives such as the Ferl Practitioners Programme (FPP) in further education and the EFFECTS project in higher education have supported practitioners to incorporate technology reflectively into their teaching and course design (Beetham and Bailey 2002; Becta 2003; Oliver and Dempster 2003).

There is evidence accumulating that this focus on working with practitioners is well placed. For example, in a systematic literature review of the use of technology in schools, Higgins (2003) reports that the effectiveness of technology is dependent on the ways teachers choose to use it. This is perhaps an unsurprising conclusion given the scope of this book and its discussion of the influential role of designing for learning in developing and delivering effective e-learning implementations. However, there is increasing evidence for the impact of the design decisions taken by e-learning practitioners; this leads us to look more closely at the staff development that is provided for them, and which may influence these decisions.

When they are asked directly about the kinds of resources that help them to develop their practice, e-learning practitioners have requested staff development materials, along with software tools and case studies in curriculum development (Beetham 2002). As e-learning practice becomes more widespread, there are interesting issues to explore around how the practice of others is represented and shared in formats such as case studies. In addition, the uptake of e-learning has led to an increasing knowledge base about the use of technology that is often codified knowledge in textual form. Conole *et al.* (2005) considered the range of different types of forms of representation that mediate between tools, theories and learning activities and that can be used to provide practitioners with advice and guidance as they make their design choices. Such mediating representations include 'illustrative examples of good practice (case studies, guidelines, narratives, etc.) or more abstract forms of representation which distil out the "essences" of good practice (e.g. specific models, use cases or patterns)' (Conole *et al.* 2005: 3).

In this chapter we consider how such representations are used by practitioners in ways that lead to changes in practice and the role that staff development and staff developers can play in supporting that process. We review the development and use of representations and use the professional learning literature to make recommendations for staff development resources and interventions.

Representations of practice

In order to understand current practice, Beetham (2002) investigated the types of representations that are used by e-learning practitioners. Data were collected from an online questionnaire (completed by a relatively expert but mixed group of 120 academics, educational developers, learning technologists and others), structured interviews and national focus groups. She found that people who had actually changed their practice reported that a crucial turning point was often the opportunity to witness the real thing, in the real context, with the real people; in other words, to actually watch a new approach or tool in action. This might be in the context of a teaching observation or a lunchtime workshop in which a colleague described and illustrated what they had done, for example. When pressed about the kinds of representation that had actually had an impact on their own practice, participants in this study were most likely to cite narratives from colleagues about what they did, what went wrong, and how they survived. Similarly, while reviewing lessons from the Embedding Learning Technology (ELT) programmes run by members of the EFFECTS project courses, Beetham (2003) notes that 'show and tell' sessions, staff seminars and case studies are influential resources for practitioners.

This is a familiar idea in the literature on communities of practice: 'war stories' serve to educate, valorize and also consolidate professional identities (Seely-Brown and Duguid 1991). In the absence of opportunities to observe real teaching situations, case studies are a valued way of providing the highly contextualized real-life stories that practitioners prefer (Sharpe 2004a). Case studies might be shared as video clips, narrative, or structured text. These richer representations are likely to be more meaningful to practitioners and offer an efficient way of giving access to real-life scenarios (see for example the video clips included in the Joint

Information Systems Committee (JISC) *Effective Practice with E-learning* booklet, JISC 2004). However, they are time-consuming and expensive to produce.

A more familiar and less expensive format is the written case study. Providing templates for case studies can help to rationalize the collecting, writing and searching processes. The e-learning practice evaluator produced for the JISC Effective Practice workshops is such an example of a case study template (see Appendix 9). This template provides prompts for practitioners to reflect quickly on their own practice. Prompts include: 'What did you ask learners to do? What resources did learners use? What was the experience like to you/the learners?' and 'What advice would you give to another teacher working in a similar context to your own?' Case studies completed using this template might be used as part of a programme of staff development or action research project.

Another quite different example was produced through collaboration between the JISC and the UK Higher Education Academy subject centres. This much longer template (see Appendix 10) has been designed to promote the collation of case studies nationally. This has a number of fields to aid the later searching of case studies in a database such as 'subject/discipline area, mode of delivery, intended learning outcomes'.

In reality, there are practical problems around the creation of case studies. The experiences from funded projects are that it can be extremely difficult to get practitioners to produce cases studies in a common format without payment or help with writing them (Harvey *et al.* 2002). It has been suggested that parts of the academic community may actually resist such explicit codification of their practice as a perceived reduction of their professional artistry (Beetham 2002). Also, practitioners are often happy enough to tell their stories of successes, but less comfortable putting their name to the failures. We do need to learn from things that don't work as well as those that do, making this reticence a particularly important issue to address.

Motivators or rewards may help with resource creation. The review of ELT programmes discussed the kinds of rewards perceived as worthy by different participants. For example, experienced academics might not want academic credit but might prepare case studies for publication as peer reviewed papers that are valued within the academic community (Harvey and Oliver 2001). Similar problems of motivation and recognition beset the sharing of learning designs (see for example Dalziel, Chapter 15).

Representations of knowledge

In previous work we have discussed how knowledge about e-learning can be represented and shared in ways that support practitioners to change their practice (Sharpe *et al.* 2004). We were concerned that the findings from the emerging e-learning research are often not used by practitioners when they are designing for learning. Building on Beetham's (2002) finding that expert practitioners expressed a preference for representations they could interact with – comment on, adapt, annotate, use in their own work, or contribute to – we suggested practical examples of ways in which knowledge resources could be enhanced to become more dynamic, contingent and owned by their readers. Such 'active' representations allow practitioners to engage with them through commentary and feedback, peer review and refinement in the light of their experience. Technology allows us to blur the boundaries between resource creation and use to create 'living' artefacts.

The role of others in such processes is important. Beetham (2002) found that practitioners' use of knowledge resources was often mediated by another person such as a mentor, staff developer or learning technology specialist. The implication of this is that staff developers, mentors and expert peers play several important roles: pointing novices to the right resource at the right time, adapting and versioning things for people, pulling out just the relevant bits and bringing the materials to life with real stories. Other studies that have asked academic staff what they found useful in professional development have confirmed the perceived importance of colleagues and collaborative strategies in changing practice (Ballantyne *et al.* 1999; Ferman 2002; Knight *et al.* 2006). Our suggestions for active representations aim to bring knowledge alive by mediating social and cultural communicative practice. Moreover, active artefacts support processes of peer learning whereby representations are constantly created, shared and tested. This leads us to think that however rich the representation of practice, or active the representation of knowledge, they are not enough on their own. In order to change practice, representations need to become part of a professional learning experience.

Professional learning: from representations to interventions

The previous discussion found that representations of both practice and knowledge are only really useful if they mediate professional activities, such as developing and delivering courses. They have little impact as sources of information but require mediation in order to make them usable. For example, learning designs need to incorporate sufficient contextual information to be reusable in new contexts and with new cohorts of learners. We also suggest that finding, interpreting, applying and adapting representations are tasks that practitioners find difficult to accomplish on their own. So a second form of mediation is required by local developers. In order to explore the process by which developers can support practitioners as they mediate between representations and their practice, we move now to consider the learning that is taking place for the practitioners and consider the role of representations within that. We argue that to understand this process fully, we must consider how professionals learn and develop (see Sharpe 2004b for review).

Learning from experience

Research in the field of adult learning has provided a large body of evidence that learning takes place in all sorts of situations, not just formal courses. Much of the work on professional learning has concentrated on the links between experience and knowledge (e.g. Schön 1983, 1987; Kolb 1984). However, experience alone may not be enough; what is required is the opportunity to move beyond just 'doing' the knowledge, to conceptualizing its value and relating it to the ideas and theories of others (Griffiths and Guile 1999).

Reflection has been promoted as the process by which people learn from experience. For professionals, reflective practice is only really a useful notion when linked to action, as Cowan suggested in his descriptions of *reflection in action*, *reflection on action* and *reflection for action* (Cowan 1998). This process is modelled as occurring in cycles of action and reflection, and recommendations have been made for professional development activities that give learners opportunities to engage in different activities at different times, such as through dialogue and facilitation (Brockbank and McGill 1998), journal writing (Moon 1999) and action learning sets (McGill and Beaty 1995).

In professional development for e-learning, cycles of learning are most clearly seen in the ELT learning outcomes that encourage practitioners to approach their embedding of learning technology in a systematic fashion. The review of these programmes concluded that while a full staff development programme wasn't necessary for all participants, they did gain from the structure provided by pursuing the outcomes (Beetham 2003).

Further implications are that representations should be available when practitioners have time and opportunity to think about their own practice. For novice practitioners this will often mean structured time, perhaps in staff development sessions, workshops and appraisals. However, even highly motivated and expert practitioners need time to engage with representations, prompts to review and reflect on their own practice, and help in translating between the theoretical and practical aspects of the situation. In developing other types of representations and interventions, we might want to think carefully about how opportunities for reflection, abstraction and generalization can be supported for various groups of staff.

Informal learning

Eraut's examination of professional knowledge has been influential (Eraut 1994, 2000). He reminds us that professional knowledge is there for a purpose – to be used when professionals need to respond effectively within professional roles. He blurs the distinction between acquiring and using knowledge, arguing persuasively that for professionals, their learning should involve application of knowledge in non-formal settings: 'Learning knowledge and using knowledge are not separate processes but the same process. The process of using knowledge transforms that knowledge so that it is no longer the same knowledge' (Eraut 1994: 25).

Studies have found that professionals consistently find it difficult to explain how they are applying their knowledge and making decisions (Polanyi 1967; Dreyfus and Dreyfus 1986) and in Chapter 4, Masterman and Vogel describe their research that attempted to capture the tacit process of designing for learning with e-learning practitioners.

The issue for our discussion of professional development is that tacit knowledge is unexpressed and so difficult to capture in the form of representations such as case studies. One interpretation is that practitioners should be encouraged to interrogate and engage with their own understanding in order to externalize and make explicit the 'knowing how', so that it can be shared and learnt from. Even if the knowledge can be captured, it could be argued that it is not the knowledge that is captured, but the practitioners' reflection on it. An alternative interpretation is that although tacit knowledge is unexpressed, it is still public, in that it can be observed. Rather than the creation of representations, we might suggest professional development that takes the form of observation, conversation or shared participation. Indeed higher education teachers report that a great deal of their learning at work has been through informal learning (Knight *et al.* 2006). Eraut (1994) and Knight (2002) both emphasize the importance of informal, social networks that allow for direct access to the tacit knowledge of colleagues.

Situated learning and communities of practice

In recent years there has been an increasing recognition of the importance of context in learning. Wenger (1998) and Lave and Wenger's (1991) work on communities of practice has been widely adopted as a conceptualization for the development and perpetuation of knowledge about professional practices. Professional learning is seen as the process of entering into that community of practice by behaving in an increasingly responsible and trusted manner. For most professions, including teaching, it is also important to consider how the values and ethical practice of the profession hold to account the uses of knowledge in practice (cf. Wenger's (1998) discussion of mutual accountability). Professional development then should be designed to account for knowledge construction both individually and collaboratively, e.g. through inquiry-based learning, problem-based learning or action research.

Communities of practice work to define what counts as 'appropriate' practices, forms of expression, and so on, and are thus powerful influences on successful development activities. However, it is likely that designing for learning is not yet a stable practice taking place in a clearly defined community (Beetham 2002). Attempts to create communities of e-learning practitioners and/or to share their knowledge have been notoriously difficult. Rather than creating a new community, it is likely that for the time being, there will be a substantial role for developers in working across already established communities. Since developers typically work across departments, disciplinary groupings and teams of managers, they are in a unique and important position to develop practice. By acting as boundary-crossing agents (in Wenger's terminology) they can represent other people's practices to each community in a way tailored to prompt reflection and development. Consequently, part of the value of this role is that the professional developer is an outsider; to 'go native' would be to lose part of the pedagogic power of such roles.

A typology of effective interventions

To build on the foundational concepts described in the previous section, four detailed reviews were undertaken as part of the JISC-funded 'Research study on the effectiveness of resources, tools and support services used by practitioners in designing and delivering e-learning activities', covering: resources (Littlejohn and McGill 2004), tools (Conole 2004), institutional services (Oliver 2004) and national services (Franklin 2004). The outcomes from each of these reports were more complex than had been anticipated. This was partly due to a deficiency in the available literature. However, it was also largely because the factors that enable or inhibit the effective use of a resource or intervention were strongly influenced by the context of use.

As a result of these background reviews, five principles for effective intervention were identified:

- *Usability*: Interventions should have a clearly defined user base, use language appropriate to those users, be known of by those users, and be functionally accessible to those users.
- *Contextualisation*: Practitioners continue to favour interventions that are contextualized for them, i.e. those that have a clear and explicit statement of purpose; acknowledge the realities of the educational setting; allow practitioners to work on their own real-life issues; and take account of the language, values, culture and priorities of their particular community.
- *Professional learning*: Changing practice requires practitioners to learn, specifically to alter their conceptions of teaching and learning through, e.g. opportunities to construct their own meanings; learning from experience through reflection; informal learning; problem-based learning; action learning; peer supported learning.
- *Communities*: There may be real advantages to working within the existing communities and networks with which practitioners are already affiliated. This links to secondary issues of authenticity and ownership: practitioners should experience interventions as genuinely sharing their concerns, and being provided or supported by people with whom they can identify.
- *Learning design*: Practitioners need to be supported in engaging with a process that starts with the educational approach. Effective interventions are dependent on an understanding of the curriculum design process and of learning outcomes.

However, it became clear that any criteria for judging the effectiveness of resources and interventions were too complex to be simplified into a bullet pointed set of guidelines. Instead, these principles were presented in a matrix structure (or 'typology') that maps how the key factors of resources, tools and services that positively influence e-learning might operate within the context of working with resources, tools and services for wider change in e-learning. This 'Typology of effective interventions' is a mapping of the key principles against each form of intervention (resources, tools and services). An extract from the matrix is presented in Table 9.1 and the full typology in Appendix 11.

The matrix structure is useful in that it illustrates how these principles might operate within the context of working with resources, individuals and groups for wider change in e-learning. The principles that render a resource or intervention effective (e.g. usability, contextualisation, etc.) are demonstrated, using evidence from real examples, against each form of intervention (resources, tools and services).

Subsequent work within the project served to refine the matrix by testing its credibility with a range of practitioners and working with their feedback (Bostock and Smith 2004). This confirmed the audience for the typology as being primarily staff and educational developers: people who would need to examine the typology and select boxes from the matrix that apply most closely to their situation (allowing that they all overlap) and use the links to project documentation to explore the issues highlighted there.

Conclusions

The previous discussion leads to recommendations about codifying professional knowledge and practice through the creation and sharing of rich, highly contextualized and adaptable forms. Wenger's idea of communities of practice may help to explain the value of such resources. This process of representing practice (in Wenger's terms, 'reifying' it) allows members of that community to comment on each other's work in a way that would not otherwise be possible. This strengthens the processes of mutual accountability that help define a community of practice, allowing it to develop. This suggests that collaborative resource development – for example sharing, enriching and commenting on learning designs – can be a highly effective way of developing shared practice. A corollary of this is that although networks need concrete representations of their shared expertise, it may often be the process of producing these rather than their reuse that is most valuable to those involved.

We have seen that representations do not just encode 'what to do' in a particular situation but are important expressions of the community's values and culture – this is how, in Wenger's terms, they can be used to hold people's practice to account. The need is not simply to distil 'the best examples' of represented practice for future use, but to establish peer processes whereby representations are constantly created, shared and tested. Interventions involving other practitioners are consistently rated positively by practitioners as forums where they can engage with peers, challenge each other and construct their own meanings. For those practitioners who are learning, it is unlikely that even a very rich resource or tool is going to be as effective as an intervention.

Although this chapter has supported many of staff development's existing practices (principally cycles of development, construction of meaning, working with others, making tacit knowledge explicit), it also calls into question the

Table 9.1 Extract from the typology of effective interventions

Principles of effective interventions 'Interventions' include a combination of resources, tools and services	Representing and sharing knowledge Supporting well-informed approaches to the use of e-learning	Developing staff Enabling individuals or groups to do something new or differently	Developing organizations Supporting change in the structure and processes of organizations
Contextualization Practitioners continue to favour tools and resources that have either been contextualized for them and/or that they can create or adapt for their context. For educators this is likely to include: • acknowledging the realities of the educational setting • tackling pertinent, real-life issues • relevance to the discipline • allowing practitioners to create, adapt, reuse or repurpose their own resources.	Representations can be contextualized by: • encouraging the sharing of authentic scenarios through, e.g. case studies, show and tell stories, narratives • offering facilities that allow for personalization, e.g. the *Virtual Learning Space* allows users to create their own profile and personalized space • offering multiple versions of resource for different disciplines, e.g. *RDN Virtual Training Suite* • presenting ideas from a variety of subject areas e.g. *Scotcit Effective Lecturing Project* • being sufficiently small to be adapted, but large enough to be educationally useful • using repurposable media and formats.	Contextualized working with individuals might involve: • establishing common ground between developers and practitioners (e.g. common discipline) • establishing and maintaining an ongoing dialogue with staff to identify what they perceive their needs to be • a better understanding of the realities of the practitioner's work, e.g. actual course design processes at work, the inequalities of the workplace or the changes in working practice • tools that provide an obvious solution to a problem • Supporting staff to develop information literacy, e.g. how to source, retrieve, use, repurpose, organize and share learning resources.	Organizational development can be supported by contextualizing development through a concerns-based approach to staff development, for example, involving: • offering a broad repertoire of approaches to support staff throughout an organization • undertaking a user requirements analysis, e.g *Connect* • reducing the time lag between analysis of user need and setting up of the service • exploiting national and institutional policies, e.g. *TechDis* or *JISC Legal Info Service* • explaining the relevance of the support for particular groups.

dominance of one or two approaches as being over-simplified solutions to the full complexity of professional learning for e-learning practitioners. Examples include the widespread use of personal reflections about practice in writing case studies; the focus from funded projects on resource-based outputs; or the use of central, generic workshops that rarely manage to connect to daily practices in any strong way, since they take place outside of the contexts of that work. Used in isolation, these all sit uncomfortably with the principles of social learning and the notion that professional knowledge is inextricably related to its use within a certain context.

Context literally embraces the processes of acquisition of professional knowledge and learning from experience. This emphasizes that we cannot focus exclusively on representing knowledge and practice in design for learning. Effective staff development tools, resources and services should encourage practitioners to develop knowledge through use; prompt learning from experience through reflection linked to action; and make the best possible use of the influence of culture, community and context. Our typology attempts to provide a guide to the tools, rules and beliefs that are likely to be most influential in developing the practices of staff in this area. It is offered as a tool to help developers explore some of the complexities of their role, and to underline the difficulties involved in the task of sharing design practice.

References

Ballantyne, R., Bain, J.D., and Packer, J. (1999) 'Researching university teaching in Australia: themes and issues in academics' reflections', *Studies in Higher Education*, 24 (2): 237–57.

Becta (2003) *Pilot Evaluation Report: The Ferl Practitioners' Programme*, Coventry: British Educational Communications and Technology Agency. Online. Available http://ferl.becta. org.uk/display.cfm?resID=6806 (accessed 30 August 2006).

Beetham, H. (2002) 'Developing learning technology networks through shared representations of practice', *Proceedings of the 9th International Improving Student Learning Symposium*, Oxford: Oxford Centre for Staff and Learning Development, pp. 421–34.

Beetham, H. (2003) 'Embedding learning technologies: lessons for academic developers', *Educational Developments*, 4 (4): 4–6.

Beetham, H. and Bailey, P. (2002) 'Professional development for organizational change', in R. Macdonald and J. Wisdom (eds) *Academic and Educational Development: Research, Evaluation and Changing Practice in Higher Education*, London: Kogan Page, pp. 164–76.

Bostock, S. and Smith, J. (2004) *Report on the Empirical Work*, Bristol: JISC (Research Study on the Effectiveness of Resources, Tools and Support Services used by Practitioners in Designing and Delivering E-learning Activities).

Brockbank, A. and McGill, I. (1998) *Facilitating Reflective Learning in Higher Education*, Buckingham: Society for Research in Higher Education and Open University Press.

Conole, G. (2004) *Report on the Effectiveness of Tools for e-Learning*, Bristol: JISC (Research Study on the Effectiveness of Resources, Tools and Support Services used by Practitioners in Designing and Delivering E-learning Activities).

Conole, G., Littlejohn, A., Falconer, I. and Jeffrey, A. (2005) *LADIE Project Report*, Online. Available www.elframework.org/refmodels/ladie/ouputs/LADIE%20lit%20review% 20v15.doc (accessed 30 August 2006).

Cowan, J. (1998) *On Becoming an Innovative University Teacher*, Buckingham: Society for Research in Higher Education and Open University Press.

Dreyfus, H.L. and Dreyfus, S.E. (1986) *Mind Over Machine*, Oxford: Blackwell.

Eraut, M. (1994) *Developing Professional Knowledge and Competence*, London: Falmer Press.

Eraut, M. (2000) 'Non-formal learning and tacit knowledge in professional work', *British Journal of Educational Psychology*, 70: 113–36.

Ferman, T. (2002) 'Academic professional development: what lecturers find valuable', *International Journal for Academic Development*, 7 (2): 146–58.

Franklin, T. (2004) *Research Study on National Services used by Practitioners in Designing and Delivering E-Learning Activities*, Bristol: JISC (Research Study on the Effectiveness of Resources, Tools and Support Services used by Practitioners in Designing and Delivering E-learning Activities).

Griffiths, T. and Guile, D. (1999) 'Pedagogy in work-based contexts', in P. Mortimore (ed.) *Understanding Pedagogy and its Impact on Learning*, London: Sage Publications, pp. 155–74.

Harvey, J. and Oliver, M. (2001) *EFFECTS External Evaluation*. Online. Available www.ilrt.org/effects/downloads/effects-evaluation-report.pdf (accessed 27 August 2006).

Harvey, J., Oliver, M. and Smith, J. (2002) 'Towards effective practitioner evaluation: an exploration of issues relating to skills, motivation and evidence', *Educational Technology and Society*, 5 (3). Online. Available http://ifets.ieee.org/periodical/vol_3_2002/harvey.html (accessed 27 August 2006).

Higgins, S. (2003) *Does ICT Improve Learning and Teaching in Schools?*, Macclesfield, Cheshire: British Educational Research Association. Online. Available www.bera.ac.uk/publications/pdfs/ICT%20PUR%20MB%20r-f-p%201Aug03.pdf#search=%22Does%20ICT%20improve%20learning%20and%20teaching%20in%20schools%3F%20%20%22 (accessed 27 August 2006).

JISC (2004) *Planning and Evaluating Effective Practice with E-learning*, Bristol: JISC. Online. Available www.jisc.ac.uk/elp_practice.html (accessed 30 August 2006).

Knight, P. (2002) 'A systematic approach to professional development: learning as practice', *Teaching and Teacher Education*, 18: 229–41.

Knight, P., Tait, J. and Yorke, M. (2006) 'The professional learning of teachers in higher education', *Studies in Higher Education*, 31 (3): 319–39.

Kolb, D.A. (1984) *Experiential Learning: Experience as a Source of Learning and Development*, Englewood Cliffs, NJ: Prentice-Hall.

Lave, J. and Wenger, E. (1991) *Situated Learning: Legitimate Peripheral Participation*, Cambridge: Cambridge University Press.

Littlejohn, A. and McGill, L. (2004) *Effective Resources for E-learning*, Bristol: JISC (Research Study on the Effectiveness of Resources, Tools and Support Services used by Practitioners in Designing and Delivering E-learning Activities).

Littlejohn, A. and Peacock, S. (2003) 'From pioneers to partners: the changing voices of staff developers', in J. Searle (ed.) *Learning Technology in Transition: From Individual Enthusiasm to Institutional Implementation*, Lisse, The Netherlands: Swets and Zeitlinger.

McGill, I. and Beaty, E. (1995) *Action Learning: A Guide for Professional, Management and Educational Development*, 2nd edn, London: Kogan Page.

Moon, J. (1999) *Learning Journals: A Handbook for Academics, Students and Professional Development*, London: Kogan Page.

Oliver, M. (2004) *Effective Support for E-learning within Institutions*, Bristol: JISC (Research Study on the Effectiveness of Resources, Tools and Support Services used by Practitioners in Designing and Delivering E-learning Activities).

Oliver, M. and Dempster, J. (2003) 'Embedding e-learning practices', in R. Blackwell and P. Blackmore (eds) *Towards Strategic Staff Development in Higher Education*, Buckingham: Society for Research in Higher Education and Open University Press, pp. 142–53.

Polanyi, M. (1967) *The Tacit Dimension*, New York: Doubleday.

Schön, D. (1983) *The Reflective Practitioner: How Professionals Think in Action*, New York: Basic Books.

Schön, D. (1987) *Educating the Reflective Practitioner*, San Francisco: Jossey-Bass.

Seely-Brown, J.S. and Duguid, P. (1991) 'Organizational learning and communities-of-practice: toward a unified view of working, learning and innovation', *Organizational Science*, 2 (1): 40–57.

Sharpe, R. (2004a) *Initial Positioning Report for E-learning and Pedagogy Research Study*, Bristol: JISC (Research Study on the Effectiveness of Resources, Tools and Support Services used by Practitioners in Designing and Delivering E-learning Activities).

Sharpe, R. (2004b) 'How do professionals learn and develop?', in D. Baume and P. Kahn (eds) *Enhancing Staff and Educational Development*, London: RoutledgeFalmer, pp. 132–53.

Sharpe, R., Beetham, H. and Ravenscroft, A. (2004) 'Active artefacts: representing our knowledge of learning and teaching', *Educational Developments*, 5 (2): 16–21.

Wenger, E. (1998) *Communities of Practice*, Cambridge: Cambridge University Press.

Chapter 10

The use of scenarios in designing and delivering e-learning systems

Chris Fowler, Joy van Helvert, Michael Gardner and John Scott

EDITORS' INTRODUCTION

This chapter offers an important bridge between the descriptions of pedagogical practice discussed in Part I (see e.g. Chapters 2, 3, 5 and 6) and the kind of formal representations that can be handled by learning design software (see Chapters 8 and 15). This chapter exemplifies design for learning within the systems design tradition, illustrating this through the use of scenarios at early stages of the design process. The authors describe the development of scenarios as a starting point for user needs analysis, and for the representation of user (learner) needs in the form of learning designs. The chapter begins with a discussion of what the authors mean by 'learning and design' and 'scenarios'. This is followed by a description of a particular Scenario-based User Needs Analysis (SUNA) method, and how it can be extended to cover evaluation activities.

Setting the scene: the role of scenarios in design and learning

In the Introduction, Beetham and Sharpe stress the importance of 'design' in the conceptualization of pedagogy within the digital age and make a distinction between different types of design activities. There is the notion of design in terms of what the teacher does – design for learning – which is concerned with designing, planning, orchestrating and supporting learning activities as part of a learning session or programme. Design for learning has also been used to describe the physical design of the learning environments or centres (Hinchcliffe, n.d.).

In contrast there is a notion of design in terms of what system designers do – designing e-learning systems. System design is concerned with understanding and improving the interaction between the learner and the technical system. This latter notion embraces the traditional design discipline, consisting of, for example, software engineering techniques, methods, tools and technical know-how.

Finally there is learning design with its focus on particular learning activities (rather than content) and how these can be modelled or described. Britain (2004) argues for three defining characteristics of learning design:

1   That learning is an active and constructive process involving activities/actions between people and not just between people and content.
2   That these activities can be systematically described in terms of sequences or flows.
3   That these sequence descriptions can be shared and thus reused.

As Britain (2004) comments, none of these ideas are new to education (indeed some are quite mature) but appear to be new to e-learning. We argue for a fourth defining characteristic:

4   That Learning Design focuses on the concept of a 'unit of learning', a bounded concept involving a defined set of actors (or roles), activities, methods and resources, but critically one that cannot be decomposed into a smaller unit. The Unit of Learning (UOL) can however be aggregated into larger units (e.g. from lectures to courses).

The three different uses of learning and design (i.e. designing for learning; design of e-learning systems; and Learning Design) described above are not mutually exclusive; they may simply exist at different levels of granularity. When designing for learning, the emphasis is on the totality of a learning experience; the designer needs to take into account a whole range of variables including the physical environment, the teacher, the learner, the context of learning, outcomes, etc. On the other hand, the system designer will attempt to describe the current experience and look for opportunities to allocate functions and activities away from people to the system. The experience is now a 'socio-technical' one – one that should help the designers of e-learning (often systems designers) to design for learning. The user of the Learning Design approach will be even more focused, modelling specific activities and specifying particular learning sequences.

A further complication is that each type of design makes direct or indirect reference to the use of scenarios. A scenario can be defined as a narrative description of a scene, normally involving actors and activities set within a given context and time frame. Scenarios have been used to support theatrical, military, foresight and educational strategic planning definitions.

In design for learning, scenarios are used mainly as case studies of effective practice (see Sharpe and Oliver, Chapter 9). In learning design the use of scenarios is closely linked with the use of Educational Modelling Languages (EMLs). EML, like its system design counterpart, Unified Modelling Language (UML), draws upon the concept of *use cases*. In system design a use case describes what the user needs to do (to the system) to achieve a particular goal (e.g. 'user log on to system') (see, for example, use cases produced by the LADIE project 2005). In learning design they describe the learning experience from which the description of what the learner needs to do within a given environment to achieve a learning outcome or objective can be derived (see Britain, Chapter 8). A number of examples are given in the IMS *Learning Design Best Practice and Implementation Guide* (2003).

Each example has the UOL title (e.g. A problem-based learning task for information sciences and technology), narrative (about a paragraph) describing the unit followed by a more detailed specification of the actors, stakeholder and interest, pre-conditions, trigger and extensions. In learning design, the use cases are abstractions whereas in system design they are decompositions. Their primary functions therefore appear to be less about supporting design and more about being a mediating form of representation (see Sharpe *et al.* 2004).

In system design, scenarios have been mainly used to support interaction design. For Rossen and Carroll (2002: 2) a 'scenario is a story about people and their activities'. Scenarios can have multiple purposes in interaction design. Quite often they are illustrative, focusing on particular novel or desirable features of a new service or product, or they may be used to compare and contrast extremes (the nightmare and dream scenarios) to help designers focus on avoiding the undesirable features (see Bodker 2000). Equally scenarios can encourage reflection among the designers by helping them make implicit the assumptions about people, tasks and objects underlying some of their design decisions (see Carroll 2000).

Rossen and Carroll go further and argue for four types of scenarios in scenario-based design. The first type is a problem scenario. The scenario is created to communicate to the different stakeholders the activities that take place in the problem domain, but not necessarily the problem itself. Critically, these are a description of current, not future practice. In writing such scenarios it is necessary to identify and describe the key stakeholders or participants. The characteristics of the participants are themselves often written in narrative form. Other input includes 'claims' about current practice. A claim is a positive or negative effect on a given stakeholder of some feature described in the scenario. For Rosen and Carroll their importance is mainly in their use to make design decisions by the trading of a positive for a negative feature (e.g. trading off functionality against cost). Both the descriptions of the stakeholders and the claims effectively scope and scaffold the problem scenario writing process.

The three subsequent types of scenarios focus less on the analysis of the current and more on the design of the future system. Activity scenarios, for example, describe the types of activities or services that people will undertake with the proposed system. These scenarios are technology independent, focusing more on the functional requirements rather than the technical implementation. Information scenarios, as their name implies, focus on what information the system needs to provide the user. Finally, Rossen and Carroll (2002) identify a fourth type of scenario – the interaction scenario. The interaction scenarios describe in detail how the user interacts with the proposed system, including the systems' responses or feedback. The interaction scenario needs to embrace the different users and tasks from the problem scenarios and the task information described in the information scenarios. This process is not prescriptive, designers will draw upon their previous knowledge (e.g. design guidelines) and experience to evolve or redesign the scenarios and the embedded design concepts.

The use of scenarios for interaction design is well covered by Rossen and Carroll. In this chapter we will focus on the use of scenarios at the early stages of the design process – that is to elicit and analyse user needs.

Scenarios and user needs analysis

User needs analysis is a front-end activity in the system design process. It attempts to ensure that the system requirements are firmly grounded in the needs of the users or learners. In more traditional software engineering models, requirements were 'captured' by using a variety of information gathering techniques (e.g. interviews) and using a set of standard descriptions to represent a system's view of what the user needs (e.g. data flow diagrams, entity models etc.). With the move to Object-Orientated Design (OOD), the aim is the same but the means, or more critically the representations, have changed. UML for example, emphasizes the importance of use cases for capturing high-level functional requirements of the user (Fowler 2000). An example of a use case would be 'User annotates a case study'. In UML, the use case descriptions need to be rich (e.g. to include descriptions of actors, triggers, dependencies, flows etc.) so that various UML diagrams (use case diagram; class diagram; interaction diagram; state diagram; activity diagram; physical diagram) can be created. Use case diagrams for example display the relationship between users and use cases, so the users or actors and relationships need to be identified.

To think of use cases as being examples of scenarios is probably misleading and certainly a use case description is more like a template than a scenario. However, these initial titles or vignettes could have been derived from a much richer and complete picture of the proposed systems, its functions and users. For example, the use case described above was derived or extracted from the following part of a scenario:

> Over the next term she uses the case study to inform her own teaching, and from her experience of using it, she annotates it with her own notes <need to annotate>, and saves the annotated version and thus 'growing the context'. Indeed, she came to the stage of being so critical of the case study that she changed it by adding some of her own material <need to edit>. Eventually she decided it would be easier to create a new one <need to create> and submit it. Later on, she notices that the University QA officer had deleted the original case study <need to delete>, and hers was now offered as the best example of effective practice in that area.

There are least two key questions about using scenarios to derive use cases. First, where do the scenarios come from? And second, how can one systematically and validly extract the needs to support the design process? SUNA (see van Helvert and Fowler 2004) was developed to help answer these two questions.

SUNA provides a simple and non-prescriptive method for creating and analysing scenarios for innovative and people-centred products and services. The method is based on workshops that bring together key stakeholders (e.g. designers, managers, practitioners, etc.). Before the first workshop the 'product or service' needs to be scoped and terms of reference defined. In a commercial environment scoping is usually achieved through a 'proposition statement' and a 'marketing requirements' document. Essentially these documents, in a formal and brief way, specify the opportunity (the proposition), who the stakeholders are, size of market, target price and so on. In a non-commercial or in-house environment, the above is usually satisfied by some form of 'project description'. Further inputs could include, for example, reports on market or technology trends, segmentation analysis, mission and vision statements, and strategy documents. The key, however, for SUNA lies less in the quality and quantity of the documentation but in the choice of workshop participants. Normally there would be five to seven participants and they would be expected to attend both workshops. Each participant is carefully chosen to represent some stake in the product. In a learning service, this could be a pedagogical expert, a designer, a senior manager, an experienced user, a practitioner and so on. Each workshop lasts about two days.

The first workshop is mainly about generating scenarios and eliciting needs. Scenarios in SUNA evolve around prospective users, and these users need to be defined. The list of users determines the number of scenarios (one for each prospective user type). In later versions of SUNA a thumbnail sketch of the user was provided and took the form of a persona that is a generic or representative description of the user's characteristics – in other words a user stereotype or archetype. Scenarios are then constructed around the persona. A library of both persona and scenarios is being collected to support the use of SUNA. Grudin and Pruitt (2002) argue that the use of personas make scenarios more engaging and memorable, a useful but not essential by-product of their use. The key to the use of personas is to ensure that they are sufficiently realistic or representative to be useful. Much work (both quantitative and qualitative) is therefore required to ensure the personas are grounded in reality (see Sinha (2003) for an interesting example of creating grounded personas), and thus reducing the possibility of the scenario being a crude representation or an over-simplification of reality.

Once the group had scoped the scenario and chosen the personas then usually one individual would write a scenario. Often more than one scenario would be written, but there is no concept in SUNA of a 'super-scenario' that links together all the subordinate scenarios. However, the scenarios are linked by the creation of one common list of user needs.

The needs are extracted by reading through the narratives and highlighting or identifying verbs and/or active software system terms or phrases. In the partial scenario example given above, the needs have been annotated into the text (<need to . . .>). Duplicate needs are removed and the remaining needs are recorded in a 'needs table'.

Before the second workshop two critical activities must take place. First the scenarios need to be checked with 'real' users. This is a form of 'early' evaluation with the scenario acting as a 'paper prototype' that users can react to, improve and generally comment on. If the scenario is deemed to be unrealistic then it can be removed, replaced, amended or the user concerns simply noted. The second activity involves the creation of a 'needs hierarchy'. Organizing the needs identified in the list into a hierarchical format is a good way of identifying missing needs (either at the same level – a missing branch, or from the process of decomposition). If new needs are identified then they should be added to the 'needs list'. Figure 10.1 is an example of a needs hierarchy for a workplace training system.

The purpose of the second workshop is to agree the scope or boundaries of the system, and begin the process of transforming needs into requirements. Scoping involves making decision about what needs will be supported by the new system. In Figure 10.1, for example, the decision was made for the proposed service to focus only on 'manage a learning contract'. The basis of that decision will be varied and complex, including available resource, requirement to focus on certain markets or opportunities, technical difficulty, 'buy or build' policies and so on. The needs identified in the 'scoped' hierarchy also provide a good starting point for producing the use cases and storyboards that can then be directly used by UML.

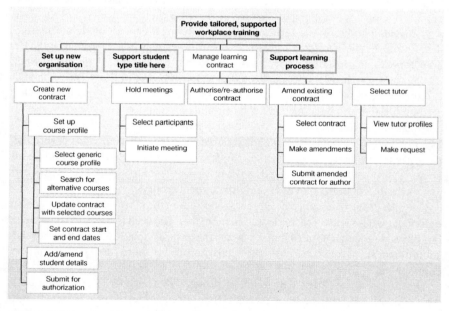

Figure 10.1 An example of a SUNA-derived needs hierarchy

Gardner *et al.* (2003) took a broader view of the design process and applied it specifically to the design of new e-learning services. Although this view includes SUNA, it makes much more explicit some of the surrounding decision-making process (see Figure 10.2). The details can be found in their paper, but there are a couple of key points. First of all they recognized that in e-learning at least, most of the functional components are generic and can be derived from pedagogical models (e.g. Laurillard 1998; Mayes and Fowler 1999), standards (e.g. Shareable Courseware Object Reference Model (SCORM); Learning Object Management System (LOMS)) and existing technical architectures (e.g. see Figure 10.3). These generically derived functions can be compared to service specific ones created via

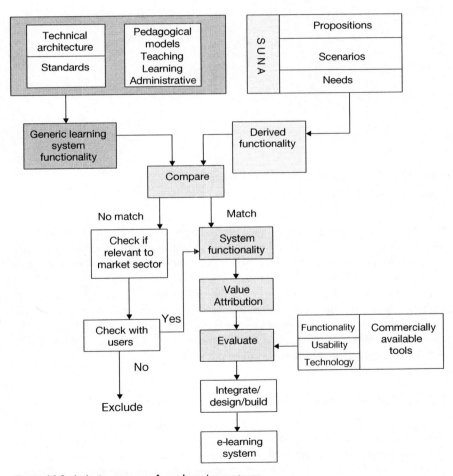

Figure 10.2 A design process for e-learning systems

Source: reproduced with permission from Gardner *et al.* (2003)

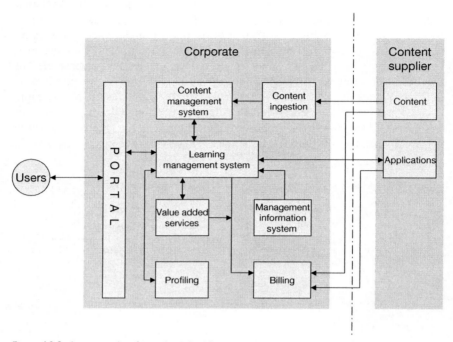

Figure 10.3 An example of a technical architecture
Source: reproduced with permission from Gardner *et al.* (2003)

a SUNA process. A second key point is supporting the 'buy or build' decision. Here we suggested an extension to SUNA called the Value Attribution Process (VAP) in which users assign values to the needs in the needs hierarchy. This identifies high-value needs (as perceived by users) and thus key functionality. Further, if investment costs are known, then it is possible to tabulate costs against value, which should help inform the decision to buy or build. So for example, if a commercial product (the buy option) fails to address a significant number of high-value needs then this would raise questions about its suitability and whether the build or a combined buy and build option should be pursued.

Scenarios and evaluation

It is useful to make a distinction between evaluation and validation. Evaluation is about measuring the perceived value of the system from the perspective of the different stakeholders. Validation is more concerned with quality assurance by checking something is right or valid, in other words the correct processes have been used and used correctly. It is therefore possible to have a valid set of requirements, but ones that are not valued by the users.

Most scenario generation does not appear to rely on an explicit creation process so validity is difficult to check. SUNA does rely on a process, albeit one involving a light touch. It is therefore possible to check that the high-level procedures (e.g. creating a needs hierarchy) have been undertaken and undertaken correctly. However, our emphasis in this section will be on evaluation rather than validation.

Evaluation also needs to be understood in terms of where in the design lifecycle the activity takes place. Traditionally evaluation took place late in the lifecycle when either the product or a high-fidelity prototype was trialled with end users. In contrast early evaluation takes place at the beginning of the design cycle, where at best only low-fidelity prototypes (e.g. mock ups or other forms of paper prototypes) are available. Other types of early evaluation techniques use analytical methods based on theories (e.g. GOMS (Goals, Operators, Methods and Selection Rules), Card *et al.* 1983) or expert inspections or walkthroughs to predict potential usability problems. In contrast late evaluation techniques adopt empirical methods that involve direct observation of users interacting with the system or prototype. They can range from controlled experiments to unstructured interviews.

In some sense analytical methods were the first of the discounted techniques as they did not require testing with real users. Discounted evaluation techniques more generally sought to reduce the costs of full-scale user trials by looking for ways to reduce the dependency on highly valid but time-consuming and expensive experimental techniques. Neilson (1992) argues that scenarios are a form of prototyping and as the 'ultimate minimalist prototype' have the qualities of a discounted technique. However, Neilson's view of scenarios is narrow partly because of his strong evaluation emphasis. For him scenarios describe a 'single interaction session' where the features and functionalities to be evaluated are limited. The limits are partly defined by focusing on a single user attempting to reach a specified goal within a certain time frame. These limited scenarios are more akin to vignettes in SUNA parlance or use case descriptions as used in UML.

What should be clear is that Rosson and Carroll's and Neilson's approaches to the use of scenarios for both design and evaluation have a strong emphasis on the user interface. Indeed the use of scenarios as part of usability engineering is now relatively well understood. In contrast, as we saw in the previous section, we have seen scenarios mainly contributing to the user needs analysis and feeding into the requirements capture stages – the very early stages of system development. At this early stage the emphasis, we would argue, should be less on usability and more on utility. However, both types of evaluation draw upon a common set of techniques, particularly the use of scenarios.

In our early scenario evaluation attempts, we simply presented the scenarios, through an animated Microsoft PowerPoint presentation, to a selected but representative group of stakeholders. The users were asked to comment on any aspect of the scenario they thought was unrealistic. This could be a misunderstanding of what people actually do, or a comment on what the system expects people to do in the future. The scenarios were discussed by the SUNA team, and then, if necessary, amended or even discarded based on the users' judgments. Due to the fact that the team included experts and other user representatives, modifications were rarely necessary. A second approach using Dervin's 'sense-making methodology' (Dervin and Foreman-Wernet 2003) is being explored, and in many respects this is a more formalized version of our earlier procedure.

Dervin argues that as we move through space and time we continually 'make sense' of our world moment to moment, drawing on a number of factors such as our past experience, knowledge of the current situation, future aspirations etc. However, when we encounter a phenomenon that does not fit the frame, that stops us in our tracks (for example an encounter in a new cultural milieu), in sense-making terms a 'gap' or discontinuity occurs. It is bridging the gap or constructing a new understanding that helps the individual move on (i.e. to cross the bridge). The method involves interviewing people and asking them to recall their 'gap' situations and recreate them, describing each step in detail. Dervin calls this a Micro-moment Timeline Interview. The interviewer then seeks out how the respondent resolved the discontinuity or bridged the gap: What sort of gap was it? What strategies were adopted? What help was used to bridge it? The sense-making methodology should work well with SUNA-generated scenarios, as these scenarios are themselves based on time lines around the notion of a 'day-in-the-life-of'. However, the use of the sense-making interviewing method will be time-consuming and perhaps should only be undertaken if there is considerable response variability or a strong negative response results from the initial PowerPoint presentation approach. It can then provide a more in depth analysis of where the problems lie and how they should be resolved.

In van Helvert and Fowler (2004) we have also alluded to another technique that could help evaluate the utility of the needs generated by SUNA. We call the technique the VAP and argue that it should be undertaken after the first SUNA workshop. We define a value as 'a feature or sub-feature that significantly enhances some aspects of the quality of our life, work, or play'. Not all needs generated by the SUNA method need to be valued, and we suggest choosing a level within the needs hierarchy. This level is usually quite high (Level 1 or 2), and a judgement has to be made that needs nested below that level are less goal orientated (e.g. manage user details) and more task or operation orientated (e.g. create and maintain diary). It is the 'goal' level that needs to be chosen. Unfortunately to date we have not applied the VAP to the design of a learning system, but Figure 10.4 is part of a needs hierarchy taken from a Device Unification Service (DUS) example.

Once a level has been chosen, a questionnaire to assess the actual value needs to be created and completed by selected stakeholders. It is important the stakeholders read and are familiar with the relevant scenario before completing the questionnaire. An example of a partially completed questionnaire for the DUS example is shown in Table 10.1. The questionnaire need to be analysed for consistency, and where inconsistent responses occur then further probing is required. For example, in the DUS questionnaire inconsistencies occurred between user ratings of certain needs because the respondents were uncertain of the question's meaning, or user

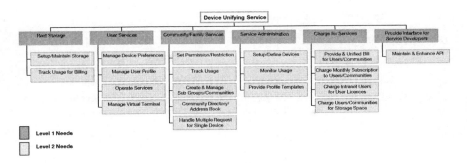

Figure 10.4 An example of a needs hierarchy (only Level 1 and Level 2 needs are presented in the diagram, lower-level needs are omitted for simplification)

circumstances led to different values being assigned. A consistency check was also done between Level 1 and Level 2 needs. Given the nature of a hierarchy, the values for the nested needs should be consistent. Again some consistency problems were caused by poor or ambiguous descriptions of the needs. In the end these consistency checks proved valuable in assessing the validity of the needs questionnaires both in terms of choosing levels and removing ambiguities, etc. in any of the need descriptions.

The mean values of the needs were then assigned to one of three levels: high, medium or low. In terms of making decisions, these values were then compared with estimated delivery or implementation cost (also using a high, medium and low classification scheme). High-level decisions could then be made on the trade-off between these two factors. In the DUS example three possible outcomes were considered:

- not to include the need in the final design (e.g. a low-value need with high implementation cost);
- include the need but reduce its prominence as it likely to be used by only a few users (but highly valued by those few);
- include as normal (e.g. high-value needs and low implementation costs).

In the DUS example, only the first 4 Level 1 needs (L1.1 to L1.4) (see Figure 10.4 – the other two did not directly affect the end user of the service), and 14 Level 2 needs (L2.1 to L2.14) were considered in making the final design decisions. Table 10.1 summarizes the final decision.

It is also possible to use the attributed values associated with groups of functions (if necessary these will have to be aggregated from the respective needs) for evaluating the goodness-of-fit between the functional specification and a commercially available offering. If any 'high-valued' functions are not supported by the commercial product then this raises serious questions about its suitability.

Table 10.1 High-level design decision table for the DUS example

Level	Value ratio (need/cost)	Design decision
L1.1	Medium/Low	Include all L2 needs but hide
L1.2	High/High	Include all but L2.3 as normal. L2.3 not included
L1.3	Variable/Low	Only L2.10 was highly valued and so should be included. Rest were rated low value, but a community address book (L1.3) as a whole would be of limited value without these features and implementation costs are low so decided to include but hide
L1.4	High/Medium	Include as normal

Conclusions

Designing for effective learning is a complex problem existing at many levels of abstraction. We have focused on the designer of e-learning systems in general and particularly at the front end of the design and evaluation process. One consequence of this early focus is to shift the emphasis away from designing for usability to designing for utility, where utility is something that is both useful and valued.

We argue that a scenario-based approach such as the one adopted by SUNA is a powerful means for supporting design and evaluation of the utility of e-learning systems. However, there is still much work to be done. The VAP and use of sense-making have only been tried on a limited number of systems. There are also other late evaluation techniques based on scenarios that need developing. One particular interesting one is Lifestyle Due Diligence, which uses scenarios to evaluate the user and task assumptions underpinning an existing system. This family of techniques, we believe, will provide some useful tools for the future design and evaluation of our e-learning systems.

Acknowledgements

The authors would like to acknowledge the work of Ivy Tung in helping to develop and test the VAP.

References

Bodker, S. (2000) 'Scenarios in user-centred design: setting the stage for reflection and action', *Interacting with Computers*, 13 (1): 61–75.

Britain, S. (2004) *A Review of Learning Design: Concept, Specifications and Tools*. A report for the JISC E-learning Pedagogy programme. Online. Available www.jisc.ac.uk/index.cfm?name=project_elearn_ped_learning_design_tools (accessed 30 September 2006).

Card, S., Moran, T.P. and Newell, A. (1983) *The Psychology of Human–Computer Interaction*, Hillsdale, NJ: Erlbaum.

Carroll, J.M. (2000) *Making Use: Scenario-based Design of Human–Computer Interaction*, Cambridge, MA: MIT Press.

Dervin, B. and Foreman-Wernet, L. (eds) (2003) *Sense-making Methodology Reader*, Cresskill, NJ: Hampton Press.

Fowler, M. (2000) *UML Distilled*, 2nd edn, Boston: Addison.

Gardner, M.R., Fowler, C. and Scott, J. (2003) 'A process for bridging technology and pedagogy for the design of e-learning systems', in Proceedings of *Online Educa 7*, Berlin, December 2003.

Grudin, J. and Pruitt, J. (2002) 'Personas, participatory design and product development: an infrastructure for engagement', in Proceedings of Microsoft's Professional Developers Conference (PDC) 2002, Palo Alto, CA, pp. 144–61.

Hinchcliffe, M. (n.d.) *Design for Learning: A Design Guide for People Who Run Learning Centres*, University for Industry. Online. Available www.ufi.com/designforlearning/ (accessed 30 September 2006).

IMS (2003) *Learning Design Best Practice and Implementation Guide*, IMS Global Learning Consortium Inc. Online. Available www.imsglobal.org (accessed 30 September 2006).

LADIE project (2005) *LADIE Project Files and Documents*. Online. Available www. elframework.org/refmodels/ladie/ouputs/ (accessed 30 September 2006).

Laurillard, D. (1998) 'A conversational framework for individual learning applied to the learning organisation and the learning society', *Systems Research and Behavioural Science*, 16 (2): 113–22.

Mayes, J.T. and Fowler, C.J.H. (1999) 'Learning technologies and usability: a framework for understanding courseware', *Interacting with Computers*, 11: 485–97.

Neilson, J. (1992) *Usability Engineering*, New York: Academic Press.

Rossen, M.B. and Carroll, J.M. (2002) *Usability Engineering: Scenario-based Development of Human-Computer Interaction*, London: Academic Press.

Sharpe, R., Beetham, H. and Ravenscroft, A. (2004) 'Active artefacts: representing our knowledge of learning and teaching', *Educational Developments*, 5 (2): 16–21.

Sinha, R. (2003) 'Persona development for information-rich domains', in Proceedings of Computer–Human Interaction Conference 2003, Fort Lauderdale, Florida, April 2003.

van Helvert, J. and Fowler, C. (2004) 'Scenarios for Innovation (SUNA)', in I. Alexander and N. Maiden (eds) *Scenarios and Use Cases Stories through the System Life-cycle*, London: Wiley.

Chapter 11

The art of design

Derek Harding and Bruce Ingraham

EDITORS' INTRODUCTION

This chapter explores the impact of arts pedagogy on the process of designing for learning, not just for the arts but for all subject areas. Given that educational thinking is largely derived from social scientific perspectives, the authors ask whether approaches valued in the arts – especially criticism and aesthetics – can provide equally valid perspectives from which to examine the new media artefacts that are central to pedagogy in the digital age. They also open up the question of how design for learning, as a creative practice, can learn from other creative subjects that are taught in our universities and colleges.

Introduction

In this chapter we explore some of the ways in which the methodologies of the arts can be brought to bear on understanding the activity of designing learning opportunities in and for the contemporary electronically mediated world of education. In the course of this exploration we will highlight some examples of interesting practice drawn from the design of learning opportunities for the arts or of artistic practice in the design of learning opportunities for other disciplines. In speaking of the arts, we are referring to those disciplines covered in the UK by the following Higher Education Academy subject network centres: Art, Design and Media; English; History, Classics and Archaeology; Languages, Linguistics and Area Studies; PALATINE – Dance, Drama and Music; Philosophical and Religious Studies.

At the heart of our position lies the assumption that while education is often studied from the perspective of the social sciences, education is perhaps more art than science. From our perspective teachers may be said to reflect on their experience of their discipline and, like an artist, create (design) opportunities upon which students can (like a critic) reflect and by so doing further their understanding of the discipline. As such, both the methods of creating and interpreting aesthetic experiences are relevant to understanding how to design for learning not only for the arts, but for many disciplines.

In addressing the aesthetics of teaching and learning, we are not confining ourselves to a consideration of the practical tuition of the creative skills of such things as music, media, art composition or performance. Quite the contrary, while in some sense the act of artistic creation inspires our thinking, the focus here is more on the activity of interpreting and understanding the significance of aesthetic and other experiences. This activity is in arts pedagogy frequently embodied in a dialogic process that leads from one set of questions to another.

Still further we see these disciplines as lying along a spectrum from the more practical and skills oriented (e.g. performing arts) to the, at times, explicitly scientific, such as archaeology, which, as Foucault (1969) reminds us, provides perhaps the most paradigmatic model of the underlying process of semiosis that characterizes all knowing and consequently all learning. Ultimately this semiotic process, this activity of interpreting, provides the key to the discipline of the arts and it is this activity that we see as the key to the art of designing for learning.

Questions and artefacts

In the arts there are similarities in approach between disciplines but there are also important differences. A key similarity that is pertinent here is the artefactual critique that is a central activity in all arts disciplines. For this to occur two things are required – artefacts to interact with and strategies through which to critically engage with them. Contemporary technology provides previously unimaginable opportunities to deploy artefacts, which can then be used as the basis for activities for students to engage in.

These artefacts might be texts, images, voice recordings or moving images and might be available in a variety of formats. They might be part of the growing collections of digitized materials provided by the Joint Information Systems Committee (JISC), the Arts and Humanities Data Service or some other provider or equally they might be provided by the lecturer. The artefacts are intended to provide a stimulus for students to engage with in some way.

Although critical reflection on artefacts can take many forms, it is highly significant that the interaction between students, scholars and the artefacts of the discipline frequently takes the form of a dialogue, written or spoken, that leads from one set of questions to another. To some degree this reflects the difference between what Giddens (1984) described as mode 1 and mode 2 knowledge. Mode 1 emphasizes objectivity, rationality and universalism and the latter emphasizes contingency, application and contextualization. Interestingly, such a division was also reflected in the language chosen by discipline practitioners to describe key curriculum issues at a recent UK Higher Education Academy Symposium on e-Learning in disciplines. In feedback from discussions arts practitioners used terms such as 'critical thinking', 'reflection', 'evaluation', and 'contextualisation' to describe key curriculum outcomes while representatives of maths and the natural sciences spoke of 'conceptualising/modelling problems', 'developing/extrapolating solutions', and 'testing and reflecting on solutions' (HEA 2006). In the context of the present discussion what we see is an emphasis on the process of thinking about a problem (of questioning) in the arts as compared with an emphasis on resolving problems, finding solutions (answers) in some other disciplines. It is this focus on the activity of questioning that is the key to the disciplines of the arts and, accordingly to designing for learning in those disciplines.

In Fine Art the stimulus may be, for example, a painting, a photograph, a critique or a body of work that students are required to respond to in some way. They may discuss the work's significance or explore a concept that it is intended to illustrate. This discussion might then inform further work. The stimulus will produce a response but not an 'answer'.

Classicists and philosophers might critically examine a set of texts (Kolb 1994) or be expressly concerned with conduct of philosophical discourse online as a subject for philosophical reflection (Carusi 2005) and, like languages, might have a concern with students being able to translate them. Languages was among the first of the disciplines of the arts to explore the potential of multimedia to enhance the process of acquiring essential language tools (see Box 11.1).

In the study of English or any other literature the focus lies on written texts and what they mean or say to different audiences. For example, in the field of English Studies in the UK the work of the Duologue project (Knights 2004) has attracted considerable attention in the area of supporting critically reflective dialogue online and Susana Sotillo (2006) reports on the use of instant messaging to provide another mechanism for freeing the dialogue from the geotemporal constraints of the classroom (see Box 11.2 for more examples from the Subject Centre for English).

The task of (re)presenting the complexity of such critically reflexive discourse has been of significant interest to the literary community, and from Landow's seminal work on hypertext (1992) and indeed earlier, many literary and other arts scholars have been interested in using hypertext as a mechanism for capturing the play of reflective discourse (e.g. Lee 1996; Kolb 2000).

Recently, Taylor (2006) reports an experiment that links the process of discussion to the use of hypertext to help students construct and represent critical thinking in/on the history of art. In this case the learners were in secondary rather than tertiary education, but the principle is readily transferable not only from one level to another, but also across a range of disciplines. Using a tool called Storyspace students were

Box 11.1 The CAMILLE project

The CAMILLE project was one of the first academically robust uses of fully featured multimedia to create a computer-mediated environment for learning (Levy 1997: 34–7). Initially a European project, CAMILLE continues at the Universitat Politècnica de Valencia. (For more information see the website www.upv.es/camille)

> ## Box 11.2 The UK subject centre for English
>
> The UK subject centre for English also provides a number of examples of projects and other resources using state of the art technology including: a project led by Stuart Lee (2006) at Oxford University using a tool called Media Stage (www.immersiveeducation.com/uk/MediaStage_Default.asp) to provide students with an opportunity to animate their interpretation of a theatrical text. Conversely, Salem (2005) reports on using the *commedia dell'arte* as a model for designing avatars to support collaborative learning. In both cases the students are being invited to reflect on a discipline through an aesthetic practice, in the first instance as directors and in the second as performers.

provided with a mechanism for visualizing the complex of relationships that emerged in a critical reflection on a particular topic. Such representations cannot only be used by students, but can also be appropriately and interesting used by scholars to represent reflective complexes (cf. Kolb 1994).

Taylor reminds us that the dialogic of learning is not limited to the student. She writes:

> According to Paulo Freire, 'Liberating education consists in acts of cognition, not transferrals of information. It is a learning situation in which the cognizable object (far from being the end of the cognitive act) intermediates the cognitive actors-teachers on the one hand and students on the other. Accordingly . . . [t]he teacher is no longer merely the-one-who-teaches, but who is him or herself taught in dialogue with the students, who in turn while being taught also teach'.
> (Freire 1994: 60–1 cited in Taylor 2006)

Similarly in History the artefacts under study may take many forms in a variety of media from photographs to letters or public records. They might, for example, be a set of marriage records (they record the occupations of the bride and groom but also the witnesses) that the students might use to examine the occupational structure of a place. Just as with discussion this activity would be unlikely to produce answers but instead would produce a set of more detailed questions designed to guide further enquiry (see Box 11.3).

Clearly there are similarities between the pedagogies of arts disciplines that we can crudely model as follows:

- stimulus – the artefact or artefacts;
- activity – critical examination of the stimulus material usually with some question(s) in mind;
- outcome – greater understanding of the artefact(s).

Box 11.3 History example

Stimulus – marriage records for a particular place.

Activity – determining the occupations of those persons in the records. The question in mind here would be whether Eric Hobsbawm's (1991) assertion that half a million hand loom weavers were left to starve to death during the industrial revolution was accurate.

Outcome – the principal occupation turns out to be weaver and this is a period after Hobsbawm's.

Evidence – observations from the official records.

Conclusions:

Observation – there are more weavers than we should expect from Hobsbawm's claim since it seems to be the principal occupation.

Questions – is this the case for other places? Is this the case for other periods? Can we say with confidence that Hobsbawm was inaccurate? What questions do we need to ask to have a greater degree of accuracy?

The outcome, however, would in practice contain a number of elements:

* evidence, i.e. observations; and
* conclusions – of two types:
  1 those which we can have some confidence about;
  2 the need for further examination.

What emerges from this process is in effect a new set of questions.

Although a similar model can be applied to each of the disciplines we are observing, the outcomes will reflect different concerns and the types of artefact will be different.

The active/act of interpretation

Understanding a work of art involves an active process during which the reader/viewer etc. interprets the semiotic structure of an object into a meaningful experience. In the arts, the term criticism is frequently used to describe the activity of reflecting on the process of interpreting the experience of reading a poem, seeing a play or whatever. At its best the role of the critic is to reflect on their experience of 'reading an object' and then to explain how and why they interpreted it as they did and, in so doing, perhaps provide some 'guidance' to help others understand their own experience of the artefact in question. This 'guidance' can and does reflect the theoretical infrastructure of the critic's discipline and can be highly contentious, or complicated, and forms the basis of much of the contemporary theoretical discourse in the arts and related disciplines. Consequently, thinking about the 'art of designing for learning' inevitably involves a consideration of such issues, but a thorough consideration of that range of issues lies well outside the scope of the present chapter.

However, we should note two things about our own perspective on this. First, the act of criticism doesn't apply only to works of art. It applies equally to the critically reflective evaluation of historical evidence, philosophical texts and, as we shall see, to the activity of understanding most things. Second, the critic's 'reading' of the art work/evidence is itself a document for interpretation. Indeed, at best, it is an independent work of art to be interpreted. Consequently any certainty about the meaning will tend to slip away in the 'semiotic drift' of interpretation and re-interpretation. However, this should not be understood as suggesting that meaning lies exclusively *in* the interpreter or to deny the intrinsic substantiality of the objects *out there*. Rather this view represents an alternative to the traditional subjectivist/objectivist dichotomy that is usually understood as the key to Western European epistemology. There is, however, a third tradition that doesn't locate knowledge either in here or out there. In fact, it isn't much interested in 'knowledge' at all. Rather it is interested in 'knowing'. That is, its locus of interest is in the interaction between in here and out there through which both become known and in the absence of which neither is known (has meaning). It is therefore the process/activity of knowing that is of interest rather than any putative learning or knowledge objects/commodities.

Although this emphasis on process rather than object has been a focus in much so-called post-modernist thinking, it should be seen not as something novel. It is part of a tradition that can be traced back in Western European thought to at least Plato. Plato's early dialogues (up to and including the *Phaedo*, *Symposium* and *Phaedrus*) can easily be seen as dramatizations of the process of semiotic interpretation that lies at the core of post-modernism. Furthermore, the activity of dialogue and dialogics is, as we shall see in the next two sections, crucial to the pedagogical processes of the arts. Still further, while early post-modernism is an important element in this tradition, it is not the only recent element that is significant. Post-modernism has its roots in the arts, but there is also a cognate theoretical perspective that has its origins in the sciences. The American pragmatist John Dewey provides a particularly useful take on this. In three books, *Experience and Nature* (1926), the *Quest for Certainty* (1929) and *Art as Experience* (1934), Dewey articulates through the imagery of the scientific method the concept of epistemology as being concerned with knowing as a process. His position is significant because it lies at the root of the intellectual movement that eventually gives rise to the constructivist/constructionist perspectives that currently dominate much educational thinking.

Dewey argues that all knowing is allied to experimentation. We build up a theoretical model and test it against our experience and then refine the theory on the basis of the results, re-test the theory and so on effectively ad infinitum because we need to constantly test the accuracy of our models. Consequently, he argues that experimental science doesn't lead to knowledge of the objective world *out there*. Experimentalism is a process of knowing through which the knower forms a better understanding *in here* of what is *out there*. This applies across the whole spectrum of the activity of knowing for human beings. In day-to-day life we mostly do this without thinking about it. It is only when we are surprised by something that we bring this to consciousness. For example, if we encounter a *trompe l'œil* or miss the last step, because the model of the world presented by our varifocals doesn't quite match the object out there, our knowledge of which is tested by a stumble. The stumble is a 'learning event'. It is the outcome of an experiment (putting our foot down expecting to find a step) from which we learn that our previous model was not entirely accurate.

What might this mean for the design of electronically mediated learning? From the perspective of the e-pedagogy researcher, it might mean that, instead of collecting statistics, they could ask students to write reflective essays on their learning experiences and then they could use those responses in order to inform their design decisions. From the perspective of the e-pedagogy practitioner, it might mean designing resources, like some of those presented below, that are structured more like the subjects of the arts in that they invite responses similar to such objects and are thus more susceptible to such analysis. This raises questions such as: How do we design interactive events through which knowing will take place? How do we create environments that allow learners not to construct their own knowledge, but to engage in the activity of knowing (learning)?

As academics we do already have one good example of a technologically mediated environment for the creation of learning experiences and a reasonably robust methodology for their critical evaluation – books and book reviewing. Writing a book is a way of designing an interactive event through which learning takes place. The book is meaningless until someone reads it. Reading it is an interpretative activity during which learning takes place. In principle, as academics we know how to write books and we know people who can design them to facilitate their capacity to engender learning events. We also know how to critically evaluate them both through the peer evaluation that is part of the publication process and through the critical reviewing process that follows it.

This is less true for other contemporary media. In 'Scholarly rhetoric in digital media' (2000) Ingraham addressed some of the issues about the kinds of expertise and literacies that may be needed by tutors and students if we are to use new technologies to create rich technologically mediated learning experiences. For example, we need better skills in the creation and interpretation of what in many respects are essentially televisual artefacts. There is an academic literature available from areas such as Media and Cultural Studies that can help us (cf. Levine and Scollon 2004). By acquiring these critical skills along with those that we already employ, we can perhaps begin to develop a methodology for what Papert (1987, 1990) called computer criticism. That is, we can move towards mechanisms for peer review and criticism akin to those through which academia monitors the quality of its printed publications. For example, *Vectors* is a relatively new academic journal publishing multimedia scholarship that can only be realized in an online format. Each of the articles in its first two issues represents a unique attempt to design the visual representation of scholarly discourse in ways that are self-evidently more aesthetic than scientific and to do so without undermining the scholarship or the learning opportunities created by engaging in such discourse.

One way of doing this may be to adopt critical strategies explicitly derived from the arts and apply them to new media learning artefacts. For example, in 'Ambulating with megafauna' (2005) Ingraham undertook a narratological analysis of a televisually mediated learning opportunity while Gouglas *et al.* (2006) report on using computer games to support the study of narratology. Similarly, we could apply such critical skills to the analysis of learning activities that we frequently seek to emulate in electronic environments. A lecture, for example, is self-evidently a theatrical performance. By better understanding what the performance elements contribute to the learning experience, we may be better able to create effective electronic analogues. Again, seminars involve a performance element and their effectiveness may owe more to the literary dialogics of Plato, Lucian or Bahktin, than we normally take into account when considering the role of a moderator in an online discussion (Ingraham and Ingraham 2006).

In short, we need to critically review both what we are publishing and what we are proposing to publish in new media to our students if we are to build up a body of good practice. Such practice can itself be critically evaluated and so inform both our practice and that of our students in much the same way that our tacit knowledge of how to read and write academic books does. And, if we aren't doing that, what are we doing? If we aren't trying to use the technology to create something at least as good as books, why bother?

Interesting design

Throughout the chapter we have noted that a focus on creative activity is typical of the arts and that the methodologies (i.e. discussion) used to study the artefactual focus of these disciplines are to some degree themselves inspired by the methodologies employed in the creation of those artefacts. This remains true when we look at what constitutes, if not good design, at least interesting design in this field. Such design comes in a variety of guises, which for convenience we can marshal into three types, the third of which may be seen as marking a transition between designing for the discipline and designing in the light of the disciplines artefactual foci. All three are valuable in their own way.

The first aspect of this is the overall design. This encompasses what it looks like and how it works.

The second level of good design is adopting practices and ideas that have been tried and tested by others in the field and adapting them for local use. The work of the Teaching and Learning Technology Programme (TLTP) phase 3-funded Courseware for History Implementation Consortium (CHIC) is a good example of adaptation for local use. A body of materials that had been created in the previous, TLTP phase 2, round of funding were used as core materials for use in other institutions and contexts. In each case they were adapted for local use and the results were evaluated with staff and students. Other initiatives have produced materials that can also be used or adapted in various ways such as the various rounds of Fund for the Development of Teaching and Learning (FDTL), JISC and Higher Education Academy initiatives and the like. These provide a wealth of ideas that lecturers can draw upon to engage in good practice and there are people in the subject centres who are willing to help spread these ideas.

The third level of good design has in a sense already been mentioned in that there are those who add to the canon by exploring the cutting and sometimes precipitously bloody edge of the pedagogical envelope. Sometimes these risks don't produce the results we hoped for but we should still applaud them for trying. In some cases quite spectacular results can arise that were not expected either. A case in point came about during the second stage of the CHIC project (see Hall and Harding 2001) when Graham Rogers of Edge Hill College was asked 'if you could do anything you wanted online what would you do?' His response was something of a surprise and a challenge. He said 'I would put my PhD online'. Once he had said it and those involved had thought it through it made so much sense. Graham had access to all of the necessary materials and the course could be designed around them in such a way that the students would follow the same steps that he did and consider the same evidence as he did but without the struggle of finding the evidence: that would be readily available online.

Graham had little experience of the technology and did not have the skills to prepare the materials but he did have the ideas and a sufficient understanding of his discipline to know which questions to ask. The project had access to skills and could fund materials production. This is how we add to the canon of e-learning. A good idea emerges at a time when the resources are available to make it happen. Graham's course was very successful and the students enjoyed doing it. It was also very cheap to produce, costing a few thousands of pounds for the data preparation and database design. Today it would be even easier and cheaper to do because the technology has moved on so far and has become more reliable.

Inconclusions

Clearly, it would be unreasonable to draw formal conclusions from the preceding discussion, but it is possible to make some observations and possibly point towards areas for further investigation. In this chapter we have observed that the disciplines of the arts tend to focus on the reflective analysis of artefacts/evidence and that it now seems likely that most arts disciplines are going to become increasingly dependent on electronically mediated artefacts to stimulate the key reflective processes of learning. This means that tutors will need to reflect on how best to design the mechanisms through which the students are invited to engage with the evidentiary base of their discipline and record their reflections on it, and we have suggested that aesthetic objects may provide valuable design models.

We have suggested that such design is occurring and is likely to occur at least three levels – basic, adaptive, cutting edge. Of these, the first is currently the best understood focusing as it does on issues of clarity and simplicity. The adaptive and the cutting edge involve more serious reflection on the capacity of the technology to support better (in the case of the adaptive) or novel and aesthetically provocative (in the case of the cutting edge) access to the evidence or mechanisms for reflecting upon that evidence or for (re)presenting those reflections.

To look at this from another perspective, the book and its derivatives have traditionally provided the primary technology for disseminating not only the evidence/artefacts upon which the discourse of the arts focuses, but also for capturing and (re)presenting that discourse. While this is likely to remain the case for the foreseeable future, it is also the case that as both the artefacts and discourse become increasingly electronically mediated in the ways we have been examining, the book is likely to become but one of many ways of mediating learning opportunities. In consequence, it is difficult to know at this stage what the primary mode of publication is likely to become and what the impact of that will be on how the discourse is conducted in the future.

Similarly, face-to-face dialogue has been and is likely to remain a key element in the conduct of the discourse of the arts. We have seen that new online models for the conduct of such interaction are emerging and these models blend into the new modes of publication. It is again difficult to predict what the hypermediated, asynchronous dialogics of the future may look like and how, if at all, they will relate to the traditional groves of Academe – except that, for the arts, the discourse, whatever its form, will always raise more questions than it answers.

References

Carusi, A. (2005) *Taking Philosophical Dialogue Online*. Online. Available http://prs. heacademy.ac.uk/documents/articles/taking_philosophical_dialogue_online.html (accessed 7 June 2006).

Dewey, J. (1926) *Experience and Nature*, Chicago: Open Court Publishing Company.

Dewey, J. (1929) *The Quest for Certainty*, New York: Capricorn Books.

Dewey, J. (1934) *Art as Experience*, New York: Capricorn Books.

Freire, P. (1994) *Pedagogy of the Oppressed*, New York: The Continuum Publishing Company. (Original work published in 1970.)

Foucault, M. (1969) *The Archaeology of Knowledge*, London: Routledge.

Giddens, A. (1984) *The Constitution of Society*, Cambridge: Polity Press.

Gouglas, S., Sinclair, S., Ellefson, O. and Sharplin, S. (2006) '*Neverwinter Nights* in Alberta: conceptions of narrativity through fantasy role-playing games in a graduate classroom', *Innovate*, 2 (3). Online. Available www.innovateonline.info/index.php?view=article& id=172 (accessed 7 June 2006).

Hall, R. and Harding, D. (eds) (2001) *Managing ICT in the Curriculum*, Middlesbrough: University of Teesside.

HEA (2006) *E-learning in the Disciplines Symposium*. Online. Available www.heacademy. ac.uk/learningandteaching/ELDisciplinesCombinedReflections.doc (accessed 7 June 2006).

Hobsbawm, E.J. (1991) *The Age of Revolution 1789–1848*, London: Cardinal.

Ingraham, B. (2000) 'Scholarly rhetoric in digital media', *Journal of Interactive Media in Education*. Online. Available www-jime.open.ac.uk/00/ingraham/ingraham-t.html (accessed 16 May 2003).

Ingraham, B. (2005) 'Ambulating with mega-fauna', in S. Bayne and R. Land (eds) *Education in Cyberspace*, London: Routledge.

Ingraham, B. and Ingraham, S. (2006) 'eQuality: a dialogue between quality and academia', *E-Learning*, 3 (1). Online. Available www.wwwords.co.uk/pdf/viewpdf.asp?j=elea&vol=3&issue=1&year=2006&article=11_Ingraham_ELEA_3_1_web&id=62.254.64.17 (accessed 7 June 2006).

Kolb, D. (1994) *Socrates in the Labyrinth*, Watertown, MA: Eastgate Systems. Online. Available www.eastgate.com/catalog/Socrates.html (accessed 7 June 2006).

Kolb, D. (2000) 'Hypertext as subversive', *Culture Machine*, 2. Online. Available http://culturemachine.tees.ac.uk/frm_f1.htm (accessed 7 June 2006).

Knights, P. (2004) *The Duologue Project*. Online. Available www.english.heacademy.ac.uk/duologue/ (accessed 7 June 2006).

Landow, G. (1992) *Hypertext: The Convergence of Contemporary Critical Theory and Technology*, Baltimore, MD: The Johns Hopkins University Press.

Lee, S. (1996) *A Case Study: Teaching on the WWW Isaac Rosenberg's 'Break of Day in the Trenches'*. Online. Available www.agocg.ac.uk/reports/mmedia/rosenbrg/rose.pdf (accessed 7 June 2006).

Lee, S. (2006) *New Tools for Creative Interpretation: An Investigative Study using Digital Video and Computer Animation*. Online. Available www.english.heacademy.ac.uk/explore/projects/archive/technology/tech16.php (accessed 7 June 2006).

Levine, P. and Scollon, R. (2004) *Discourse and Technology*, Washington, DC: Georgetown University Press.

Levy, M. (1997) *Computer-assisted Language Learning*, Oxford: Clarendon Press.

Papert, S. (1987 and 1990) 'Computer criticism vs. technocentric thinking', published as 'M.I.T. media lab epistemology and learning memo no. 1' (November 1990). (Another version appeared in *Educational Researcher* (vol. 16, no. I) January/February 1987.)

Salem, B. (2005) 'Commedia virtuale: from theatre to avatars', *Digital Creativity*, 16 (3): 129–39.

Sotillo, S. (2006) 'Using instant messaging for collaborative learning: a case study', *Innovate*, 2 (3). Online. Available www.innovateonline.info/index.php?view=article&id=170 (accessed 7 June 2006)

Taylor, P. (2006) 'Critical thinking in and through interactive computer hypertext and art education', *Innovate*, 2 (3). Online. Available www.innovateonline.info/index.php?view=article&id=41 (accessed 7 June 2006).

Chapter 12

Discipline-based designs for learning

The example of professional and vocational education

Rachel Ellaway

EDITORS' INTRODUCTION

Designs for learning for professional and vocational education are often rich and deeply contextualized in specific forms of practice yet they often remain unseen and unknown outside their particular contexts of use. This chapter exemplifies how learning designs have developed to promote the principles of the teaching of a particular subject domain. Professional and vocational education is dominated by teaching and assessing practice-based knowledge, designing for complex integrated curricula and the influence of external requirements. This chapter considers a range of exemplars and discusses the implications for design in the context of the new educational paradigms associated with e-learning.

Professional and vocational education

The separation between professional and vocational education and the rest of the post-compulsory sector reflects its uniqueness and exclusivity (Eraut 1994) and its heterogeneity (Bines and Watson 1992). Common characteristics of professional and vocational education include relatively narrow post-qualification vectors (most graduates of a particular programme will go into a narrow range of similar professions, often with much better job prospects than non-professional and vocational education colleagues), a dependence on workplace learning and external regulation and accreditation, and a requirement for practitioner educators. Not only does this create technical obstacles for designs for learning (such as difficulties in reusing learning materials from outside the domain), but it also tends to obscure what kinds of designs for learning are required and their function and importance within different professional and vocational domains. By considering the issues, solutions and ways of working that have developed in professional and vocational education using examples from medicine, nursing, veterinary medicine, dentistry and allied health professionals ('ideal type' professions, Eraut 1994: 1), a number of essential designs for learning in these domains will be identified and reviewed.

Knowing in practice

Professional and vocational education involves a range of different forms of knowledge. These have been conceptualized in many different ways. For instance Miller (1990) in considering clinical competence proposes a continuum between 'knowing what' and 'doing'. At the core of this debate Eraut identifies the 'distinction between propositional knowledge which underpins or enables professional action and practical know-how which is inherent in the action itself and cannot be separated from it' (1994: 15).

However, in joining a profession a student is required to do far more than learn about being a practitioner, they must actually become a practitioner, adopting both its culture and ways of working as a means of joining its community of practice (Lave and Wenger 1991; Wenger 1998). This socializing process involves the negotiation and acquisition of broader and often quite different forms of knowledge from those required in non-professional and vocational education contexts. For instance, Lincoln et al. (1997) identify technical competence, professional interpersonal skills, professional standards of conduct and personal ethical competence as a way of modelling these practitioner knowledge domains, while Harter and Kirby (2004) propose a more holistic model with students developing a sense of appropriate limits, responsibilities, team working, ethics and behaviour in practice as well as technical knowledge and skills.

It is clear that while designs for learning for professional and vocational education may encompass knowledge acquisition, at its core must be its application in a context of practice. In this respect professional and vocational education should be considered in the context of 'situated learning' discussed by Mayes and de Freitas in Chapter 1. Furthermore, design for learning for professional and vocational education clearly needs to be as close to real-world practice as possible while simultaneously affording effective educational opportunities and activities. This is the basis of Schön's conception of a practicum, 'a setting designed for the task of learning a practice. In a context that approximates a practice world, students learn . . . by undertaking projects that simulate and simplify practice; or they take on real-world projects under close supervision ' (Schön 1987).

However, for Schön the practicum should 'usually fall short of real world practice' and be 'relatively free of the pressures, distractions and risks of the real' (Schön 1987). In professional and vocational education, although students may not (for instance for reasons of licensure) actually practice within a professional context they must be able to experience and learn from situations that are either real or as close to reality as they can be; the pressures, distractions and risks associated with such real-world practice being essential components of the experience. In the case of vocational apprenticeships, the context is authentic but learners engage in what Lave and Wenger term 'legitimate peripheral participation' (Lave and Wenger 1991): their responsibilities, while 'real', are less demanding than those required of a fully fledged expert and they are not expected to work without support.

In terms of e-learning a particularly effective and widely used class of designs for learning is the simulator, game or virtual world (Aldrich 2005; Quinn 2005).

Following the concept of Schön's practicum, students engage in meaningful scenarios where their skills and knowledge are either developed or assessed. The use of simulators is well established for technical domains such as pilots, architects, navigators of large vessels, and managers of industrial installations. Increasingly the use of simulation is being extended to less technical aspects of professional and vocational education such as urban planning (Beckett and Shaffer 2005), healthcare, business and law. Employing key aspects of 'game-informed learning' (Begg *et al.* 2005) these simulators can provide highly immersive, valid and interactive learning and assessment opportunities for both individual and collaborative designs for learning, reflecting both formal and naturalistic projections of professional practice.

In healthcare education, for instance, it is the use of virtual patient simulators that has demonstrated utility in teaching, learning and assessment (Issenberg *et al.* 1999). Furthermore, virtual patients can be used within a wide range of designs for learning (see Box 12.1). To an extent virtual patients have also developed from the now well-established use of problem-based learning (a core heuristic for many professional and vocational education programmes of study), which is based on

---

Box 12.1 Virtual patient modalities

A virtual patient has been defined as 'an interactive computer simulation of real-life clinical scenarios for the purpose of medical training, education, or assessment' (Ellaway et al. 2006b). There are many ways in which virtual patients can be used as designs for learning, as follows (adapted from Ellaway 2004):

- The learner may take many different roles (role modes).
- The learner may work within an existing virtual patient (player mode) or they may create one from scratch (author mode).
- The learner may act independently, under the guidance of a tutor or instructor, or in a collaborative setting with their fellow students or other students from intersecting curricula (independent, tutor or peer modes).
- The learning process may be naturalistic where uncertainties of real practice are key or formalized where the activity is more structured (naturalistic or formalized mode).
- The learner may build up the virtual patient themselves (blank mode), or they may explore an existing patient or scenario (critique or rehearsal modes).
- The virtual patient may be used to address particular topics (context mode), to explore personal/professional dimensions (reflective mode), or banks of patients or scenarios may be used to address broader issues such as public health (pattern mode).

prepared problem scenarios (Wood 2003), and role-play often with simulated patients – usually actors.

Virtual patients, although lacking the sensorial richness of embodied encounters, can potentially support many different kinds of designs for learning such as critical decision making, exploring alternative strategies and metrics-based assessment, as well as providing triggers and resources for problem-based learning activities and, where appropriate, the environments through which problem-based learning activities are conducted. Virtual patients are also conceptually well aligned with Carroll's ideas of 'minimalist instruction' (Carroll 1990) in that they allow for rapid engagement with meaningful tasks, can encourage reasoning and improvisation, support error recognition and recovery, and build upon prior learning using realistic situations.

However, it should be noted that while technical issues such as creating and negotiating high-fidelity 3D environments often require much time and effort, simpler low-fidelity simulations (mostly text-based and following the principles of action mazes or 'build your own adventure' narrative hypermedia) are proving just as effective and very much easier to produce and sustain (see for instance http://labyrinth.mvm.ed.ac.uk). In legal and other professional contexts, online debate (rather than discussion) and role-play scenarios using simple computer-mediated communication systems are successfully used.

Despite the clear benefits of using simulators as designs for learning a great many challenges remain. Not least of these challenges is how to connect and aggregate discrete simulation designs for learning into whole simulated practice worlds while ensuring their educational efficacy.

Box 12.2 Simulating legal negotiations

Since 2000, the Diploma in Legal Practice programme in the Glasgow Graduate School of Law has run a personal injury negotiation project using text-based computer-mediated communication (CMC). Students are divided into 'virtual firms' of four students, with half the firms acting for claimants, and the other half acting as solicitors for the insurers. Originally run using Microsoft Mail Client on Windows 3.1.1 at Glasgow Caledonian University, the project has evolved to provide a polyphonic and flexible CMC architecture that can support a student year group of around 288. The architecture involves FAQs (frequently asked questions), discussion forums for internal communication within the firms, web-based correspondence for fact-finding and negotiations, real-time correspondence with characters and institutions in a virtual town (Ardcalloch) and tutors acting as actual practice managers to the virtual firms. This environment has been found to accommodate the communicational requirements of the students as well as the complex relationship between simulation and reality (see Maharg 2006).

Whole-programme online learning environments

It has already been noted that professional and vocational education subjects tend to be both exclusive and heterogeneous, requiring higher levels of synthesis across their curricula than non-professional and vocational education subjects. Thus, while they may still include some discrete modules or courses, there is a much higher requirement for whole-programme learning environments that allow all participants to negotiate a common and integrated learning experience. This echoes both the importance of trajectories between novice and expert status in communities of practice (Lave and Wenger 1991; Wenger 1998), and Bines and Watson's observation that 'many professional courses require dedicated specialist accommodation' (1992: 64). Despite this, in recent years quite a number of professional and vocational education programmes have been required to discontinue their own purpose-built environments in favour of common institutional systems, often despite there being little actual cost difference between the two models (Cook 2005). Such normalization of professional and vocational education can often be quite destructive in that users' abilities to organize designs for learning within a specific discipline context, to manage programme-wide integration of designs for learning, and to reify and align the requisite cultural, symbolic and ethical aspects of that discipline, can be lost or significantly diminished in the process.

Where dedicated specialist online environments have been allowed to flourish they are often better able to support a holistic view of the learning environment, mediating any aspect of the environment that needs it (Ellaway *et al.* 2003; Ellaway *et al.* 2005b). For instance, a key success factor for the systems used for medicine and veterinary medicine in the author's own institution was improving the management of the complex logistical, coordination and communications issues associated with their respective programmes of study. Once a reliable programme-wide information and service scaffold was established, the development and provision of more educationally oriented services proved very much easier and effective than if they had been attempted in the absence of such a framework (Ellaway *et al.* 2004). In this respect, solving environmental management problems in professional and vocational education can be the 'killer app' around which a comprehensive learning environment can be built. Certainly engaging with the broad needs of the community of practice engaged in a subject-specific context can be a highly effective approach to designing online professional and vocational education environments (Ellaway *et al.* 2006a). By so doing both the designs for the learning environment and those essential domain-specific designs for learning can be better accommodated and integrated into the learning environment as whole.

Modelling the curriculum

Because professional and vocational education curricula are often large, complex, internally integrated and subject to external professional as well as internal educational change, they can be difficult to comprehend by both students and staff, thereby making them hard to manage with a resulting loss of meaning and cohesion. One solution to this has been the use of curriculum mapping (English 1980) by which all learning opportunities, participants, locations, resources, events and any other discrete curricular entities can be linked to the required procedural learning objectives and the exit learning outcomes and to each other.

Curriculum maps can serve both as powerful designs for learning in their own right and as meta-designs for learning that link all the constituent aspects of a programme of study together. A student can use a curriculum map to orientate themselves within the curriculum, seeing how what they are currently doing relates to what they have already done and will do subsequently, checking how they will be assessed, reviewing what learning opportunities (including designs for learning) are available to them and following the ways these aspects relate to future professional practice (Harden 2001). Curriculum mapping can also support alignment between designs for learning and their intended objectives and outcomes. Combining this kind of alignment with a constructivist educational philosophy is the basis of constructive alignment (Biggs 1999).

Considering a curriculum map as a design for learning has implications for the model of the learner in such an environment in that it implies a self-directed and significantly autonomous entity directly engaged in negotiating their own paths through the available affordances of their learning environment(s). This echoes many of the assumptions in Knowles' conception of adult learning or 'andragogy' (Knowles *et al.* 1998). Although conceptually predating the information and communication technology (ICT) revolution, it is with the use of online database-driven curriculum mapping that dynamic designs for learning based upon these maps become possible.

Assessing professional and vocational education

Assessment cannot and should not be disassociated from learning and as such there are important and distinctive professional and vocational education designs for learning that involve assessment. Given the importance of skills in practice, professional and vocational education assessment must be able to test a student's performance as well as their knowledge. An ideal way to test performance is to test it in practice and despite a continuing need for embodied face-to-face assessment in professional and vocational education there remains a significant role for new paradigm e-learning solutions.

Knowledge-based assessment in professional and vocational education can use computer-aided objective testing. This is a common way of testing the theoretical aspects of vocational courses in further education. For example, catering and hairdressing students can currently access such tests on their mobile phones (see TestVQ at www.testvq.com). Extensions to the usual multiple-choice and extended-matching (best answer) formats have been developed to include formats such as multiple 'grey-answer' question types and data grids (such as used in completing a drug chart or a project plan). However, technical challenges are faced in this context due to relatively poor support from commercial software for non-standard question types.

The objective standard clinical examination (OSCE) is one of the most common performance-based summative exam formats in healthcare education (Marks and Humphrey-Murto 2005). OSCEs involve students moving through a series of discrete 'stations', each of which tests a different clinical skill, knowledge or other performative task. Although much of this still needs to be embodied to retain its validity, many aspects of OSCEs are being moved online (Begg *et al.* 2005b) and as a result they become reified as e-learning designs for learning, both in their own right and as a template or starting point for further developments.

Portfolios

Portfolios represent a major professional and vocational design for learning, often with a higher assessment profile than those found in non-professional and vocational education subjects. Given the professional and vocational focus on the development of praxis rather than knowledge alone, the portfolio can act as both a developmental log and as a tracking mechanism to assure key outcomes and signifiers (of for instance fitness to practice). Indeed, while portfolios in science or humanities subjects often sit 'outside' the teaching, learning and assessment process and are likely to be student owned and controlled, professional and vocational portfolios are more often directly integrated into teaching and assessment and involve higher levels of scrutiny and structure. These structures (as well as the portfolio as a whole) can also be considered as designs for learning. Specific portfolio designs include logbooks and critical event analyses, personal and professional development planning, written case reports, progress tests, professional CVs, individual objectives and curriculum mapping as well as more personal and formative diary entries. All of these portfolio designs are increasingly being mediated and stored online, either as integrated parts of a virtual learning environment (VLE) or as a standalone system typified by the ePortfolio system developed at the University of Newcastle upon Tyne (see www.eportfolios.ac.uk).

The portfolio is also an increasingly key component in continuing professional development and (re)accreditation, where an individual's activities are rarely linked to a formal curriculum or context of study. In these situations requisite evidence, such as reflections on papers written or read, presentations given, meetings attended or training activities completed, are often best stored (and checked) in an online portfolio. This focus tends to influence earlier stages in professional and vocational education and as a result there will be growing pressures to integrate student and practitioner portfolios and their associated activities. This in turn tends to reinforce particular subject perspectives on lifelong learning and their vertical alignment to the profession thereby weakening their horizontal alignment to portfolio designs for learning within their host institutions.

The online medium as message

In addition to the remediation of existing methods and practices in new ways (e.g. online papers and textbooks, timetables, coursework submission) and affording new forms of teaching and learning (simulations, collaborative and distance working, personalization), there is a third dimension (echoing McLuhan's 'the medium is the message' (1964)), where the use of ICTs is an essential part of the experience, and therefore the design for learning.

Many professions have been fundamentally changed by the 'information revolution' of the past few decades and as a result informatics has become a core theme in contemporary curricula (Coiera 1998). The rise of the Internet has also diminished the professions' control of information and knowledge while compounding the growth of the professional knowledge base thereby driving Miller's professional cognitive shift from 'knowing what' to 'doing'.

In terms of designs for learning and beyond the relatively ephemeral (though essential) acquisition of computing skills lie broader professional issues such as information literacy, evidence-based practice, the conduct of professional practice online and the use and critical appraisal of online sources of information.

Drill and practice

Despite the unfashionable behaviourist aspects of 'drill and practice', much professional and vocational education still requires the acquisition of essential practical skills as part of a practitioner's knowledge base. Typical drill and practice designs for learning make use of online resources to demonstrate and exemplify essential practical skills.

Video clips and Flash movies can be particularly valuable in supporting drill and practice as they allow learners to experience an expert performance as often as they need to, and in their own time. For healthcare students these include exemplars of measuring and recording (such as taking blood pressure or ECGs) or administering and doing (such as venepuncture or handwashing), while for hospitality students this can include exemplars of napkin folding and fish filleting. In other professions architects need practical exemplars of how to survey, lawyers need to understand courtroom protocols, accountants need to be able to prepare financial reports and hairdressers need to be able to cut hair. An additional advantage is to be had where these exemplars can be delivered on handheld devices (such as PDAs (personal digital assistants)) to support students within the workplace itself.

All of these exemplars involve aspects of drill and practice and can be equated to the 'part-tasks' in the 4C/ID model of designs for learning (Merriënboer et al. 2004). Where these tasks are mediated online they should follow a close cognitive mapping between the simulated and actual aspects of drill and practice to be of practical benefit and retain validity (see Figure 12.1) as well as being well integrated into their appropriate contexts of use.

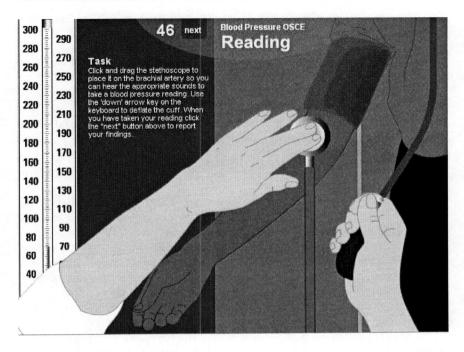

Figure 12.1 Screen from an online OSCE station on taking blood pressure exemplifying cognitive mapping in e-learning professional and vocational education activities. The student needs to place their 'left hand' holding the stethoscope over the brachial (elbow) or radial (wrist) arteries to hear the Korotkoff sounds while deflating the pressure cuff with their 'right hand', and watching the mercury column in the sphygmomanometer to identify the systolic and diastolic pressure readings at the appropriate points

Discussion

This chapter has outlined the principles of professional and vocational education and reviewed some of its key e-learning designs for learning. The extent to which these principles and designs can be generalized across the rest of professional and vocational education depends on a number of factors; not least of which how much 'knowing in practice' is required, how much of it is formalized and is how much of it is academicized. A particular instance may for instance use e-learning purely for knowledge acquisition while pursuing the performative aspects in a traditional face-to-face context. An interesting example of this is the Joint Information Systems Committee (JISC)-funded REHASH project that repurposed materials developed for medical education for use in other contexts such as nursing (see www. etu.sgul.ac.uk/rehash/). Most reuse focused on didactic instruction while the richer more discursive aspects of learning did not involve the reused materials.

This phenomenon was described by Bines and Watson as following three stages (1992: 12–17):

- pre-technocratic – an apprenticeship model where learners deliver an actual service and educational episodes are undertaken outside the work context;
- technocratic – a phased model moving from acquiring the requisite knowledge base to applying it in practice;
- post-technocratic – competency-based integration of knowledge and action from the outset – essentially Schön's conception of the practicum.

Thus while a curriculum may be post-technocratic overall it still may use e-learning in a particularly technocratic fashion.

Other influences on the designs for learning for particular professional and vocational education subjects include professional regulations and other external requirements, the extent to which the programme is separated from others around it, and the risks and/or legislation associated with malpractice or incompetence. Nevertheless, there are clear similarities across many if not most professional and vocational education domains. For instance, practica and simulators, portfolios, competency assessment, curricula coordination and integration and professional informatics are essential to and require appropriate designs for learning (albeit in many different guises).

One other key difference between professional and vocational education and other domains is its relationship with a client base. For example, the primary beneficiaries of healthcare education are not students but patients, for hospitality education it is their customers and for architects it is those that inhabit or use their buildings. This adds a further dimension to the relationships and conceptions of the learning situation. In terms of design for learning there is a continuous underlying theme of service in all professional and vocational education. A key, but as yet relatively unexplored, aspect of design for learning is clearly its application to its professional engagement with its client communities (excepting teacher education), for instance, the use of virtual patients to better inform a patient about their condition, or using virtual models to support client choice in hairdressing.

It should also be noted that the growing focus on multiprofessional education (when students from different professions learn side by side) and interprofessional education (when students from different professions learn from and about each other) (CAIPE 1997) both introduce significant new challenges, not least of which are concerns over the kinds of designs for learning that are appropriate for students from mixed curricula and educational cultures.

Conclusions

In responding to Mayes and de Freitas' imperative to only ascribe that to the new paradigm that which could not have been accommodated before, the key question would seem to be: 'What is the difference that makes the difference?' The designs for learning presented in this chapter are a response to that question but are clearly not all 'new paradigm' either in their conception or execution. It remains a problem, resulting from professional and vocational education's inherent exclusivity, that what is normative within a professional and vocational education discipline is often unknown or misunderstood by those outside it. By reifying these essential designs, the designs for learning movement would seem to offer substantial benefits to professional and vocational education by increasing transparency and utility both within and beyond their domains of use (Ellaway *et al.* 2005a). One apparent effect that the consideration of new paradigm designs for learning is having is the placing of much greater value on face-to-face educational encounters.

Although design for learning can be seen as prescriptive and algorithmic, this developing field offers significant promise in those areas, such as professional and vocational education, where learner autonomy and developing 'knowing in practice' is ill-suited to over-structured designs. In these cases looser, more practicum-like approaches are better aligned with more attention paid to the holistic nature of both the participants and their contexts of practice. In this way well-aligned designs for learning also follow some of the key trends in contemporary professional and vocational education regarding holistic practice, such as challenging practitioners' tendency to treat a problem rather than a person (or community).

A useful model (beyond the curriculum map) is to consider professional and vocational education programmes as 'information ecologies' among whose key aspects are 'keystone species' (Nardi and O'Day 1999: 49), equating to the essential designs for learning for any given professional and vocational education domain. The learning technology research and development agenda has tended to focus on generic approaches that are presented as solutions for all (Laurillard 2002; Jochems *et al.* 2004). The effect of this has been to diminish or sideline the consideration of domain-specific designs for learning in professional and vocational education, despite their importance as 'keystone species' within their particular contexts of use. It is to be hoped that the emerging designs for learning discourse will facilitate better understanding of the nature and importance of these designs and facilitate a more aligned and proximal approach to e-learning across the professional and vocational education spectrum as a whole.

Acknowledgements

Thanks to Paul Maharg and David Sugden for comments and additions on an earlier version of this chapter.

References

Aldrich, C. (2005) *Learning by Doing*, San Francisco: Pfeiffer.

Begg, M., Dewhurst, D. and MacLeod, H. (2005a) 'Game informed learning: applying computer game processes to higher education', *Innovate*, 1 (6). Online. Available http://innovateonline.info/index.php?view=article&id=176 (accessed 30 August 2006).

Begg, M., Scollay, J., Cameron, H., Dalziel, L. and Parks, R. (2005b) *The Online System for Clinical Assessment (OSCA)*, Amsterdam: AMEE.

Beckett, K.L. and Shaffer, D.W. (2005) 'Augmented by reality: the pedagogical praxis of urban planning as a pathway to ecological thinking', *Journal of Educational Computing Research*, 10: 129–37.

Biggs, J. (1999) *Teaching for Quality Learning*, Milton Keynes: SRHE and Open University Press.

Bines, H. and Watson, D. (1992) *Developing Professional Education*, Milton Keynes: Open University Press.

CAIPE (1997) 'Interprofessional education – a definition', *CAIPE Bulletin*, 13.

Carroll, J.M. (1990) *The Nurnberg Funnel: Designing Minimalist Instruction for Practical Computer Skill*, Cambridge, MA: MIT Press.

Coiera, E. (1998) 'Medical informatics meets medical education', *The Medical Journal of Australia*, 168: 319–20. Online. Available www.mja.com.au/public/issues/apr6/coiera/coiera.html (accessed 30 August 2006).

Cook, J. (2005) 'Review of virtual learning environments in UK medical, dental and veterinary education', Higher Education Academy, Subject Centre for Medicine, Dentistry and Veterinary Medicine, Newcastle-upon-Tyne. Online. Available www.meder.cc.uk/docs/cook_vle/cook_vle_final.pdf (accessed 20 January 2007).

Ellaway, R. (2004) *Modeling Virtual Patients and Virtual Cases. MELD*. Online. Available http://meld.medbiq.org/primers/virtual_patients_cases_ellaway.htm (accessed 30 August 2006).

Ellaway, R., Dewhurst, D. and Cumming, A. (2003) 'Managing and supporting medical education with a virtual learning environment – the Edinburgh Electronic Medical Curriculum', *Medical Teacher,* 25 (4): 372–380

Ellaway, R., Dewhurst, D. and McLeod, H. (2004) 'Evaluating a virtual learning environment in the context of its community of practice', *ALT-J, Research in Learning Technology*, 12 (2): 125–45.

Ellaway, R., Dewhurst, D., Mills, E., Hardy, S. and Leeder, D. (2005a) *ACETS: Assemble, Catalogue, Exemplify, Test and Share*, Newcastle-upon-Tyne: The Higher Education Academy Subject Centre for Medicine, Dentistry and Veterinary Medicine.

Ellaway, R., Pettigrew, G., Rhind, S. and Dewhurst, D. (2005b) 'The Edinburgh electronic veterinary curriculum: an online program-wide learning and support environment for veterinary education', *Journal of Veterinary Medical Education*, 32 (1): 38–46.

Ellaway, R., Begg, M., Dewhurst, D. and MacLeod, H. (2006a) 'In a glass darkly: identity, agency and the role of the learning technologist in shaping the learning environment', *E-Learning*, 3 (1): 75–87.

Ellaway, R., Candler, C., Greene, P. and Smothers, V. (2006b) *An Architectural Model for MedBiquitous Virtual Patients'*, Baltimore, MD: MedBiquitous.

English, F.W. (1980) 'Curriculum mapping', *Educational Leadership*, 37 (7): 558–9.

Eraut, M. (1994) *Developing Professional Knowledge and Competence*, London: The Falmer Press.

Harden, R.M. (2001) 'AMEE guide no.21. Curriculum mapping: a tool for transparent and authentic teaching and learning', *Medical Teacher*, 23 (2): 123–37.

Harter, L.M. and Kirby, E.L. (2004) 'Socializing medical students in an era of managed care: the ideological significance of standardized and virtual patients', *Communication Studies*, 55 (1): 48–67.

Issenberg, S.B., McGaghie, W.C., Hart, I.R., Mayer, J.W., Felner, J.M. *et al.* (1999) 'Simulation technology for health care professional skills training and assessment', *Journal of the American Medical Association*, 282 (9): 861–6.

Jochems, W., van Merriënboer, J. and Koper, R. (eds) (2004) *Integrated E-learning: Implications for Pedagogy, Technology and Organization*, London: RoutledgeFalmer.

Knowles, M.S., Holton, E.F. and Swanson, R.A. (1998) *The Adult Learner: The Definitive Classic in Adult Education and Human Resource Development*, Houston, TX: Gulf Publishing.

Laurillard, D. (2002) *Rethinking University Teaching – A Conversational Framework for the Effective Use of Learning Technologies*, London: RoutledgeFalmer.

Lave, J. and Wenger, E. (1991) *Situated Learning: Legitimate Peripheral Participation*, Cambridge: Cambridge University Press.

Lincoln, M., Carmody, D. and Maloney, D. (1997) 'Professional development of students and clinical educators', in L. McAllister, M. Lincoln, S. McLeod and D. Maloney *Facilitating Learning in Clinical Settings*, Cheltenham: Stanley Thornes, pp. 65–98.

McLuhan, M. (1964) *Understanding Media: The Extensions of Man*, Cambridge, MA: MIT Press.

Maharg, P. (2006) 'On the edge: ICT and the transformation of professional legal learning', *Web Journal of Current Legal Issues*, 2006 (03). Online. Available http://webjcli.ncl.ac.uk/2006/issue3/maharg3.html#_Toc138138224 (accessed 4 October 2006).

Marks, M. and Humphrey-Murto, S. (2005) 'Performance assessment', in J.A. Dent and R.M. Harden (eds) *A Practical Guide for Medical Teachers*, Edinburgh: Elsevier, pp. 282–92.

Merriënboer, J.V., Bastiaens, T. and Hoogveld, A. (2004) 'Instructional design for integrated e-learning', in W. Jochems, J.V. Merriënboer and R. Koper *Integrated E-learning*, London: RoutledgeFarmer, pp. 13–23.

Miller, G.E. (1990) 'The assessment of clinical skills/competence/performance', *Academic Medicine*, 65 (supplement): S63–7.

Nardi, B.A. and O'Day, V.L. (1999) *Information Ecologies: Using Technology with Heart*, Cambridge, MA: MIT Press.

Quinn, C.N. (2005) *Engaging Learning: Designing E-learning Simulation Games*, San Francisco: Pfeiffer.

Schön, D.A. (1987) *Educating the Reflective Practitioner*, San Francisco: Jossey-Bass.

Wenger, E. (1998) *Communities of Practice*, Cambridge: Cambridge University Press.

Wood, D. (2003) 'Problem based learning', in P. Cantillon, L. Hutchinson and D. Wood (eds) *ABC of Learning and Teaching in Medicine*, London: BMJ Books.

Chapter 13

Designing for practice

Practising design in the social sciences

Chris Jones

EDITORS' INTRODUCTION

This chapter is concerned with design for learning within the social sciences, and out of the social scientific tradition. It sets out from a consideration of what the social sciences might encompass and an identification of some core issues for design in the social sciences. In accordance with the overall approach of the book, the chapter considers design at what is described as a meso level, clarifying that the focus is on activities within programmes and not on the macro level of learning infrastructure or environments, nor on the micro level of the detailed interactions of specific episodes of learning. Like Harding and Ingraham (Chapter 11) the author takes a deliberately dual view of design, examining both examples of design within the pedagogy of social science and some key lessons from the social sciences that impact on the practice of design.

Introduction

The social sciences are a complex domain that includes a range of applied and pure sciences. The Economic and Social Research Council (ESRC) – the UK funding body for this area – has this comment on its web site:

> Social science is, in its broadest sense, the study of society and the manner in which people behave and impact on the world around us. Some experts however argue that no single definition can cover such a broad church of academic disciplines, deploying a wide range of approaches to gathering evidence. Instead they simply define the sciences by listing the subjects they encompass.
>
> (ESRC 2004)

I agree that the social sciences cover a broad range of subject areas and there is no simple way to define the area. As an example of what the social sciences might cover, I have taken the range of subject areas covered by the UK-based Intute (www.intute.ac.uk) (previously Resource Discovery Network and Social Science Information Gateway (SOSIG)), which provides a database of web resources for

Table 13.1 Subjects covered by Intute under the title social sciences

Subjects listed by Intute under the title social sciences

Anthropology	Human Geography	Social Welfare
Business and Management	Hospitality and Catering	Sociology
Economics	Law	Sport and Leisure Practice
Education	Politics	Statistics and Data
Environmental Sciences	Psychology	Travel and Tourism
European Studies	Research Tools and Methods	Women's Studies
Government Policy		

education and research. One of the main hubs of this network is based on the longstanding SOSIG. Any classification that divides knowledge into discipline and subject areas will create anomalies and differences with other classifications, and the list of subsidiary subject areas provided by Intute under the heading of social science is no exception. The subject areas identified by the gateway are shown in Table 13.1.

The anomalies you may identify here are the inclusion of Psychology (a human science), the exclusion of Cultural and Media Studies (Arts), the inclusion of Statistics and Data, and the division of Geography between Human Geography and other geographical areas, which are found under the Intute subject heading of Science and Technology. Perhaps more importantly for our purposes, the subject areas are diverse between each other and internally with regard to the kinds of knowledge they are dealing with and the disciplinary traditions of teaching and learning. Having made this point, it remains the case that social sciences are a recognized and recognizable research field in international terms, and there are social science bodies that promote the field through research and scholarship at national level (e.g. Academy of Social Sciences in Australia, Standing Committee for the Social Sciences in the European Union and the Social Science Research

---

Box 13.1 The Higher Education Academy subject centres

The UK Higher Education Academy (www.heacademy.ac.uk) provides another taxonomy of subjects and disciplinary areas in the organization of their 24 subject centres. Social sciences are covered by the Centres for Social Policy and Social Work (SWAP), Sociology Anthropology and Politics (C-SAP), Law (UKCLE), Education (ESCALATE), Economics (Economics Network and Business, Management, Accountancy and Finance). There is also a separate Centre for Psychology. These centres are a good source of information on developments in e-learning in particular subject areas.

Council in the US) and faculties and schools organized on this basis at university level. It may be, therefore, that it is possible to define broad features of a design tradition within the social sciences. An alternative classification is provided by the Higher Education Academy subject centres in Box 13.1.

Designing for the social sciences

We have already identified those subject areas that might be considered part of the social sciences in Table 13.1. It is clear from the range of subjects that there is no single approach that could encompass design in this disciplinary area. We begin this section with a brief consideration of what might be common design questions that affect most, if not all, of these subject areas.

Common concerns in social sciences might include:

- *Information literacy skills*. From the earliest contact with tertiary education social science students are generally required to engage with large bodies of evidence and/or secondary sources.

  - How do students search for, distinguish and select valid and reliable sources?
  - What primary sources are available and what means are there to manipulate these sources?

- *Communication, dialogue*. The social sciences tend to be discursive and this is connected to the type of knowledge that social sciences are concerned with.

  - How do course and programme designers select from available communication media – asynchronous, synchronous, conferencing, wikis, blogs, etc.?
  - If communication is essential, is face-to-face communication essential?

- *Employment-related skills*. While there are a range of subject areas and not all are vocational in character, social sciences have a strong link to key employment skills including teamwork, information management, the evaluation of sources of all types and time management. For a critical examination of these pressures see Wolf (2002).
- *Progressing from learning to independent research*. Progression in the social sciences often involves a move from reading other people's research to conducting some primary research of one's own. By the end of an undergraduate degree students may be expected to have undertaken an independent or research-based study resulting in a substantial dissertation. For a useful article on critical thinking and progression, relevant to the social sciences, see Moon (2005).

The first two of these concerns are perhaps the most characteristic of the social sciences as distinct from other subject areas, and have received the most attention: I will therefore consider them in more detail.

The use of digital resources in the social sciences

The UK-based Joint Information Systems Committee (JISC) Distributed National Electronic Resource (DNER), later known as the Information Environment (Brophy *et al.* 2004a, 2004b), recently funded a study of digital resources. As part of this work we interviewed teaching staff identified as innovators in their subject areas about their use of digital resources. Two areas of variation in the use of digital resources stood out: disciplinary differences in the level and types of resources used, and a difference in terms of progression. By progression I mean the way the student is expected to change over time during the course of their studies, most particularly between years and levels (e.g. undergraduate to postgraduate) of study.

In social science subjects, students were expected to make use of journal articles, whether electronic or paper based, early in their studies. This was not the practice in other subjects, for example in some of the sciences and mathematics. They were also expected to keep up to date and make use of ephemeral and sometimes 'dangerous' source materials as part of their studies. For example, Social Work students were asked to search for and view pro-Ana web sites. These web sites were written by and for anorexics, often advocating an anorexic lifestyle. The sites were regularly removed by service providers. They provided a view into issues that future social workers might meet, but they were not the kinds of quality-assured resources that providers of educational materials, such as the JISC Information Environment, would offer.

As a general rule social sciences are concerned with access to current materials, unlike historians, for example, who may be interested in access to archived material. Two general concerns that affect the design and provision of learning environments are the supply of good access to journals and books, including digital editions accessed electronically, and the supply of good and reliable ephemeral sources. These may be government web sites and news or other contemporary sources. As an example of these concerns here are the views of a Politics lecturer:

> [W]e are encouraging students to look at, to look in detail at what is going on in Contemporary Conflicts and who is intervening in them, who is doing what to try to sort them out and for example to look at, if it was the Kosovan conflict we would encourage them to look at what the Foreign Offices view is, what the Russians view is, what the American view is and you often can't do that from resources in the Library because they are bound to be several years out of date and so developing a kind of critical but kind of probing use of internet resources is a very important skill for supporting people's essays and generally supporting people's current awareness.
>
> (Politics lecturer in Jones and Goodyear 2003: 15)

An issue in design that arises from this use of ephemera is who maintains such links and resources. Often the library will store and maintain subscription resources but the kinds of contemporary materials often used in social sciences will stand out from the library's concerns.

Cooperation, collaboration and networked learning

Cooperation and collaboration are stronger terms than communication, implying activities that are essentially social, and that depend fundamentally on the interactions between participants. The technological changes that have enabled computer-mediated communication (CMC), however, have combined with social and situated views of learning to generate a powerful research paradigm known as Computer Supported Collaborative Learning (CSCL) (Koschmann 1996, 2001). The move to CSCL is related to but not entirely the same as a much longer tradition of cooperative or collaborative learning. It also has surprisingly loose links to developments related to new technology in work and the research area called Computer Supported Cooperative Work (CSCW) that has an active research community, journal and related international conferences.

Social science research and practice in the area of pedagogy and new technology is closely related to the development of social and situated views of learning and the cultural turn in the social sciences (Vygotsky 1986; Engeström 1987; Lave and Wenger 1991; Hutchins 1995; Jameson 1998). The key feature of this re-orientation of the social sciences has been the central focus on social and cultural factors rather than the individual and their psychology, or on the biological bases of learning. These factors had previously been heavily emphasized in behaviourist and cognitivist theories of learning. Compare Mayes and de Freitas (Chapter 1), or for a fuller discussion of this area see Jones *et al.* (2007).

Many advocates of CSCL who hold a social or situated view of learning (for example Koschmann 2001 and Stahl 2003) do not claim that it is a more efficient or a more effective learning process. Others, however, do see collaborative learning as superior to other forms of learning (see for example Johnson *et al.* 2000). For some writers, collaborative learning comes close to meaning 'learning' in general, as from a social or situated perspective *all* learning can be described as a social activity. Collaborative learning understood as social learning is not an approach that can be argued for; it is more like a descriptive enterprise setting out how people learn *in* and *through* social activity.

Recently Strijbos *et al.* (2004) provided an overview of CSCL in higher education. CSCL is a growth area of research supported by an international conference series, a book series of which the Strijbos *et al.* volume is one part and a new journal published under the auspices of the International Society for the Learning Sciences.

In the conclusion Strijbos *et al.* set out both a list of what we know about CSCL (summarized in Box 13.2) and a list of what we don't know. In relation to what we don't know, the research issues they identified as significant included:

- providing a basis for making choices of when and how to use different technologies;
- a revisiting of social psychology as a valuable resource for understanding the small-group dynamics that are essential to CSCL;
- a move from surface analysis of content to a deeper understanding of the nature of communication;

Box 13.2 What we know about CSCL

It's all about learning – The authors argue for what they call a 'probabilistic perspective' on design. That is they argue that we know that causal approaches to design do not work but that design is still possible in CSCL environments.

Learning, collaboration and assessment – The probabilistic nature of design carries over into assessment and the understanding, sharing of knowledge and learning that takes place.

What is meant by 'support' – 'CSCL implementation is not limited to introducing a new technological environment, but rather that it requires the alignment of technology with learning/teaching objectives which is not readily accomplished in technical environments used by higher education institutes' (Strijbos *et al.* 2004: 250).

Technology and interaction – The focus of design requires a shift from interface design to interaction design, and the focus on usability may need to expand to include the utility of a system in a specific setting.

Learning through collaboration supported by computers – The aim should be to increase the alignment of the various elements in a CSCL setting by systematic design so that the *probability* of desired outcomes is increased.

(summarized from Strijbos *et al.* 2004)

• a move towards what Strijbos *et al.* call prospective analysis, the testing of falsifiable hypotheses, and away from a reliance on 'retrospective' analysis of events that are 'usually *not planned*' (2004: 254).

I strongly disagree with the last of these points: we still know far too little about what happens in the day-to-day practice of teaching and learning, and more retrospective analysis is exactly what we need. Where I think they are right is in their focus on how good research might inform practice so that we can achieve more predictable and/or reproducible results.

An alternative formulation to CSCL is networked learning, advocates of which argue that learning emerges from relational dialogue with online resources and others in learning networks or communities (McConnell 2000). The Centre for Studies of Advanced Learning Technology (CSALT) group at Lancaster University in the UK has been associated with the following definition of networked learning: 'Learning in which information and communication technology (ICT) is used to promote connections: between one learner and other learners, between learners and tutors; between a learning community and its learning resources' (Goodyear *et al.* 2001: 155). The key element of this definition is the term *connections*. The notion of learning emphasized in this definition is a relational view in which learning takes place in relation to others and also in relation to an array of learning resources. Networked learning does not privilege any particular types of relationships between people or between people and resources and in this it differs from CSCL. CSCL arose out of the reaction to cognitivist and individualist notions of learning (Koschmann 1996, 2001).

For CSCL the relationship between people is one of cooperation or collaboration, and though CSCL includes learning resources it does not draw particular attention to them. A danger that is present in CSCL is that the description of learning in terms of collaboration becomes a moral imperative, so that collaboration *ought* to be the way we learn. For these two reasons networked learning has been suggested as an alternative way of dealing with the concerns that gave rise to CSCL. Networked learning does not discard the outlook formed by research and practice in CSCL: it sees cooperation and collaboration as special cases of the wider phenomena of networks. The idea of networked learning has been explored from this perspective, drawing on recent developments in network analysis (Jones 2004; Jones and Esnault 2004; Jones *et al.* 2006). A practical guide based on the idea of networked learning was developed several years ago and is freely available as a web-based resource (Goodyear *et al.* 2001).

Design and levels of design

The rest of this chapter considers how the fields of social science can contribute to an understanding of design, in a learning context. Design can be understood in a variety of ways and takes place at a variety of levels (see Beetham and Sharpe, Introduction). The design level I intend to focus on I describe as meso level (Liljenström and Svedin 2005; Jones *et al.* 2006). That is, I am not concerned with the design of broad (virtual) learning environments, university, national or global infrastructures, nor am I concerned with the immediate micro-level interactions in and through which teaching and learning take place in locally situated conditions.

The meso level indicates a relational position in a spectrum of activity but I am proposing a more analytic use of the term to identify interactions in and with settings beyond the small group, but still with a local focus that remains open to routine control and intervention. Meso also implies a time frame that is beyond the immediate interaction but not fixed for extended periods of time. Micro in this set of related concepts points to the contingent and highly local whereas macro points to the level of interaction that has a general character, not open to routine control and persistent over the long term. Meso points to *social practice* as the locus in which broader social processes are located and contingency is moderated by organization and planning (Schatzki 1996; Schatzki *et al.* 2001).

Cooley (1999) has remarked that the notion of design, as it is understood today, arose during the fourteenth and fifteenth centuries in Europe and implies the separation of thinking and doing:

> This is not to suggest for a moment that designing was a new activity. Rather it was separated out from a wider productive activity and recognized as an

activity in its own right. Design can be said to constitute a separation of hand and brain, of manual and intellectual work, of the conceptual part of a work from the labour process.

(Cooley 1999: 59)

He goes on to suggest that the scientific method has influenced the characteristics that a process or design must display to be regarded as scientific: that design must be predictable, repeatable and quantifiable in mathematical terms. Such a view of design, he claims, diminishes the role of intuition, tacit knowledge, imagination and dreams (Cooley 1999: 60). In contrast ethnographic studies of the design process suggest a view that places design and designs as part of situated action (Suchman 2007). Design as situated action cannot have the characteristics that Cooley describes as the scientific method. From the perspective of situated action, design is an iterative process and the products of design are part of a deeply social and situated set of work practices. Design and the products of design – plans, representations, etc. – do not have a determining role, rather they form resources for action available to inform the working practices of those involved in the designed process.

The practice of design for learning generally involves making a large number of decisions guided by assumptions about the nature of knowledge and learning (Boot and Reynolds 1984). Reynolds (1997) suggests the process of design is concerned with the beliefs and values held by designers rather more than it concerns the selection of methods and contents considered to be appropriate for achieving intended purposes. A common view is that design for learning requires the ability to be *critically reflective* about practice (Burgoyne and Reynolds 1997). The *critical* aspect encourages practitioners to be aware of the larger social processes, assumptions and hidden issues that are part of any design for learning activity. The *reflective* aspect encourages practitioners to question and revise their practice, including the working theories that underpin the design and may not match with their expectations or outcomes. Burgoyne and Reynolds argue the critically reflective practitioners play an important role as: 'they are aware that with every practical action they take they are "fixing (temporally) their belief" and acting on their current best working theory, but they realise that this may also be open to challenge and improvement' (Burgoyne and Reynolds 1997: 2).

Indeterminacy – the indirect nature of design

This distinction between tasks and activities (see Beetham, Chapter 2) forms part of a broader design philosophy. In brief, tasks are what designers set, they are prescriptions for the work the students are expected to do, activity is what people actually do. Because students constitute their own learning context it should be expected that students' activity will often differ from the task that initiated it. The distinction between task and activity is mirrored by two further distinctions between space and place and between organization and community. Together these three

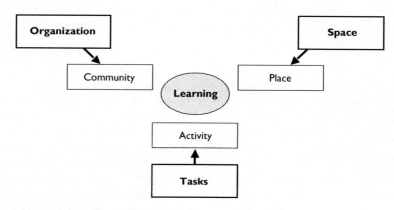

Figure 13.1 Design: an indirect approach
Source: Goodyear *et al.* (2001)

distinctions are referred to as an indirect approach to learning and their relationships are shown in Figure 13.1.

As an example of this approach, Jones and Asensio (2001) examined a distance learning course and reported a post-assessment series of interviews within one tutorial group. The group had been divided up into sub-sets that had the task of preparing their final assessment in the form of a group project with an individually prepared component. Students interpreted their instructions in highly contingent ways that depended on the particular context each student found themselves in. The responses to the set assessment task could be grouped into two broad understandings of the task, but they were affected by highly specific factors in each case. It is worth emphasizing that this course and assignment were extremely well designed: the problems arose not from the design of the task itself but from factors affecting the students that were outside the course design process and indeed in some cases outside of the learning environment.

An example of the two contrasting interpretations is illustrated in the following quotations (interviewer in italics):

1 What did you conceive that task to be?
I would assume that it was more to continue the computer mediated conferencing as an exercise in itself for people to work together to sort of exchange ideas and irrespective of what the particular project was to work on. (Daniel)

2 What do you think the emphasis was?
Your personal individual um your personal big 500 words or whatever

So the individual submission was . . . .
Was more important than the group work.

And how about content and process if we split it that way?
Content.

Rather than process. . .
Rather than process and yet it's, I would argue the process probably took as much time as writing the content if not more. (Lillian)

The two students were part of the same group working together to produce a joint report yet they had different understandings of the task they had been set. This was despite extensive documentary guidance provided in a 12 page assessment booklet. When prompted to re-read the booklet Daniel, who had identified the task as being to conduct group work, revised his view and conceded that content may indeed have been more important. There were two reasons offered by students in the group that shed light on why the group process dominated over the intention of the assessment criteria. First, the group process was novel and pervasive as they used the conferencing system throughout the course and were expected to work collaboratively using the system for two assessments. Second, the ability to communicate between students was a valued and novel element within the distance learning setting.

The point I am making here is that there is no simple way out of this design problem. There is no special kind of design that will make every student or even most students read instructions or any other text in the same way. It points towards a social and iterative process of design in use that makes the artefacts and products of design only one part of the design process. In particular it points to the need for good processes to take place during the enactment of a design to ensure its success. In the case of assessment instructions, checks can be made on students' understandings as the task is undertaken and an assumption made that design is not a once and for all activity of preparation but a process that includes the enactment of the design in use.

Process and structure

This chapter set out to describe design at the meso level, a level at which most academics work beyond their immediate classroom practice that involves the art of interaction and the tactics or didactics of teaching. This level above micro day-to-day interactions is open to planning and a planfulness that can be described as design. The types of planning teaching academics are involved in varies considerably according to institutional factors that are generally beyond the immediate control of both individual academics and small course teams and even the department or faculty. I am thinking here of the kinds of virtual learning environments (VLEs) selected for use by the institution, the institutional procedures for course validation and assessment, the technical control of access to university networks and the overall library provision. The designs that academic staff can achieve are necessarily within relatively fixed parameters at any one time. The type of design is also affected by

---

**Box 13.3 The Open University – design in
an industrial model**

Courses at the Open University are designed by a course team considerably
in advance of the course going live. Each course team is composed of full-
time academics who write activities and in many cases key texts relevant to
the course. The course teams have a chair who organizes meetings and when
the course goes live the chair will liaise with and support part-time associate
lecturers who are recruited as tutors for the course. Course materials are read
by critical readers beyond the course team and there is a relatively formal
system of quality control. Robin Mason has described this system as the
industrial model (Mason 1989). It relies on scale, with courses generally
recruiting hundreds if not thousands of students and having a course life of
about five years. Without this scale the resources required for this amount
of planning would not be cost effective.

Consider the position in your own university or one you know well. What
resources are there for planning ahead? How many students are there likely
to be on the courses and how long will they run for? Do academic staff work
in formal course teams with administrative support? Do the core academic
staff teach on the course or are others such as graduate students or part-time
and sessional staff doing the teaching? All these factors impact on the level
and nature of the planning and design process.

---

issues such as scale and the nature of the core student population such as in the
example of the UK Open University in Box 13.3.

The whole question of design for the social sciences touches on a core question
at the heart of modern social sciences, the question of agency and structure. This
chapter is not the place to resolve an issue that is so complex and central to the
social sciences. Having said that, a chapter dealing with design cannot fail to
mention how this core issue reflexively impacts on thinking about design.

Conclusions

The social sciences have a lot to offer and a lot to learn about the relationships
between pedagogy, technologies and the social practices of education. Social
science has deep knowledge accumulated about the way technologies are related
to social change. In particular studies in the social shaping of technology and social
studies of science and technology indicate that technology cannot simply determine
social change. A key support for this can be found in CSCL research that illustrates
that technology is not an independent factor and cannot in any simple sense *cause*
educational effects or any particular pedagogical responses. Design in the social
sciences and design for the social sciences is an exercise in choice, a way of setting

the parameters within which technologies will be deployed. Design could be a response to perceived social pressures – the need for team working in the workplace for example – or it could be a choice to stand opposed to the general social trend that has been called networked individualism. Technologies do not decide such issues; rather these are the issues that can be central to design if it is thought of as more than simply a technical task.

Design choice can be exercised at many levels. I have introduced the analytic distinction between micro, macro and meso levels. At a macro level design is outside of the control of individuals and small groups and takes time to enact. The decisions and design choices made at the macro level are national, institutional and corporate. These are choices about national and local infrastructures, equivalent to roads and utilities. Which VLE will your institution choose, what educational policies for e-learning will be developed and what will the organization of digital resources look like? These are choices typically made by collective bodies over time, and are not subject to local design until they are deployed in use.

At the micro level precise designs can be developed for very particular inter-actions. CSCL has generated a great deal of empirical work in this area, either examining individual systems in highly specific settings or studying close micro interactions. At this level design can be very detailed but it is subject to a high degree of contingency. The danger is that research can find it hard to move beyond the particular to the general. However, this is a fundamental problem that affects all levels of design, as we will note below in relation to indirect design.

The level that I argue educational practitioners might need to focus upon is the meso level of design. At the meso level we are focused on the medium term, and decisions that small groups and individuals can easily make or influence. In universities this might mean the department or course team, the design of a course rather than an individual interaction, and design that involves the use of systems and tools selected elsewhere.

The one fundamental point that a social scientific understanding can contribute to this field is the indirect nature of design. This is not a problem that can be dealt with by developing 'situated' designs or by setting up processes of design that can eliminate uncertainty. The cultural turn and the many varieties of social theories that flow from it, from post-modern and ethnomethodological to feminist, post-colonial and critical theory, point to a simple but hard-to-digest foundational issue. Every time a technology is deployed, every time a design is enacted, every time a plan is put into use, its meaning has to be disinterred from the technology, design or plan by those putting it into use for their own purposes. Design of the tasks we provide for students, the spaces we place students in and the organizations we set up for them can only indirectly affect the activities they generate from tasks, the places they make from spaces and the communities they build within organizations. Worse than that for those who believe in a formal design process: the active process of enactment means that not only can design never be *of* learning only *for* learning, but also learning itself is only loosely related to the activities, places and communities our students create.

References

Boot, R. and Reynolds, M. (1984) 'Rethinking experience based events', in C. Cox and J. Beck (eds) *Management Developments: Advances in Practice and Theory*, Chichester: John Wiley & Sons.

Brophy, P., Fisher, S., Jones, C.R. and Markland, M. (2004a) *Final Report of the EDNER Project: EDNER Formative Evaluation of the Distributed National Electronic Resource*, Manchester: CERLIM (Centre for Research in Library & Information Management). Online. Available www.cerlim.ac.uk/edner/dissem/x3.doc (accessed 24 July 2006).

Brophy, P., Markland, M. and Jones, C. (2004b) *Final Report of the EDNER+ Project: EDNER+ Information Environment Formative Evaluation*, Manchester: CERLIM (Centre for Research in Library & Information Management). Online. Available www.cerlim.ac.uk/projects/iee/reports/final_report.doc (accessed 24 July 2006).

Burgoyne, J. and Reynolds, M. (ed.) (1997) *Management Learning: Integrating Perspectives in Theory and Practice*, London: Sage Publications.

Cooley, M. (1999) 'Human-centred design', in R. Jacobson (ed.) *Information Design*, Cambridge, MA: MIT Press, pp. 59–83.

Engeström, Y. (1987) *Learning by Expanding: An Activity Theoretical Approach to Developmental Research*, Helsinki: Orienta-Konsultit Oy. Online.

ESRC (2004) *What is Social Science?* Online. Available www.esrc.ac.uk (accessed 30 September 2006).

Goodyear, P., Jones, C., Asensio, M., Hodgson, V. and Steeples, C. (2001) *Effective Networked Learning in Higher Education: Notes and Guidelines*, Lancaster: CSALT, Lancaster University. Online. Available http://csalt.lancs.ac.uk/jisc/ (accessed 24 July 2006).

Hutchins, E. (1995) *Cognition in the Wild*, Cambridge, MA: The MIT Press.

Jameson, F. (1998) *The Cultural Turn: Selected Writings on the Postmodern 1983–1998*, London: Verso.

Johnson, D.W., Johnson, R.T. and Stanne, M.B. (2000) *Cooperative Learning Methods: A Meta-analysis*. Online. Available www.co-operation.org/pages/cl-methods.html (accessed 30 August 2006).

Jones, C. (2004) 'Networks and learning: communities, practices and the metaphor of networks', *ALT-J, Research in Learning Technology*, 12 (1): 82–93.

Jones, C. and Asensio, M. (2001) 'Experiences of assessment: using phenomenography for evaluation', *Journal of Computer Assisted Learning*, 17 (3): 314–21.

Jones, C. and Esnault, L. (2004) 'The metaphor of networks in learning: communities, collaboration and practice', in S. Banks, P. Goodyear, V. Hodgson, C. Jones, V. Lally *et al.* (eds) *Networked Learning 2004: Proceedings of the Fourth International Conference on Networked Learning 2004*, Lancaster: Lancaster University and University of Sheffield, pp. 317–23.

Jones C. and Goodyear, P. (2003) *EDNER: Formative Evaluation of the Distributed National Electronic Resource: Pre-1992 University Institutional Case Study* (Deliverable Z7-C-1, EDNER Project), Lancaster: CSALT (The Centre for Studies in Advance Learning Technologies) Lancaster University. Online. Available www.cerlim.ac.uk/edner/dissem/dissem.html (accessed 2 October 2006).

Jones, C., Dirckinck-Holmfeld, L. and Lindström, B. (2006) 'A relational, indirect, meso-level approach to CSCL design in the next decade', *International Journal of Computer-Supported Collaborative Learning*, 1 (1): 35–56.

Jones, C., Cook, J., Jones, A. and de Laat, M. (2007) 'Collaboration', in G. Conole and Oliver, M. (eds) *Contemporary Perspectives in E-learning Research*, London: RoutledgeFalmer.

Koschmann, T. (ed.) (1996) *CSCL: Theory and Practice of an Emerging Paradigm*, Mahwah, NJ: Lawrence Erlbaum Associates.

Koschmann, T. (2001) 'Revisiting the paradigms of instructional technology', in G. Kennedy, M. Keppell, C. McNaught and T. Petrovic (eds) *Meeting at the Crossroads. Proceedings of the 18th Annual Conference of the Australian Society for Computers in Learning in Tertiary Education*, Melbourne: Biomedical Multimedia Unit, The University of Melbourne, pp. 15–22. Online. Available www.ascilite.org.au/conferences/melbourne01/pdf/papers/koschmannt.pdf (accessed 24 July 2006).

Lave, J. and Wenger, E. (1991) *Situated Learning: Legitimate Peripheral Participation*, Cambridge: Cambridge University Press.

Liljenström, H. and Svedin, U. (eds) (2005) *Micro Meso Macro: Addressing Complex Systems Coupling*, Hackensack, NJ: World Scientific Publishers.

McConnell, D. (2000) *Implementing Computer Supported Cooperative Learning*, 2nd edn, London: Kogan Page.

Mason, R.D. (1989) *A Case Study of the Use of Computer Conferencing at the Open University*, PhD, Milton Keynes: Open University.

Moon, J. (2005) *We Seek it Here . . . a New Perspective on the Elusive Activity of Critical Thinking: A Theoretical and Practical Approach that Examines Critical Thinking in Education*, ESCALate discussion series. Online. Available http://escalate.ac.uk/2041 (accessed 10 September 2006).

Reynolds, M. (1997) 'Learning styles: a critique', *Management Learning*, 28 (6): 115–33.

Schatzki, T.R. (1996) *Social Practices: A Wittgensteinian Approach to Human Activity and the Social*, Cambridge: Cambridge University Press.

Schatzki, T.R., Cetina, K. and von Savigny, E. (eds) (2001) *The Practice Turn in Contemporary Theory*, London: Routledge.

Stahl, G. (2003) 'Meaning and interpretation in collaboration', in B. Wason, S. Ludvigsen and U. Hoppe (eds) *Designing for Change in Networked Learning Environments: Proceedings of the International Conference on Computer Supported Collaborative Learning 2003*, Dordrecht: Kluwer Academic Publishers.

Strijbos, J.-W., Kirschner, P. and Martens, R. (eds) (2004) *What We Know About CSCL: And Implementing it in Higher Education*, Boston: Kluwer Academic Publishers.

Suchman, L. (2007) *Human-Machine Reconfigurations: Plans and Situated Actions, 2nd Expanded Edition*, New York and Cambridge: Cambridge University Press.

Vygotsky, L.S. (1986) *Thought and Language*, A. Kozulin (trans.), Cambridge, MA: The MIT Press.

Wolf, A. (2002) *Does Education Matter? Myths about Education and Growth*, London: Penguin Books.

Chapter 14

Designing for mobile and wireless learning

Agnes Kukulska-Hulme and John Traxler

EDITORS' INTRODUCTION

The previous chapters explored design in different disciplinary contexts. This chapter looks at how new technical opportunities can change what is considered effective in pedagogic design. There is much interest in the possibility that mobile and wireless technologies can support greater choice in how learners engage with learning activities, and, from the educator's point of view, that this might enable more flexible approaches to learning design. Developments in mobile learning could therefore have a significant impact on learning and teaching practices. In this chapter, the authors examine how the potential is being realized and suggest constructive ways of thinking about design for these new technologies.

Introduction

At the heart of this chapter is the relationship between the design *for* learning, which plays to the strengths of mobile and wireless technologies (learning that is essentially situated, spontaneous, personalized, inclusive, and so on), and the design *of* aspects of learning such as content, activities and communication. We also consider how design should take account of both physical space layout and the networking capabilities of the new technologies.

It must be said that some of the most interesting examples of mobile learning are technologically sophisticated and logistically complex. They give us a glimpse of learning scenarios we are likely to see more of in the future, as the technologies become more commonplace. Simpler, everyday devices such as mobile phones can be highly effective and easier to adopt into practice, provided there is a good match between the technology and the learning that it is intended to support. In the next section, we reflect on the nature of mobile learning by examining its attributes, its emerging categories and the reasons why it is being adopted or trialled.

The nature of mobile learning

Mobile learning is characterized by pilots and trials where the technologies are being tested in a variety of learning contexts. These are demonstrating that mobile learning has considerable pedagogic potential, in some cases a unique pedagogic potential, and that many of the technical limitations are being overcome. Mobile learning is now gradually moving from small-scale, short-term trials to larger, more sustained and blended deployment, but within institutional constraints such as budgetary and human resources, institutional practices, procedures and priorities. The idea of a 'wireless campus' has been catching on quite rapidly, with institutions such as the University of Twente in the Netherlands, the University of Kentucky in the US and Singapore's Nanyang Technological University leading the way in large-scale implementations involving laptops and personal digital assistants (PDAs) (Weber *et al.* 2005; University of Kentucky 2006; University of Twente 2006). The drive to move towards a wireless world has also been apparent behind developments at Ealing, Hammersmith and West London College, a sixth form and further education institution, where wireless Tablet PCs have been used by teachers as a way of gaining 'anywhere, anytime' access to student records and performance data, and to the college's online managed learning environment (JISC 2005).

There are obviously conceptualizations of mobile education that define it in terms of its technologies, its devices and its hardware, namely that it is learning delivered or supported solely or mainly by mobile technologies. These include handheld computers, PDAs, mobile phones, smartphones, wireless laptop PCs and personal media players such as the iPod™. The core platforms are often enhanced by location-sensing functionality such as the Global Positioning System (GPS), by video, audio and image capture and playback functionality, such as digital cameras, and by data entry functionality such as virtual keyboards and voice-activation. Such a definition is however constraining and technocentric, and tied too closely to specific existing technologies. We should therefore explore other conceptualizations that look at the underlying learner experience and ask how mobile learning differs from other forms of education, especially forms of e-learning.

If we take the characterizations of mobile learning found in the literature (the proceedings from major conferences dealing with this theme, for example), we find words such as: 'personal', 'spontaneous', 'opportunistic', 'informal', 'pervasive', 'situated', 'private', 'context-aware', 'bite-sized' and 'portable'. This may be contrasted with words from the literature of conventional, sometimes called 'tethered', e-learning such as: 'structured', 'media-rich', 'broadband', 'interactive', 'intelligent' and 'usable'. We can use these two lists to make a fuzzy distinction between mobile learning and e-learning. This distinction is however only temporary. Many of the virtues of e-learning are the virtues of the power of its technology (and the investment in it) and soon these virtues will be accessible to mobile and handheld devices too, as market forces drive improvements in interface design, processor speed, battery life and connectivity bandwidth. Nevertheless, this approach underpins a conceptualization of mobile learning in terms of the learners' experiences with an emphasis on device ownership, informality, movement and context that will always be inaccessible to conventional e-learning.

There is now a large number of case studies documenting trials and pilots in the public domain (Attewell and Savill-Smith 2004; JISC 2005; Kukulska-Hulme and

Traxler 2005). In looking at these, we can see some categories of mobile learning emerging:

- *Technology-driven mobile learning* – some specific technological innovation is deployed in an academic setting to demonstrate technical feasibility and pedagogic possibility.
- *Miniature but portable e-learning* – mobile, wireless and handheld technologies are used to re-enact approaches and solutions already used in 'conventional' e-learning, perhaps porting some e-learning technology such as a virtual learning environment (VLE) to these technologies or perhaps merely using mobile technologies as flexible replacements for static desktop technologies.
- *Connected classroom learning* – the same technologies are used in classroom settings to support collaborative learning, perhaps connected to other classroom technologies such as interactive whiteboards (see Box 14.1).
- *Informal, personalized, situated mobile learning* – the same technologies are enhanced with additional functionality, for example location-awareness or video-capture, and deployed to deliver educational experiences that would otherwise be difficult or impossible.

Box 14.1 Examples: connected classroom learning

A great deal of 'mobile and wireless' work is being done inside classrooms and lecture halls, where mobility may in fact be relatively limited. Electronic voting systems in large lecture theatres are one form of wireless technology that allows learners to interact via handheld devices and can promote active and collaborative learning. It has been found to lead to improved understanding and retention (JISC 2005).

In a review of projects using handheld computers (specifically PDAs) in classrooms, Finn and Vandenham (2004) noted positive effects ranging from improved willingness to participate in group work, to increased rates of homework completion, to opening up new possibilities in a specific discipline, namely music composition.

A study on the use of Tablet PCs in schools in England (Sheehy *et al.* 2005; Twining *et al.* 2005) showed that a key benefit of using these portable devices was the in-built support for handwriting recognition, but they were also very useful for sharing information among the children. Presentation and sharing of work was done either via a wireless network to other pupils' Tablet PCs or through a projector for whole-class display and teaching. Tablet PCs could also be used outside on sports fields or during field trips.

- *Mobile training/performance support* – the technologies are used to improve the productivity and efficiency of mobile workers by delivering information and support just-in-time and in context for their immediate priorities (for an early account, see Gayeski 2002).
- *Remote/rural/development mobile learning* – the technologies are used to address environmental and infrastructural challenges to delivering and supporting education where 'conventional' e-learning technologies would fail, often troubling accepted developmental or evolutionary paradigms.

The documented accounts give a range of reasons for adopting mobile learning techniques (Traxler and Kukulska-Hulme 2005) and include:

- *Access* – for example improving access to assessment, learning materials and learning resources or increasing flexibility of learning for students.
- *Changes in teaching and learning* – for example guiding students to see a subject differently than they would have done without the use of mobile devices or exploring whether the time and task management facilities of mobile devices can help students to manage their studies.
- *Alignment with institutional or business aims* – for example making wireless, mobile, interactive learning available to all students without incurring the expense of costly hardware; or delivering communications, information and training to large numbers of people regardless of their location; or harnessing the existing proliferation of mobile phone services and their many users.

This overview gives some indication of the current activity and potential in mobile and wireless learning. In the next sections we explore the issues of design *for* and *of* mobile learning, with reference to a number of examples and case studies.

Design *for* learning

This section focuses on the ways in which design *for* learning can exploit the affordances (Norman 2004) or characteristics of mobile and wireless technologies. These technologies offer unique possibilities to design for learning that are unlike any afforded by other e-learning technologies. They also offer unique possibilities to support designs for learning where access, inclusion, opportunity and participation are priorities.

Mobile and wireless technologies support designs for learning that are personalized, situated and authentic; for each of these, we give further clarification and examples below. It is more difficult to design intentionally for learning that will be spontaneous and informal; however mobile and wireless technologies do have affordances that support these types of learning. For example, mobile and wireless devices are usually by their nature private and personal, and so suited to spontaneous reflection and self-evaluation; the current e-portfolio technologies (see for example, www.pebblepad.co.uk/) are expected to migrate to mobile devices. An example of 'designed' informal learning is given later in this section.

By *personalized learning*, we mean learning that recognizes diversity, difference and individuality in the ways that learning is developed, delivered and supported. Personalized learning defined in this way includes learning that recognizes different learning styles and approaches (though perhaps this should not be related too literally to the established literature of 'learning styles', see Coffield *et al.* 2004), and recognizes social, cognitive and physical difference and diversity.

Learning designed for mobile and wireless technologies offers a perspective that differs dramatically from personalized e-learning designed for networked desktop computers. It supports learning that can potentially recognize the context and history of each individual learner (and perhaps their relationships to other learners) and delivers learning to each learner when and where they want it. Prototypes exist for learning designed on the basis of knowing

- where the learner is;
- how long they have been there;
- where they were before;
- who else was learning nearby;
- their progress and preferences as learners;

and moreover for the design of the learning delivered by the system to evolve with the learner and their learning (see Box 14.2 for example).

By *situated learning*, we mean learning that takes place in the course of activity, in appropriate and meaningful contexts (Lave and Wenger 1991). The idea grew up by looking at people learning in communities as apprentices by a process of increased participation. It can however be extended to learning in the field (in the case of botany students for example), in the hospital ward (in the case of trainee nurses), in the classroom (in the case of trainee teachers) and in the workshop (in the case of engineering students). Box 14.3 shows examples of how mobile learning

---

Box 14.2 Example: personalized learning

At Bletchley Park in the UK (Mulholland *et al.* 2005) researchers decided to use mobile technology to encourage follow-up activities among recent visitors to the Bletchley Park museum. As they wander around the museum, visitors can express their interests in particular exhibits by sending text messages containing suggested keywords, using their mobile phone. This information is subsequently used to create a personalized web site for each visitor to use when they get home, so that they can explore information about their chosen exhibits as well as semantic connections between them.

Box 14.3 Examples: authentic and situated learning

In a higher education context in the Netherlands, the Manolo project (2006) has amassed a good deal of experience in mobile fieldwork in subjects such as archaeology, biodiversity and vegetation science. Archaeology students have used PDAs with GPS for field surveys. This has allowed them not only to collect field data in electronic form but also to be more involved in processing and interpreting the data than was previously possible. The PDA's mobile phone function has been used by these students to communicate with their group leader in the field and the texting and email functions for other types of support.

In a project called Mudlarking in Deptford (Sutch 2005), schoolchildren have used PDAs to take part in, and to co-produce, a guided tour of the riverbed at Deptford Creek. The handheld device with GPS capabilities delivers location-sensitive information when the child walks into node areas indicated on a map. Children are also able to create multimedia content during their tour and alert other users to that content. The project aims to engage young learners in responding creatively to an environment that blends physical experiences with the history of the area.

In the Savannah project (Facer *et al.* 2005) a mobile game was designed for use by groups of children moving around in the school playing field, aimed at encouraging the development of children's conceptual understanding of animal behaviour in the wild. This 'learning experience' involves the use of GPSs linked to PDAs through which the children 'see', 'hear' and 'smell' the world of the Savannah as they move around various zones in the playing field, acting like a pride of lions. There is also a special designated indoors area where they can reflect on how well they have succeeded in the game, develop their strategies and access resources to support their understanding.

can be designed to support this context-specific and immediate 'situated' learning (Sariola and Rionka 2003; Seppala and Alamaki 2003; Kneebone and Brenton 2005; Wishart *et al.* 2005).

By *authentic learning*, we mean learning that involves real-world problems and projects that are relevant and interesting to the learner. It means that learning should be based around authentic tasks, that students should be engaged in exploration and enquiry, that students should have opportunities for social discourse, and that ample resources should be available to them as they pursue meaningful problems. There is a clear overlap between authentic learning and situated learning. Mobile learning enables these conditions for authentic learning to be met, allowing learning tasks designed around content creation, data capture, location-awareness and collaborative working in real-world settings (Chen *et al.* 2003 and Hine *et al.* 2004 describe this approach in natural history).

Informal learning may be deemed to occur spontaneously and independently of formal education – but in mobile learning the term is frequently used to describe forms of learning where the technology supports a specific activity that has been designed in advance with a particular user group in mind. For example, Fallahkhair *et al.* (2005) have developed a system to support informal mobile language learning; Corlett and Sharples (2004) describe the use of Tablet PCs with software designed to support informal collaboration among engineering students; while Bradley *et al.* (2005) report on the development of materials for a mobile local history tour. Various informal, contextual or location-based learning experiences are being trialled in art galleries, gardens and museums, for example at the Uffizi art gallery in Florence and Birmingham's Botanic Garden (see Box 14.4). These are often experimental projects that are imaginative in terms of their epistemological and pedagogical approaches as much as in the technology that is used.

Much of the potential is only now becoming apparent as technological and pedagogical expertise builds up. Case studies in our book (Kukulska-Hulme and Traxler 2005) and elsewhere in the literature make it clear that progress in designing for learning with mobile and wireless technologies is hampered not only by the current state of the technologies but also by the diversity of educational objectives.

Mobile and wireless technologies can also deliver learning specifically designed for learners' wider social and economic contexts. In particular, the widespread acceptance and ownership of sophisticated mobile phones allows educators to design learning that encourages participation in e-learning among groups often under-represented in formal learning (see for example, Attewell and Savill-Smith 2003). Increasingly in the UK, students in formal learning are under a range of growing pressures, most obviously those of time, money, resources and conflicting/

Box 14.4 Example: informal learning

There is increasing interest in exploring the territory where informal learning can be enhanced. In Birmingham's Botanic Garden (Naismith *et al.* 2005) a system has been developed to support visitors with location-based information that reflects their interests and needs. Content and activities are presented to them through PDAs with GPS capability. Visitors are presented automatically with audio content upon entering different parts of the garden; they can then view additional multimedia content for that particular location, or capture their own observations if they wish to do so. Using the PDAs has been found to increase participants' engagement with their physical surroundings.

competing roles. Learning designed around mobile and wireless technologies can allow these students to exploit small amounts of time and space for learning, to work with other students on projects and discussions, and to maximize contact and support from tutors (Traxler and Riordan 2004; Sharples *et al.* 2005).

Finally, mobile and wireless technologies also allow unique opportunities to design learning for students who might have difficulty fulfilling their potential with other e-learning technologies. One example is students with dyslexia since mobile devices can support time management (Rainger 2005).

Design *of* learning

Having identified the opportunities and priorities that justify the use of mobile and wireless learning, specifications of learning activities can be worked out, along with some thought being given to the physical settings in which these activities are likely to take place. Typically from the educator's point of view, there will be three key designs to consider: design of content, of activities and of communication. In many cases at least two of these areas will be involved.

Content

In terms of the ability to view and interact with educational content, the use of very small devices may initially seem unpromising. By looking at how the technologies are changing our approach to content, however, we can come to a better understanding of what would be appropriate on mobile devices. Our focus here is not on the content itself, but rather on ways of thinking about content. We suggest that the following aspects are worth considering:

- *Open-endedness*: if students are expected to construct some of the content as part of their learning, this could be done in various locations and mobile devices can facilitate it.
- *Personalization*: mobile devices can cater to individual needs by enabling learners to receive, assemble and carry around personally useful resources.
- *Time-critical nature*: content updates may be more easily delivered to mobile devices when learners are highly mobile.
- *Portability*: content such as portfolios might be best developed on mobile devices and physically owned and carried around by learners.
- *Measured delivery*: when content needs to be accessed by learners little by little over a period of time, mobile devices can make this easier.
- *Aural medium*: if the content is aural, a personal listening device is often the best way to access it.
- *Prioritizing medium*: when some content is made available for mobile devices, this can prioritize or reinforce it over other content, which may be a useful deliberate teaching strategy.

- *Alternative medium*: learners can appreciate having the option of mobile access to electronic learning materials and resources, even if they generally prefer desktop access.

Activities

The second area to consider is the design of learning activities. Naismith *et al.* (2004) have demonstrated that mobile technologies can relate to six different types of learning, or 'categories of activity':

- For *behaviourist*-type activity, the quick feedback or reinforcement element is facilitated by mobile devices.
- For *constructivist* activity, immersive experiences are provided by mobile investigations or games.
- For *situated* activity, learners can take a mobile device out into an authentic context, or use it to access information while moving around an environment in a specially equipped location such as a museum.
- For *collaborative* learning, mobile devices provide a handy additional means of communication and a portable means of electronic information sharing.
- For *informal and lifelong* learning, mobile devices accompany users in their everyday experiences and become a convenient source of information or means of communication that assists with learning, or records it on the go for future consultation.
- *Support*, or *coordination* of learning and resources, can be improved by the availability of mobile technologies at all times for monitoring progress, checking schedules and dates, reviewing and managing – activities that teachers and learners engage in at various times during the day.

Research has also shown that at a more detailed level there are particular tasks that are well suited to mobile learning, e.g. activities that involve data collection, tests and quizzes, consolidation of learning, personal reflection and skills acquisition. There is further scope to develop learning activities that combine the use of mobile devices with other learning resources; for example this can be done by providing a commentary accessed on a personal device as a means of motivation or orientation within a set of learning materials. Mobile devices can also be used as a way to facilitate remote, 'on the move' participation in online activities that might be continued or completed at a desktop PC.

As mentioned earlier, mobile and wireless technologies seem very well suited to learning that has been variously described as informal, opportunistic, 'bite-sized' and spontaneous (Colley and Stead 2003; Bull *et al.* 2004) – and also 'disruptive' (Sharples 2003). This is a major challenge for the design *of* learning especially the design *of* formal learning since the two seem inimical or at least, very difficult to reconcile.

Communication

This is often the most problematic aspect of design due to worries about the costs incurred by learners if communication and connectivity become additional financial burdens. Within this constraint, mobile and wireless devices can support:

- spontaneous communication and collaboration, e.g. one-to-one or one-to-many by texting on mobile phones, by sending a message to a forum or blog while travelling,
- beaming of stored information from device to device;
- portable sound-recording, voice-recording, photos and video clips that are used in communication.

Many mobile phones support not only voice and texting but also email, and connected PDAs support instant messaging, email and web-based conferencing. Experience of m-moderating (moderating of mobile conferences) is limited but it can be expected to follow the same trajectory as e-moderating, moving from an early model based on administrative support and reacting to individual content queries, to a more mature model of pastoral support and proactively supporting new forms of learning. Mobile learning communities are still at an embryonic stage; some recent projects have designed informal learning for groups of homeless people and for travellers (Keefe 2003).

Space design

Physical learning spaces, in other words buildings, must also be designed for learning and fit for purpose. In UK post-compulsory sectors this is enormously problematic since the vast majority of their estate is ageing and over-crowded. There is a need for greater exploration and recognition of the relationships between the location and layout of learning and the nature and success of learning, and to integrate virtual learning spaces, that is the design and practice of e-learning, more closely. Mobile learning and handheld and wireless technologies are increasingly important in these relationships. At the moment, there is a number of points at which these intersect and there is a tension between the (re)design of spaces for learning and the design of learning for spaces.

There are some specialist classrooms designed to support collaborative learning based on wireless connectivity, handheld computers and interactive whiteboards. These require high investment in dedicated and purpose-built rooms in either new buildings or dramatically refurbished old ones and also require a substantial commitment in staff development and curriculum design. Highly specialized learning can be designed for these spaces.

On the other hand, wireless laptops for general academic work are increasingly available for loan to students and for issue to staff. They have the potential to free up substantial amounts of estate currently dedicated to ranks of networked desktop

PCs and also to change the working lives of academic staff and thus change the demands these staff make on their accommodation.

In a wider sense, universities and colleges are public sector agencies indirectly and sometimes directly funded to deliver elements of any current government's education agenda and policy objectives. These have recently included community education, lifelong learning and widened participation. The interaction of mobile learning development and physical learning space design has the potential to carry these issues forward since both can challenge the arbitrary division between academic institutions and their hinterlands and catchment areas. Mobile learning developments have the potential to carry education into communities including their most marginal and disaffected members while physical learning space design has the potential to entice and welcome communities into academic institutions.

Conclusion

Compared with other aspects of learning design tackled in this book, the design *of* learning using mobile and wireless technologies and the design *for* learning with these technologies is still tentative and exploratory. Much valuable work is not consolidated for financial reasons and much else fails to reach its educational potential for technical reasons. We have nevertheless attempted to identify trends and possibilities from the existing accounts and expect the increasing power and diversity of the devices to support more powerful and diverse learning designs.

Earlier, we outlined the emerging categories of mobile learning. Each of these has implications for learning design. If the technologies are only used to support 'miniature but portable e-learning' then the learning design will be correspondingly conservative; if they are used to support 'technology-driven mobile learning' then learning itself may be secondary to technology; if they are used to support 'connected classroom learning' then the learning designs will draw heavily on classroom pedagogy whereas if the technologies are used to support 'informal, personalized, situated mobile learning' then the learning designs are much more likely to be exciting, innovative and challenging.

References

Attewell, J. and Savill-Smith, C. (2003) 'Mobile learning and social inclusion: focusing on learners and learning', paper presented at mLearn 2003 – 2nd World Conference on mLearning, London, May 2003.

Attewell, J. and Savill-Smith, C. (eds) (2004) *Learning with Mobile Devices: Research and Development*, London: Learning and Skills Development Agency.

Bradley, C., Haynes, R. and Boyle, T. (2005) 'Adult multimedia learning with PDAs – the user experience', paper presented at mLearn 2005 – The future of learning in your hands, Cape Town, October 2005.

Bull, S., Bridgefoot, L., Corlett, D., Kiddie, P., Marianczak, T. *et al.* (2004) 'Interactive logbook: the development of an application to enhance and facilitate collaborative working within groups in higher education', paper presented at mLearn 2004 – Mobile learning anytime everywhere, Bracciano, Italy, July 2004.

Chen, Y.S., Kao, T.C. and Sheu, J.P. (2003) 'A mobile learning system for scaffolding bird watching learning', *Journal of Computer Assisted Learning*, 19 (3): 347–59.

Coffield, F., Moseley, D., Hall, E. and Ecclestone, K. (2004) *Should We Be Using Learning Styles? What Research Has to Say to Practice*, London: Learning and Skills Research Centre. Online. Available www.lsneducation.org.uk/pubs/ (accessed 23 June 2006).

Colley, J. and Stead, G. (2003) 'Take a bite: producing accessible learning materials for mobile devices', paper presented at mLearn 2003 – 2nd World Conference on mLearning, London, May 2003.

Corlett, D. and Sharples, M. (2004) 'Tablet technology for informal collaboration in higher education', paper presented at mLearn 2004 – Mobile learning anytime everywhere, Bracciano, Italy, July 2004.

Facer, K., Stanton, D., Joiner, R., Reid, J., Hull, R. and Kirk, D. (2005) 'Savannah: mobile gaming and learning?', *Journal of Computer Assisted Learning*, 20: 399–409.

Fallahkhair, S., Pemberton, L. and Griffiths, R. (2005) 'Dual device user interface design for ubiquitous language learning: mobile phone and interactive television (iTV)', paper presented at IEEE International Conference on Wireless and Mobile Technology for Education (WMTE) in Tokushima, Japan, November 2005.

Finn, M. and Vandenham, N. (2004) 'The handheld classroom: educational implications of mobile computing', *Australian Journal of Emerging Technologies and Society*, 2 (1): 21–35.

Hine, N., Rentoul, R. and Specht, M. (2004) 'Collaboration and roles in remote field trips', paper presented at mLearn 2003 – 2nd World Conference on mLearning, London, May 2003.

Gayeski, D. (2002) *Learning Unplugged – Using Mobile Technologies for Organisational and Performance Improvement*, New York: AMACON – American Management Association.

JISC (2005) *Innovative Practice with E-learning: A Good Practice Guide to Embedding Mobile and Wireless Technologies into Everyday Practice*, Bristol: Joint Information Services Committee.

Keefe, T. (2003) 'Mobile learning as a tool for inclusive lifelong learning', paper presented at mLearn 2003 – 2nd World Conference on mLearning, London, May 2003.

Kneebone, R. and Brenton, H. (2005) 'Training perioperative specialist practitioners', in A. Kukulska-Hulme and J. Traxler (eds) *Mobile Learning: A Handbook for Educators and Trainers*, London: Routledge.

Kukulska-Hulme, A. and Traxler, J. (eds) (2005) *Mobile Learning: A Handbook for Educators and Trainers*, London: Routledge.

Lave, J. and Wenger, E. (1991) *Situated Learning: Legitimate Peripheral Participation*, Cambridge: Cambridge University Press.

Manolo project (2006) Project website. Online. Available http://130.37.78.10/Projecten/Manolo/ (accessed 23 June 2006).

Mulholland, P., Collins, T. and Zdrahal, Z. (2005) 'Bletchley Park text: using mobile and semantic web technologies to support the post-visit use of online museum resources', *Journal of Interactive Media in Education*. Online. Available http://jime.open.ac.uk/2005/24/ (accessed 23 June 2006).

Naismith, L., Lonsdale, P., Vavoula, G. and Sharples, M. (2004) *Literature Review in Mobile Technologies and Learning, Report 11 for Futurelab*. Online. Available www.nesta futurelab.org/research/lit_reviews.htm#lr11 (accessed 23 June 2006).

Naismith, L., Sharples, M. and Ting, J. (2005) 'Evaluation of CAERUS: a context aware mobile guide', paper presented at mLearn 2005 – The future of learning in your hands, Cape Town, October 2005.

Norman, D. (2004) *Affordances and Design; Affordance, Conventions and Design (Part 2) – Two Essays on Design*. Online. Available www.jnd.org/dn.pubs.html (accessed 23 June 2006).

Rainger, P. (2005) 'Accessibility and mobile learning', in A. Kukulska-Hulme and J. Traxler (eds) *Mobile Learning: A Handbook for Educators and Trainers*, London: Routledge.

Sariola, J. and Rionka, A. (2003) 'Mobile learning in teacher education – the LIVE project', in H. Kynaslahti and P. Seppala (eds) *Mobile Learning*, Helsinki: IT Press.

Seppala, P. and Alamaki, H. (2003) 'Mobile learning in teacher training', *Journal of Computer Assisted Learning*, 19 (3): 330–5.

Sharples, M. (2003) 'Disruptive devices: mobile technology for conversational learning', *International Journal of Continuing Engineering Education and Lifelong Learning*, 12 (5/6): 504–20.

Sharples, M., Corlett, D., Bull, S., Chan, T. and Rudman, P. (2005) 'The student learning organiser', in A. Kukulska-Hulme and J. Traxler (eds) *Mobile Learning: A Handbook for Educators and Trainers*, London: Routledge.

Sheehy, K., Kukulska-Hulme, A., Twining, P., Evans, D., Cook, D. and Jelfs, A. (2005) *Tablet PCs in Schools: A Review of Literature and Selected Projects*, Coventry: Becta. Online. Available http://publications.becta.org.uk/display.cfm?resID=25889&page=1835 (accessed 22 January 2007).

Sutch, D. (2005) 'Bossing adults and finding spotty bras: learners as producers within mobile learning contexts', paper presented at mLearn 2005 – The future of learning in your hands, Cape Town, October 2005.

Traxler, J. and Kukulska-Hulme, A. (2005) 'Evaluating mobile learning: reflections on current practice', paper presented at mLearn 2005 – The future of learning in your hands, Cape Town, October 2005.

Traxler, J. and Riordan, B. (2004) *Using Personal Digital Assistants (PDAs) to Support Students*, Belfast: Higher Education Academy Resources. Online. Available www.ics.heacademy.ac.uk/italics/vol4–2/PersonalDigitalAssistantsmeansofsupportingstudents.pdf (accessed 25 January 2007)

Twining, P., Evans, D., Cook, D., Ralston, J., Selwood, I. *et al.* (2005) *Tablet PCs in Schools: Case Study Report*, Coventry: Becta. Online. Available http://publications.becta.org.uk/display.cfm?resID=25914&page=1835 (accessed 22 January 2007).

University of Kentucky (2006) *The University of Kentucky Wireless Evolution – Frequently Asked Questions*. Online. Available www.uky.edu/Wireless/faq.html (accessed 23 June 2006).

University of Twente (2006) *Wireless Campus*. Online. Available www.utwente.nl/wireless-campus/en/ (accessed 23 June 2006).

Weber, I., Choong Yow, K. and Soong, B.-H. (2005) 'Tuning in to students' mobile learning needs: a Singapore interactive initiative', in A. Kukulska-Hulme and J. Traxler (eds) *Mobile Learning: A Handbook for Educators and Trainers*, London: Routledge.

Wishart, J., McFarlane, A. and Ramsden, A. (2005) 'Using Personal Digital Assistants (PDAs) with Internet access to support initial teacher training in the UK', paper presented at mLearn 2005 – The future of learning in your hands, Cape Town, October 2005.

Chapter 15

Building communities of designers

James Dalziel

EDITORS' INTRODUCTION

This chapter describes the origins, design and development of the Learning Activity Management System (LAMS) Community. It begins with the history of LAMS as a new kind of e-learning design tool, instantiating in practice many of the principles and possibilities explored in this book. The author – the original developer of LAMS – goes on to discuss new principles for the development of Learning Object Repositories (LORs) as a means of sharing designs and communicating about the practice of design. Again, the LAMS Community is used to explore these principles through a practical and living example. The chapter concludes with some reflections on tools and communities for the future.

Overview

As at June 2006, the LAMS Community (www.lamscommunity.org) was the largest online community sharing Learning Designs. In the nine months since its launch, it achieved over 1,300 registered members from 86 countries, an average of 2,000–3,000 requests per day, approximately 100 shared Learning Designs down-loaded 2,000 times, and 1,500 discussion forum postings. These membership, daily request and forum posting figures are modest compared to those of the e-learning community formed around the Moodle virtual learning environment (VLE), and the number of shared objects and downloads are modest compared to those of LORs such as MERLOT and ARIADNE. However, as one of the first examples of a website that integrates both community and repository elements in the one location, it illustrates new approaches to the sharing of educational resources and experiences. More particularly, the LAMS Community provides an indication of the potential for building communities explicitly focused on sharing Learning Designs.

The fundamental driver for the development of LAMS, and subsequently of the LAMS Community, was my belief that if educators from around the world could freely share and adapt 'runable' good practice then the education sector would be transformed by improved educational quality combined with reduced preparation workloads. This belief runs through much of the work on sharing e-learning materials (although often implicitly), but despite hundreds of millions of dollars in public and private investment, it is clear that the dream is in trouble – not many educators use repositories of educational content, and very few share back improved versions. For me, there are two fundamental problems: (1) education is more than just content, so any attempt to share good practice requires e-learning systems capable of replicating the pedagogy of a typical classroom – that is, a structured flow of content and collaborative tasks; and (2) the sharing of good practice requires a community of educators to discuss ideas and practice – a searchable content dump is not sufficient. LAMS and the LAMS Community are an attempt to address these problems, because despite the difficulties to date, the dream still seems worth believing in.

Frustration I

I have been involved in e-learning since the mid-1990s when the Internet and the World Wide Web became household terms. During that time, I saw the rise of the early VLEs (now also called Learning Management Systems and perhaps most aptly, Course Management Systems) such as FirstClass, TopClass and WebCT. In the late 1990s I marvelled at the rapid adoption of VLEs by universities around the world, and like many had high hopes for how these platforms could transform pedagogy through innovative online tools.

By 2001 I had become concerned about the state of pedagogical innovation in VLEs. After the promising years of the late 1990s, the pace of innovation seemed to stall, and the same cluster of educational tools (forum, chat, document sharing, quiz, assignment dropbox, etc.) kept appearing with little real difference across a range of VLEs. Much of the focus of using VLEs was on content development (see also Britain, Chapter 8), and while this might be an important part of e-learning, it lacked any collaborative dimension – the online analogues of classroom debate, small group discussion, teamwork, Socratic dialogue, etc. It was as if e-learning had become synonymous with the library (a repository of content), rather than the classroom (a collaborative learning experience of rich, structured interaction). While a few innovative educators used discussion forums (and very rarely, chat) to foster collaboration, VLE use seemed to be driven by content delivery (course information, lecture notes, past exam papers, etc.) and 'e-administration' (calendars, student email, assignment dropboxes, etc.). While useful, this was not the pedagogical transformation that many of us had hoped for.

My concern ran deeper than the way in which VLEs were used: it seemed that some fundamental dimension was missing – the 'process' of education. At the heart of most successful classroom experiences, whether they are K-12 school lessons or university tutorials, is some careful planning by the teacher/lecturer to structure the flow of tasks. This involves structuring the delivery of content as well as interleaving appropriate student activities, such as discussion, debate, small-group work, etc. Whether explicit or implicit, the educational process usually involves a flow of content and collaborative tasks over time, and it was this 'flow' that seemed absent from VLEs. If the only educational aspect of universities was lectures, this might have been understandable, but tutorials and seminars have been integral to university education for many years: most K-12 school classes illustrate the importance of a flow of content and collaboration on a daily basis. My concern was not just at the absence of what would later be called an 'education workflow engine'. It was that until educators could easily capture the process and content of education together, there would be no way of sharing the heart of the teaching process, no way of building on good practice and adapting it in the way that school teachers develop and share (paper-based) lesson plans. Why didn't technology facilitate both the sharing and running of these activity structures?

I discussed the need for this dimension of education with senior members of several VLEs and similar initiatives. Some literally could not understand what I was saying; others indicated that this kind of feature was a 'pedagogical nice to have', but did not really matter to the bulk of their users, or, for that matter, to the managers who actually paid the VLE licence fee. For a while I thought the problem was that I had not explained the importance of this concept in a sufficiently persuasive way, but over time I came to recognize that no amount of persuasion was going to break this impasse soon. So I decided that if I believed as passionately as I did in this dimension of education, and its importance to the dream of sharing and improving good practice, then I would have to find a way to create a system that was based around the structured flow of content and collaborative tasks. And I would need to ensure that these 'flows' of tasks would be shareable, exportable, adaptable and reusable.

LAMS

LAMS was a direct response to the frustrations outlined above. From its inception, it set out to provide educators with an easy-to-use authoring environment for creating structured flows of content and collaborative tasks (called 'sequences'). One pivotal aspect of this environment was a simple 'drag-and-drop' interface that allowed educators to choose and connect a set of generic activity tools such as chat, forum, questions and answers (Q&A), voting, resources, and then configure each tool to suit their particular subject area (see Figure 15.1). While some of these tools would be familiar to VLE users, others had new features that emphasized the collaborative dimension. For example, the Q&A tool allowed students to type in an answer, but on the next page it collated the answers from all students in the group, so that they could also reflect on the ideas of others. However, it was the structured flow of collaborative tasks (and content) that set LAMS apart from VLEs.

Once an educator has saved a sequence, it can be run for a designated group of students, and students can access the sequence of activities from a learner area. As students progress through the sequence, the educator can monitor both group and individual activity, and a record of all activities is kept to allow each student (and the educator) to see how they are progressing.

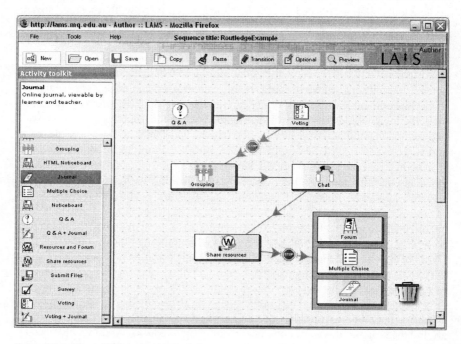

Figure 15.1 The LAMS authoring interface

To share a sequence, the educator can export a simple file that can be emailed to colleagues or placed on a web site or in a repository. The LAMS software also provides internal areas for sharing among educators who use the same LAMS server. Once another educator has received a sequence, it can be run with their students, or opened in the authoring area to be reviewed and modified. LAMS built on the concept of Learning Design, but extended it in a number of ways, particularly the close integration of activity tools. For a more detailed discussion of the development of LAMS, and the concepts of Learning Design, see Dalziel (2003, 2005).

During 2004, I was struck by an insight into the concepts behind LAMS that had not yet occurred to me despite several years of software development. I had thought we were building an e-learning system that focused on structured flows of collaboration and content. However, the 'e' was not a necessary requirement – it was possible to conceptualize most sequences as a generic set of educational activities that could be delivered either online or face to face (see Box 15.1).

Based on this insight, new features have been added to the second version of LAMS so that it has become a generalized educational activity planning environment, with 'e-delivery' as simply one option depending on context, pedagogy, etc. In the case of face-to-face delivery, the authored sequence can be set to

Box 15.1 A sequence of generic educational activities

Consider the following example: the teacher introduces a topic that has different views, each student then answers a question about this topic, then students break into small groups and debate their answers, then all students consider some new ideas from an expert, then the teacher and all students have a whole-class discussion of the initial individual and group ideas compared to those of the expert, then each student writes an essay about their final view of the topic. This example could be conducted face to face in a classroom/tutorial without any online component. Alternatively, the entire sequence of tasks could be run online by LAMS using tools such as Q&A, grouping, chat, resource sharing and assignment submission, combined with the presentation of these tasks in a structured flow by the LAMS 'workflow engine'. Another option would be to create a sequence where some tasks were online, but others were face to face (perhaps the sequence starts in the classroom with the first three tasks run face to face, but continues online over the following week for the remaining tasks).

replace the online environment with printed instruction sheets for the educator (and where relevant, worksheets for students); for online delivery, it creates the relevant environment (chat, forum, quiz, etc.) and 'runs' the activity for the relevant group of students, including presentation of instructions and resources as appropriate.

In terms of the dream of capturing and sharing good practice, this new approach provides a mechanism for describing and running educational practice of all kinds, as well as making it easily shareable and modifiable. It represents a response to the first of my frustrations. But LAMS itself was not built to provide an environment for community discussion and sharing of sequences – it merely made the creation of sequences possible. The second part of the vision meant addressing a second set of frustrations – the difficulty of developing a Learning Object Repository (LOR) that appealed to educators (not just LOR builders).

Frustration 2

LORs are online facilities for collecting learning objects so that they can be searched for and obtained by educators. Some (but not all) allow for the submission of learning objects by typical educators (rather than specialist developers), and some allow for easy adaptation and resubmission by fellow educators. So some but not all LORs support the dream of sharing and improving good practice outlined at the beginning.

Whether a Learning Design is called a Learning Object or not is less important than the recognition that a Learning Design as a sequence of collaborative activities is a radically different thing to an aggregation of content. In theory, Learning Designs could have been included in LORs; in practice, almost all LORs are content-centric – they contain individual content resources, or aggregations of content, or both.

In addition to the absence of Learning Designs, I was frustrated by a different set of concerns about how LORs were set up and managed. In September 2005, when I first presented the idea of the LAMS Community, I summarized the nine principles of its design as a response to these concerns (Dalziel 2005).

1 Learning Designs/activities' focus, rather than content

As discussed above, the sharing of good educational practice requires more than content, it requires the description of structured flows of collaborative activities (as well as content). An LOR that only shares content demonstrates a quite limited concept of what constitutes education. The challenging prior condition to the creation of the LAMS Community was the development of a new category of e-learning technology to support structured activity flows (Learning Designs).

2 Community focus, rather than repository focus

Most LORs are simply a searchable dump of content – they lack the explicit voice of educators about how the materials have been used, what did and didn't work, and how and why educators have adapted resources to suit their requirements. In many cases the truth is that few educators have used the content from the LOR, so there is little community to build on. However, even if there is a large community of users, the technical design of most LORs focuses heavily on the management of content, with little if any support for community discussion around it.

For the LAMS Community, we started with an Open Source software system built for supporting online communities (.LRN – based on OpenACS), and then added repository functionality to this system. This allowed the LAMS Community to inherit all the mature community features of .LRN, such as the ability to have sub-communities, discussion forums for each community, delegation of sub-community management and many other community-centric features. The repository functionality was then added so that each sub-community could have its own area for sharing Learning Designs. This approach allowed sub-communities to build different kinds of collection, complemented by different kinds of discussion.

3 Search based on free-text, not metadata

Within the LOR field, an appalling amount of time has been spent fighting over descriptive metadata to aid searching. This might be defensible if educators used metadata regularly to find useful resources, but in reality most educators are satisfied with free-text searching in the style of Google. Even in other fields where extensive metadata is available (such as library catalogues), I understand from private discussions with library colleagues that very few search queries are based on metadata or other advanced search options (usually less than 5 per cent). A related problem is the cost of creating good metadata, which most LORs fail to factor into their operation (Currier 2004). Educators are often expected to create extensive metadata records themselves, which they generally refuse to do (due to lack of time) or do poorly (due to lack of expertise). In either case, the outcome is such that even if metadata searching was a natural habit of educators, in practice it would be of little value due to the absence or poor quality of the metadata.

One important but challenging exception to this is the mapping of educational resources to specific curriculum requirements. This is most common in K-12 schools (rather than universities), and while this kind of metadata is highly valued by teachers, it has the downside of being very expensive to implement across a set of resources even for a single educational jurisdiction, let alone the thousands of jurisdictions throughout the world who all define their curriculum differently. From the perspective of any LOR that applies to many educational jurisdictions, this requirement is simply unattainable. In my experience, when this issue is discussed with typical teachers, they quickly recognize the problem, and use free-text searching as an alternative strategy, and then use their own professional judgement to determine the appropriate curriculum area for a selected resource. There is a strong case to be made that educational metadata would benefit from more cost/benefit analysis prior to implementation.

In the LAMS Community, based on lessons learned from the COLIS project (especially Goodacre and Rowlands 2003) we decided to provide a simple, Google-style search interface with as few metadata fields as possible to encourage easy submission (see p. 202). The main field used was 'Description' for entering narrative text about the sequence, along with a number of optional explanatory items (Keywords, Subject, Audience, Run-time, Delivery Mode, Resources, and Outline of Activities). By including these as plain text within the Description field, we supported free-text searching that included this information, without making these mandatory metadata fields for submission. Having watched the lengthy fights over terminology for other LORs, and given the principles outlined, we decided not to define any of these terms formally, nor provide particular vocabularies – instead, we left it to the community to evolve this terminology through practice.

4 Automated usage tracking/rating systems

One simple way of building a community around a repository is tracking usage and ratings, such as the number of views/downloads of a resource, and simple scoring of resource quality. These kinds of community features have become very popular across the Web in the past 12 months with the rise of 'Web 2.0' approaches such as photo sharing at Flickr, video sharing at YouTube, etc. Some LORs have implemented complex quality control approaches, such as formal peer review processes. While these 'heavy-weight' community processes are often cited as desirable, they can have the significant downside of slowing the rate of publication of resources, which in a web context can be fatal to widespread use (as illustrated by the history of Wikipedia, which only grew rapidly once prior peer review of materials was discontinued).

For the LAMS Community, we adopted the simple community measures of counting the number of downloads, and allowing any registered community member to rate a sequence on a scale of 1 to 5. Rating data are collected automatically, and the averaged score is presented. While not supporting any formal peer review process, an asynchronous forum is added to each individual sequence to allow for community discussion.

5 Small set of simple licences

Few LORs are explicit about the rights of users in relation to resources, and their silence on usage rights leaves educators unclear whether resources can be freely used or modified, and what restrictions may exist. In some cases, LORs have attempted to encode usage rights into technical languages, but as almost none of the software that 'plays' resources is able to act on this information, it is of little value (and the encoding can only be understood by technical specialists). In other cases, complex special purpose licences have been developed to cover the appropriate usage of objects, but these licences are so long and difficult to understand that educators either fail to read them, or ignore the LOR itself.

The LAMS Community decided to use the now widely adopted Creative Commons licensing scheme (www.creativecommons.org) as a recommended approach for explaining usage rights for sequences. One of the most attractive features of Creative Commons is the use of 'human readable' rights descriptions – that is, simple summaries of the main usage conditions of a licence that do not require legal expertise to understand. After discussion with potential LAMS Community users of their expectations of appropriate usage rights, the 'attribution, non-commercial use only, share alike' licence was selected (see http://creativecommons. org/licenses/by-nc-sa/2.5/). While educators are free to choose other Creative Commons licences (or even to enter the text of an alternative licence), a default licence was provided to encourage consistency among the sharing of sequences.

6 Learning software and learning content are free

If educators themselves need to pay a fee to access either learning software or learning content, then this is likely to greatly diminish its rate of adoption, particularly given the quantity of no-cost software and content already available on the Web as an alternative. Going further, many educators have concerns about the commercialization of educational software and content, and this can act as a barrier to adoption and use. Going one step further again, the principles of free software ('free' as in 'free speech', not as in 'free beer', Free Software Foundation 2004) and

Open Source software require that software can always be modified, and the modifications freely distributed, and this requirement may undercut some traditional commercial models.

The decision to provide both the LAMS software itself and the LAMS Community without cost was made for both philosophical and practical reasons. Practically it was a way to encourage widespread adoption and use; philosophically it ensured that benefits that may arise from the LAMS approach were not confined only to those who could pay a software or content licensing fee. While a part of the wider LAMS initiative is the commercial services and support company 'LAMS International', which offers fee-based technical support and content, there is no requirement on anyone to use these fee-based services – the software and the community are open to all who have the determination and skills to use them.

7 Resources can be easily adapted by others

One of the great failures of some LORs is that they provide packaged content that cannot be modified or localized by educators: either the package itself cannot be disaggregated to allow for modification, or if it can, the nature of the content is beyond the technical abilities of most educators to modify. This is a significant failing, as the opportunity for modification/localization is highly valued both practically (real-world teaching situations may differ from the one for which the object was originally designed) and philosophically (not all educators may actually modify resources, but they want to know that they can if they choose). In the field of content aggregations, there are important techniques for externalizing key 'properties' such as simulation variables, instructional text, quiz items, etc., from aggregated objects to make these properties easy to edit independently (e.g. Dolphin and Miller 2002). Sadly, many expensive learning objects created in the past five years have failed to implement this approach, and hence the objects are little better than web-viewable versions of the multimedia courseware of the mid-1990s.

The easy adaptation principle informed the original development of the LAMS software – particularly the emphasis given to the drag and drop authoring interface, and its necessary simplification of the concepts of Learning Design into easily understood activity tools. The LAMS Community, in this case, acts as the conduit for easy sharing and modifying of complex objects (structured flows of content and collaborative activities) via the existing features of the LAMS software.

8 Close integration of learning platform and the community for sharing

Many educators would prefer information about LOR materials delivered directly into their main online education workspace (typically their VLE), rather than treating the two as separate systems. In many cases, however, LORs have been quite separate from the software used to deliver learning experiences, which makes it difficult for educators to find and integrate relevant content, as well as causing problems for students (for example requiring multiple log-ins and passwords). While some integration work has been conducted between LOR products and VLEs, LORs that arise from a single institution or government initiative have generally been poor at this. It should be noted that even when LORs conform correctly to appropriate technical standards (such as IMS Content Package or SCORM (Sharable Courseware Object Reference Model)), some VLEs have not implemented these standards correctly, and hence packages acquired from an LOR may not 'run' in the VLE. This problem has been particularly acute with school and university VLEs and the use of IMS Content Package, whereas corporate e-learning use of SCORM and its predecessor AICC specification has been less problematic due to more rigorous certification of SCORM players in relevant VLEs as well as certification of SCORM content.

To support close integration with the LAMS Community, the LAMS software was given special integration features that allowed an individual's LAMS Community account to appear in summary form on the bottom half of the LAMS welcome page (with full access available in a new window by clicking a 'Full Screen' option on the summary page). This integration included the option of storing a user's LAMS Community name and password within their LAMS software account to allow direct access to both systems from one log-in.

9 Easy to share

For LORs with the goal of sharing good practice among educators, a key barrier to the sharing of creations/modifications is a lengthy and complex repository submission process. The LAMS Community used a minimalist metadata scheme (see pp. 198–9) to encourage rapid and easy sharing of resources, complemented by automated fields included author (based on log-in information) and date of submission, and 'secondary usage metadata' collected automatically such as downloads, ratings and asynchronous forum comments.

In summary, these nine principles represent the basis on which the LAMS Community website was designed and launched in September 2005. Most principles are relevant to any LOR, regardless of whether they focus on content or Learning Designs; a few are specific to the dream of sharing and improving good educational practice, which requires not only content but also structured flows of activities. While not all LOR designers would accept all of these principles, they represent a considered response to the failure of the first generation of LORs to achieve significant uptake. Given the amount of money spent in this field, a critical reappraisal of fundamental assumptions and the exploration of alternative approaches are surely justified.

The LAMS Community – one year on

It is almost a year since the launch of the LAMS Community, and while it has achieved some important milestones, a number of significant goals remain as open questions. This section reflects on our experiences to date and concludes with directions for the future.

Given the dream of sharing and improving good educational practice, perhaps the most important observation to make is that so far there has been little sharing back of improved sequences. While the repository has received approximately 100 sequences to date, only a few of these are explicitly based on other existing sequences from the LAMS Community. So at first glance it may appear that the dream remains in trouble.

In reality, the situation is more nuanced. Having discussed these issues with both experienced and novice members of the LAMS Community, it appears that although direct adaptation is fairly rare to date, members do use the work of others as an inspiration for their own creations. Community members describe the experience of seeing a great idea in someone else's sequence, which they use or adapt later when they come to create their own.

It is also worth noting that not all LAMS users make use of the LAMS Community – indeed, many users of the software are not even aware of its existence, as the software itself provides an area for sharing sequences among those with accounts on that particular server. In one of the few quantitative studies of this issue, a study of LAMS users in UK schools (Becta 2005) found that of a total of 565 sequences created by teachers during the project, 106 were adaptations of an existing sequence by the same teacher, and 36 of these were reuse of an existing sequence by a different teacher. It may be that teachers are more prepared to share and reuse sequences created by people they can readily identify as colleagues.

These observations resonate with another experience from the past year – the problem of developing generic rather than topic-specific sequences. In two separate contexts I have spoken with authors who have tried to developed generic sequences (that is, sequences whose main purpose is to capture some general pedagogic idea that could be adapted for many discipline areas).While it is still anecdotal at this stage, the early evidence is that generic sequences can seem boring and lifeless, whereas topic-specific sequences can bring alive both the topic and the capabilities of LAMS. While in theory the generic pattern should be easier to reuse than the discipline-specific example, in reality designers rarely get excited by generic designs. As we have observed, discipline-based patterns *can* lead to reuse even if it is only providing people with good ideas for building new sequences.

A further relevant observation is the nature of discussion in the different LAMS sub-communities. The technical community (which covers software development and installation/system administrator issues) has been the most active community since the launch, with a regular stream of postings throughout this period: typically more than one per day. This behaviour is unsurprising – software developers and system administrators are familiar with the use of online communities for discussion and support. The nature of Open Source development makes communities of kind necessary to coordinate the development effort, and this has been par noticeable over the past few months as translations of LAMS V2 in other than English have been underway (19 in progress as at Au e-learning development communities have observed high levels of activity in technical forums: for example, an analysis of the Sakai VLE mailing lists indicated that over 70 per cent of all discussion arose from the Developer list, whereas the Pedagogy list generated less than 2 per cent (Masson 2006).

The various educational communities have engaged in more irregular patterns of discussion, with specific topics sparking participation for a few days or weeks before going quiet. It may be that a single education community would have created a greater sense of *esprit de corps*, leading to more regular, sustained discussion. Another possibility is that although the technology required for participating in online discussion is not particularly complex, it still may present challenges to educators who are unfamiliar with this style of community and discourse. The still relatively small size of this community, combined with the busy lives of most participants, may be limiting its potential for involvement. Or we may just conclude that current behaviour is exactly as to be expected: that different issues arise in different areas, and spawn a discussion only as long as is appropriate to the particular debate.

One promising dimension of discussions with the LAMS Community is the sense of a shared language about the educational process. My own experience of pedagogical discussions has been that almost no communication occurs between the participants about what really happens in the classroom (this can easily be tested by asking one teacher to conduct a lesson based on the narrative descriptions of another). This may be due to the lack of a shared descriptive framework for the component parts of the educational process. The LAMS Community, building on the visual representations of the LAMS software, provides a forum where educators do have a shared language, at least inasmuch as it relates to things that LAMS can represent.

In terms of the nine principles, these have been noticeably unproblematic to date within the community. For example, almost every sequence has been licensed using the default licence (Creative Commons BY-NC-SA), and there has been no real debate about licensing within the community to date. Similarly, the approach to metadata has been accepted without significant debate, and the few comments I have received (priv⌐   are from users who wish there were even less fields to complete wʰ   ʼquence. In both cases, my sense is that community
me⌐ʼ   ʒmatic approach of just 'getting on' with using the
                                ʼs principles. The one area of significant concern has
                              hile download counts are popular, ratings have
                              A number of users indicates that they would like
                              sequences – particularly those which are shared
                              ctice examples, but rather as works-in-progress
                              f this feedback, it is likely that ratings will be

                              ɪmunity web site deserve mention. First, the
                              ttractive, and this may have discouraged
                              ɾance is important. Second, it is not (yet)

possible to preview a sequence directly from the web site – educators must download a sequence from the web site to their desktop, then import it into their LAMS authoring environment to view it. This somewhat cumbersome process takes around seven steps (instead of the ideal single step – a preview button on the sequence details page that directly opens the sequence in LAMS authoring). In both cases, these issues will be addressed in the near future.

The future

The LAMS Community illustrates how a new approach to e-learning technology, combined with new approaches to LORs, can foster communities of designers in education. Its usage statistics to date support the basic principles of its creation – and yet the wider significance of the dream of sharing good education practice remains open to interpretation. Important unanswered questions remain, such as: 'Do educators really want more than content?', 'Do educators really want to share?', 'Do educators really want to use and adapt the work of their peers?' In one sense the answer is a modest yes, as illustrated by the LAMS Community. But the reason that many of us continue to devote our lives to e-learning is the challenge of improving education through the widespread transformation of the teaching and learning process – and this challenge remains.

Acknowledgements

I'm deeply indebted to Ernie Ghiglione for an extraordinary development effort to make the LAMS Community possible.

References

Becta (2005) *Learning Activity Management System Specialist Schools Trust Pilot*. Online. Available http://partners.becta.org.uk/page_documents/research/lams.pdf (accessed 4 September 2006).

Currier, S. (2004) *Metadata Quality in E-learning: Garbage In – Garbage Out?* Online. Available www.cetis.ac.uk/content2/20040402013222 (accessed 4 September 2006).

Dalziel, J.R. (2003) 'Implementing learning design: the Learning Activity Management System (LAMS)', in G. Crisp, D. Thiele, I. Scholten, S. Barker and J. Baron (eds) *Interact, Integrate, Impact: Proceedings of the 20th Annual Conference of the Australasian Society for Computers in Learning in Tertiary Education*, Adelaide, December 2003. Online. Available www.lamsfoundation.org/CD/html/resources/whitepapers/ASCILITE2003% 20Dalzie%20Final.pdf (accessed 4 September 2006).

Dalziel, J.R. (2005) 'From re-usable e-learning content to re-usable learning designs: lessons from LAMS', in *Proceedings of the EDUCAUSE Australasia Conference, 2005*, Auckland, New Zealand. Online. Available www.lamsfoundation.org/CD/html/resources/ whitepapers/Dalziel.LAMS.doc (accessed 4 September 2006).

Dolphin, I. and Miller, P. (2002) 'Learning objects and the information environment', *Ariadne*, 32. Online. Available www.ariadne.ac.uk /issue32/iconex/ (accessed 4 September 2006).

Free Software Foundation (2004) *The Free Software Definition*. Online. Available www. gnu.org/philosophy/free-sw.html (accessed 4 September 2006).

Goodacre, C. and Rowlands, D. (2003) *Real World Metadata Management for Resource Discovery: Proof of Concept across Education and Library Sectors in Tasmania*. Online. Available www.colis.mq.edu.au/COLIS_CD/content_COLIS_Phase2/Education%20 Research%20Reports/Tasmania%20Final%20Report.pdf (accessed 4 September 2006).

Masson, P. (2006) 'Who are we?', posting to internal Sakai mailing list, 5 July. Online. Available http://collab.sakaiproject.org/access/content/attachment/f767a7de-0f13–436c-80a6–440490560a73/SakaiDiscussionsPie.jpg (accessed 4 September 2006).

Chapter 16

New horizons in learning design

Andrew Ravenscroft and John Cook

EDITORS' INTRODUCTION

This final chapter explores new horizons in learning design, based on findings from a series of case studies in successful e-learning innovation, and on current projects that test the definition of learning designs and the concept of reuse. The authors question the current orientation towards content and instruction, and suggest a paradigm shift towards more contextualized, process-oriented and personalized (learner-centred) frameworks for the future of learning and interaction design.

Background

The discipline of learning design is emerging in a context where the implementation and integration of e-learning applications is becoming widespread in all sectors of education in many countries of the world. But we have seen that most of these initiatives fail to address questions such as: What can these innovations actually do in terms of *teaching-learning processes*? What improved *pedagogical practices* will be supported? And, how will *practitioners learn about and adopt useful e-learning innovations*? To address these questions we describe a set of case studies in successful e-learning innovation that have served as enabling representations to researchers and practitioners. The case studies represent a range of innovations, pedagogical approaches and educational contexts. They were selected to give a flavour of the scope of current e-learning innovations and also to highlight cases that have been of recognized value. They have been described in greater detail in Ravenscroft *et al.* (2005): here we present a concise rationale and description of each, followed by a synthesis and critique that considers what made these innovations successful and what the implications are for the field of learning design.

Case 1 – 'Arguing for the sake of it': using AcademicTalk to scaffold critical discussion and reasoning between peers

This activity was based on social constructivist (Vygotsky 1978) concepts of internalization and the acquisition of socially grounded dialogical practice. It also drew on well-established models for collaborative working (e.g. Johnson and Johnson 1991; Soller and Lesgold 1999). A mediating tool, called AcademicTalk, was used to scaffold collaborative argumentation through structured dialogue (McAlister *et al*. 2004a). Dialogue took place in a synchronous, text-based environment, within a broader Activity Model of preparation, interaction and summary stages. The preparation stage included phases that cover confidence and community building as well as critical discussion.

This e-learning activity was evaluated with Open and Distance Learners (ODLs) studying through the Institute of Educational Technology at the UK Open University, on a course called 'You, your computer and the net' (T171). The evaluation (McAlister *et al*. 2004b) found that the activity supported academic argumentation and debate among the mixed ability students, who had not met face to face and often lacked confidence in their ideas prior to the dialogue exercises. Specifically, when compared with chat, the scaffolded dialogues contained deeper, extended and more varied discussion and argumentation, and the students spent more time on topic. Students also rated their experience as highly valuable and a useful complement to their other teaching-learning activities.

Case 2 – Using learning objects to enhance blended learning

In this case a course team developed learning objects for introductory programming in Java. Each learning object focused on one learning objective, and was designed to support a constructivist pedagogy. Multiple media were used to elicit engagement, visualize abstract processes and scaffold learning.

These learning objects were used across three relevant modules at London Metropolitan University, and in a year 1 module at the University of Bolton, being accessed by over 1,000 students in the first two years of implementation (2002–4). This initiative has been extensively reported in journal and conference papers (e.g. Boyle 2003; Boyle *et al*. 2004) and the learning objects themselves won a European Academic Software Award (EASA) in 2004. Marked improvements were noted in student pass rates across the four modules, of between 12 to 23 percentage points in year 1, and 12 to 27 percentage points in year 2. These improvements are attributed to: a collaborative team approach to the development and use of high-quality materials; the use of multimedia learning objects, based on constructivist pedagogy; and a blended learning environment that structures access to these learning objects.

Case 3 – Continuing and professional development (CPD) at a distance

This case formed part of a project sponsored by the British Council and run jointly with Middlesex University and the Islamic University Gaza (IUG). A six-week online workshop series, accredited by the National Centre of Work Based Learning Partnership (NCWBLP) at Middlesex University, provided IUG academic staff with CPD in the area of e-learning. Specifically, the course examined the curriculum design and pedagogical models for virtual learning environments (VLEs). During one two-hour learning episode, the Induction Event, learners produced individual learning agreements, and negotiated assessment criteria for peer review presentations. The pedagogical model for this episode was highly learner-centred and went beyond a 'transmission design' to include higher levels of cognitive interaction and communication. Flexibility was also a key component, with contingency plans built into every phase.

This project was the co-winner of 2004 UK Higher Education Academy's e-Tutor of the Year Award. Follow-up work with the teaching team and the British Council has led to the development of a framework for dialogue-led e-learning (Cook *et al.* 2006).

Case 4 – 'Digital Threads': training British Asian women in the use of advanced computerized sewing machines

This case involved students at a Community Centre in the North of England (Wardleworth) taking part in a Workers Educational Association (WEA) course as part of the 'Digital Threads' project. The course, 'Digital embroidery', involves the use of digital sewing machines, acquisition of basic information and communication technology (ICT) skills, searching the Internet for design patterns, digitizing the patterns using a scanner, and interfacing new patterns with the sewing machines. Learners are predominantly Bengali, Asian Pakistani and Asian Kashmiri women, 99 per cent of them on income support (an entitlement provided by the UK government for people who are seeking employment). In this context there is a fluid response to learner and community needs by the project staff.

The students started by making use of the Disney materials provided with the digital sewing machines (e.g. Mickey or Minnie Mouse designs). However, they quickly began using search engines and a Community Grid for Learning (CGfL) initiative (a game linked to digital embroidery) to find culturally more appealing material. One of the participants has already gone on to set up in business, and many are taking advantage of the study support (literacy) that is provided in additional sessions at the centre.

This case supports earlier work in adult and community learning (Cook and Smith 2004), which found that if community centres can tap into the goals and motivations of centre users, and if they provide crèche and other facilities that suit users, then confidence building and community participation is possible for those who are otherwise digitally excluded.

Case 5 – Historical e-learning: using an intranet and First Class to support the teaching of history

In order to support their classroom activity, history students at a further education and sixth form college (Richard Huish), were encouraged to make use of an intranet and First Class conferencing system to access a variety of resources. These resources helped them in preparatory work for the classroom session, were used during the session, and were also then used to reflect on sessions and for assessment tasks. Students could access the resources from the classroom, the Learning Resources Centre (LRC), from college workstations and remotely from home. The activities used an associative approach, with an emphasis on organized activity and clear goals with constructive feedback. There was a progressive sequence of component-to-composite skills with a clear instructional approach for each part of the course.

These students have seen the use of learning technologies as an enhancement that has enabled them to improve their results. Remote access to resources has been successful with figures showing usage to be much higher outside college hours. Now that this approach is integrated it has become vital to learning outcomes, and has a positive effect on motivation. Both staff and students have seen the tangible benefits of using learning technologies to enhance the learning process.

Case 6 – Keeping to the beat

This case studied the use of a VLE on Music Performance and Promotion courses at a further education college in Scotland (Reid Kerr in Paisley). The VLE-based activities mainly related to the organization and promotion of gigs (music events), and so could be described as 'authentic' activities within a situated or Community of Practice (CoP) approach. Students build group relationships and undertake their own research. The VLE offered a safe environment for participation and facilitated learning dialogues and community building. The organization and promotion of an actual gig involved assessment not just by peers on the course, but also by fellow students from the college, and others who purchased tickets.

The advantage of using the VLE was that students could choose a time and place for participation, without having to be co-present with other students. This resulted in virtually all students contributing to the collaborative working process, which had not been true of previous collaborative activities. The use of the VLE helped to engage and motivate learners, allowed the cohort to 'gel' quickly, and resulted in increased retention and achievement.

Insights and synthesis

This section identifies key insights from the case studies and distils out the generic messages and implications for e-learning researchers and practitioners.

First, in all cases the use of e-learning within realistic and appropriate limits improved teaching-learning practice. In each case there was either a serious and well-defined teaching-learning problem to address (e.g. Cases 2 and 3) or a similarly well-defined opportunity to improve the teaching-learning process (e.g. Cases 1, 4, 5 and 6), or both. This 'fit' between an existing problem or opportunity and the e-learning solution has been described by Draper (1998) as 'niche based success'. The technologies used were easy to integrate with the existing teaching-learning landscape, i.e. they built on existing technological and pedagogical practices.

Second, none of the cases were ostensibly technology-led or knowledge-based, and most (i.e. except Cases 2 and 5) used e-learning to support or mediate 'human-to-human' processes. Cases 1, 3 and 6 show this quite clearly. The innovation in Case 1 mediated critical discussion and reasoning between learners, Case 3 facilitated and supported a dialogue-based approach to professional development, and Case 6 improved participation and collaboration around an assessed event.

Third, most of the cases demonstrated the thoughtful integration of e-learning activities within complex learning contexts where significant social, organizational and cultural features had to be addressed. So it was interesting that a number of the cases were essentially communicative or community oriented (e.g. Cases 1, 3, 4 and 6) in their focus. In brief, the technologies and e-learning activities acted as catalysts for human learning and development.

Fourth, although the cases emphasized different learning processes (e.g. interactive engagement for knowledge acquisition (Case 2); the development of critical reasoning and dialogical skills (Case 1); and, confidence building and empowerment to acquire practical skills relevant to a specific community and culture (Case 4)), there was arguably no clear separation of these concerns. For example: the learning objects delivered individual cognitive benefits in a blended situation that addressed the organizational prerequisites and features necessary for pedagogical innovation; the AcademicTalk exercises delivered improvements in discussion and reasoning skills in line with an existing emphasis on community and confidence building; and, the 'Digital Threads' case demonstrated that cultural dimensions needed to be addressed in fostering the development of a practical skill. Collectively, these cases demonstrate that cognitive, social and cultural dimensions all interplay during successful teaching and learning (Ravenscroft 2004) and that the emphasis shifts during successful learning trajectories.

At the horizon: towards more contextualized, process-oriented and personalized approaches

Through considering the case studies described in this chapter we have been forced to realize that current approaches to learning design are arguably in a state of crisis, and we need a paradigm shift in the discipline. The insights offered below are meant to be interpreted as lenses through which we should re-focus our approach to learning design, and technology-enhanced learning more generally.

Can we 'design' for learning?

The very notion of 'learning design' may be a problem in itself. The approaches that tend to define it are usually more representative of 'instructional design' than 'learning design'. Arguably, most current initiatives are actually setting up the conditions for learning, either by organizing and packaging content within repositories and VLEs or sequencing learning activities. In these approaches the key processes of learning are treated as almost incidental or epiphenomenal to the creation, packaging and management of content. However, learning, conceived as the refinement or development of skills, knowledge and understanding, is achieved through a complex orchestration of content, tools and communicative processes. The nature of this orchestration cannot be easily pre-specified. It emerges 'in action', and so we should be aiming to *catalyze* or *amplify* effective learning processes towards favoured educational outcomes, rather than thinking we are 'designing learning'.

Content is not the problem

Why have most learning design approaches to date focused on content? Large sums of money have been invested into creating digital content, marking it up according to standards and making it available via repositories, VLEs and the like. But making content easily available and accessible does not lead to learning in the same way that opening a library does not lead to a literate local community. Content can only become 'alive' when it is integrated and related to meaningful learning and pedagogical processes. An analogy of this point can be made through a comparison with our everyday use of a search engine such as Google. With Google we nearly always find some relevant content that has not undergone any complicated technical preparation to make it 'findable', they are just other web pages. Its power rests in the way it operates as an ambient and accessible technology that allows us to get what we want when we need it in a way that seamlessly links with our everyday behaviour. What we need for e-learning are tools that link as seamlessly with our teaching-learning behaviour as Google does with our everyday digital behaviour.

Use before reuse

Many approaches to learning design have focused on the technical mechanisms for content reuse before thinking about how adoption, adaptation and reuse actually come about within rich and varied educational contexts (see Masterman and Vogel, Chapter 4). The reuse of e-learning content or activities will be promoted by representations of their integration into effective learning and teaching practice, i.e. contextualized examples of meaningful and powerful adoption. Case studies such as those reported in this chapter can present the pedagogical 'why' and the educational 'how', with a lesser emphasis on the technical 'how to', as the latter can only be tackled when the former are understood.

Learning is interaction

Underlying most of the arguments developed in this chapter is the notion that learning occurs through interaction between people and with content, using tools within communities. The converse of this is content that does not facilitate or afford meaningful interaction is virtually useless for learning. Also, content does not have to be separately created and stored. Meaningful learning interactions can create and refine content during the flow of activity, and this content is often more 'alive' than pre-stored content, because it is involved with engaging inter-human activity. Therefore, learning design cannot be separated from interaction design, accepting that interaction is by its nature contextualized and therefore difficult to design, store and 'reuse'.

Teaching practitioners are the bottleneck

Although most learning design approaches have focused on providing tools or content for 'the teachers', teachers are the stakeholders with arguably the least time, and perhaps the lowest level of new media fluency. In a context where the underpinning technology and related practices change so quickly, it is very ambitious to expect the teaching practitioner to constantly adopt innovative methods within a high-pressured and somewhat unforgiving organizational context.

Designing for personalization and the 'world of the learner'

A partial answer to the problem above is to shift our learning design emphasis away from the 'world of the teacher' to 'the world of the learner'. Unlike most teachers, learners typically have more time to experiment, are under less pressure, and are highly fluent in using new media technologies. But to design for the world of the learner we need to shift control of the learning situation to them, and build links between e-learning and their everyday digital behaviour. This means building on and integrating with their personalized technologies and preferences, rather than providing experiences that are prepared, managed and controlled through an organizational mechanism or artefact such as a VLE. Personalization and learner-centredness mean starting from the learner's own devices, preferences and behaviours. We must design meaningful and relevant interactions for a generation of technology-enabled learners, instead of imposing externally designed experiences.

New foci for learning design

This work reported in this chapter argues that we need to move beyond content and administrative practices to consider how we can design and reuse community-centric and learner-centric processes, linking these with learning design technologies. We hold that this can be achieved through adapting, or 'tuning', relatively generic yet flexible tools and models within authentic contexts of use. Similarly, we have argued for 'use before reuse' in the context of learning design, emphasizing the importance of thoroughly analysing the influence, impact and value of innovative e-learning activities before assuming they are ripe for wider exploitation.

Two significant lines of work are pushing the current boundaries of the reuse of learning designs and related technologies. A large-scale Centre for Excellence in Teaching and Learning (CETL) in Reusable Learning Objects (RLOs) has been established in the UK, with an overarching goal to develop a learning object economy, making significant savings in costly e-learning developments. A second line of work explores the reuse of advanced pedagogical processes or practices, mediated through a flexible Open Source tool called InterLoc (based on Academic-Talk, Case 1). We now turn to the implications of these two developments for the future of learning design.

RLOs: the reality of designing reusable content

The RLO-CETL see (www.rlo-cetl.ac.uk) started work in April 2005 and is developing and evaluating over 90 learning objects every year. RLOs are being used in such diverse areas as Maths, Nursing, Language Learning, Business Studies and Study Skills to address known problems. For example, many students in institutions such as London Metropolitan University perform paid work in excess of 20 hours a week, and many – entering the University through widening partici-pation policies – also have childcare or other family commitments. At the University of Nottingham there is an emphasis on provision for mature learners returning to study Nursing or Medicine. Flexible RLOs allow these diverse student populations to study any time, any place and at their own pace.

A major challenge for the RLO-CETL is to build cross-institutional communities for reuse. Students, tutors and multimedia developers are being placed at the heart of the RLO design approach: an innovative and extensive staff reward programme has been designed; expert knowledge is being harnessed; the student voice is being captured and heard; and these perspectives are being translated into engaging interactive shareable RLOs. Building communities of people with different roles and institutional identities is complex, but by actively engaging students in the design and development process (Holley et al. 2006) RLOs are being seen as a Trojan horse for improving blended learning more generally.

In building the RLO-CETL community, the distinction between reusable objects and reusable tools has become an important one. Of course this distinction is hardly new: it was made for example by the SoURCE project (www.source.ac.uk/), a UK Teaching and Learning Technology Programme (TLTP) project, which investigated the reuse of educational software (tools) in higher education. SoURCE confirmed that reuse of software is possible if academic staff autonomy can be retained. The granularity of resources explored by SoURCE (i.e. software products and tools) was probably too large for easy reuse. Nevertheless, the RLO-CETL can be said to be picking up the challenge where SoURCE left off. Key questions remain much as SoURCE defined them: What, in practice, do practitioners reuse? What might they reuse, given the right incentives? How far are the barriers to reuse cultural and capable of being overcome and how far are they intrinsic to the contextualized practices of teaching and learning?

One way to tackle these issues is to advance our conceptual model of learning objects as follows. A major mechanism in the CETL is the development of generative learning objects (GLOs) where it is the pedagogical pattern inherent in the object that provides the primary focus for reuse, rather than its content (see McAndrew and Goodyear, Chapter 7). A GLO authoring tool is being developed that will enable tutors to adapt existing learning objects or construct new ones based on successful patterns (Boyle 2006). Thus a content-oriented approach is evolving into an approach with a reusable tools orientation.

Reusable e-learning tools: the reality of designing reusable learning and pedagogical processes

The InterLoc tool (Ravenscroft and McAlister 2006a, 2006b, www.interloc.org) is a 'state of the art' dialogue tool that reuses interaction designs (i.e. dialogue games for critical discussion and reasoning), and also reuses the broader pedagogical practices that wrap around the interactive activities. It is a tool-based approach that links highly engaging learning activities to the pedagogical conditions that support them. It has also been extensively pedagogically evaluated and disseminated, and in the process of undergoing wider adoption within practitioner and researcher communities (Ravenscroft *et al*. 2006).

Our experience with this process-oriented approach has taught us that educational activities and interaction designs need to be 'tuned' to the context of use and cannot simply be reused 'from the box'. Digital dialogue games also need to be relevant to and involve the experiences of individual learners: content cannot be imposed upon them. A particular strength of the approach is the degree to which it supports scaffolds and engages students in pedagogical activities that are often associated with emotional barriers, such as a lack of confidence in discussion.

Dialogue games have been shown to help students develop their dialogical and cognitive skills, leading to more students learning to think and to think together. These benefits are achieved without significant effort on the part of the tutor or learning manager, who typically just needs to set up, adapt or reuse existing learning activities, and to sanction the approach to learning that InterLoc embodies. However, a tool such as InterLoc, which embodies a well-defined pedagogical philosophy, has the potential to disrupt the pedagogical context in which it is implemented. In extreme cases, evaluations have shown that it may be considered a 'disruptive technology' that questions tutors' views of teaching and students' views of learning. This questioning can only add spice to the educational context, and promote reflection on the broader frames of pedagogical practice.

Further work is planned in two related areas. The first is integrating InterLoc with the academic practices of tutors by making it interoperable with learning design tools and VLEs. The vision is to make digital dialogue games easier to adopt, by linking InterLoc's capacity for interaction design (what Jones, Chapter 13 calls the 'micro' level of design) with learning design tools at the 'meso' level, such as LAMS or Moodle, creating hybrid tool-sets. The second area of work is making dialogue games more attractive to learners and more integrated with their everyday digital devices, behaviours and practices. Ongoing design studies are improving the multimedia and multimodal features of the InterLoc tool-set, to extend its attraction for learners used to gaming and mobile devices. Specific design areas we are exploring include improving the coordination of multimedia materials (e.g. music and sound, video, 3D graphics and other games), and providing speech input via mobile devices. Through this gaming paradigm, we are bridging highly communicative learning with the common digital behaviour of students, making dialogue games easier for students to adopt and adapt directly.

The InterLoc tool-set lies deliberately at the intersection of technologies that are personalized and used by the technology enabled learner, such as MySpace, flickr and del.ic.ious, and those that are typically managed by a tutor or organization, such as VLEs (e.g. Web-CT and Moodle) and Learning Design tools (e.g. LAMS and Reload). It is unique in the sense that it can operate within either paradigm, with the degree of personalization, a dimension that varies across contexts. The aim is to have dialogue games that are ambient and yet integrated, and also pervasive – in the sense that they operate through the technologies that are favoured by students. We anticipate that this somewhat ecumenical approach to personalization will be the next trend with learning technologies, as the degree of student-centredness will vary based on the context of use. While some students and some cultural contexts will favour a highly personalized approach, e.g. informal studies based on interest, others will be linked to carefully planned curricula, e.g. planned exercises based on specific course topics. It is naive to see personalization as the only option that should be considered when some institutions successfully organize engaging student learning. In brief, we need to accept that some students will always be interest-driven and self-motivated whereas others will prefer to be managed. Indeed, an awareness of the degree of personalization that the learner is comfortable with should be seen as part of the personalization process itself.

Summary and conclusions

Considering these six cases and two developments collectively, there is no 'factor x' that makes e-learning effective. Instead, e-learning solutions work well when they satisfy a pedagogical need within a complex socio-cultural context, either solving a problem or amplifying a learning opportunity. Indeed, e-learning is most effective when the technology recedes into the environment and facilitates 'human-to-human' teaching-learning processes.

Building on these insights, learning design needs to address itself centrally to the role of the teaching-learning context and the learner experience if it is to mature from a field of research and development and contribute in a practical way to educational practice. The activities of learning design and the resultant designs for learning have to be meaningful and useful in terms of the teaching-learning community and the learners' own experience. The tools used need to add interest, engagement and transformative potential, rather than simply making design more cost-effective.

Arguably, the most important factor in ensuring that learning designs are reused is a belief in the central pedagogical idea – that students should learn to think and to think together. In the case of InterLoc, this focus on collective enquiry and critical thinking has produced a tool that can be pedagogically tuned to local learning problems and opportunities. We hold that an interesting and sound pedagogical idea, implemented through a flexible e-learning tool, will provide the own impetus for its adoption and use. A corollary of this is that learning designs will be adopted and reused by learners because they do something interesting, engaging and 'cool', rather than because they merely simplify or commodify instruction.

Acknowledgements

The authors are grateful to James Clay, who performed the Case studies 5 and 6, and Professor Tom Boyle who performed the Case study 2. Some of the work that has been reported was carried out with the support of the UK Joint Information Systems Committee (JISC) in the framework of the 'E-learning and Pedagogy' and 'E-tools' programmes. The content of this paper does not necessarily reflect the position of the JISC, nor does it involve any responsibility on the part of the JISC.

The case studies of innovative e-learning practice are available at: www.jisc. ac.uk/elp_innov_casestudies.html

References

Boyle, T. (2003) 'Design principles for authoring dynamic, reusable learning objects', *Australian Journal of Educational Technology*, 19 (1): 46–58.

Boyle, T. (2006) 'The design and development of second generation learning objects', *Proceedings of ED-Media*: World Conference on Educational Multimedia, Hypermedia and Telecommunications, Orlando, Florida, June 2006.

Boyle, T., Bradley, C., Chalk, P., Jones, R. and Pickard P. (2003) 'Using blended learning to improve student success rates in learning to program', *Journal of Educational Media*, 28 (2–3): 165–78.

Cook, J. and Smith, M. (2004) 'Beyond formal learning: informal community e-learning', *Computers and Education*, 43(1–2): 35–47.

Cook, J., Basiel, A.S., Mitchell, W.L., Mohammed, T.H. and Commins, R. (2006) 'Blending formal and informal learning within an international learning network', paper presented at *Networked Learning 2006*, Lancaster, April 2006.

Draper, S. (1998) 'Niche-based success in CAL', *Computers and Education*, 30: 5–8.

Holley, D., Andrew, D. Cook, J., Celik C. and Mitchell, A. (2006) 'Elements of expectancy: incorporating the student voice in the online design process', paper presented at *Networked Learning 2006*, Lancaster, April 2006.

Johnson, D. and Johnson, R. (1991) *Learning Together and Alone*, Englewood Cliffs, NJ: Prentice Hall.

McAlister, S., Ravenscroft, A. and Scanlon, E. (2004a) 'Combining interaction and context design to support collaborative argumentation using a tool for synchronous CMC', *Journal of Computer Assisted Learning*, 20 (3): 194–204.

McAlister, S., Ravenscroft, A. and Scanlon, E. (2004b) 'Designing to promote improved online educational argumentation: an evaluation study', in S. Banks, P. Goodyear, V. Hodgson, C. Jones, V. Lally *et al.* (eds) *Networked Learning 2004: Proceedings of the Fourth International Conference on Networked Learning 2004*, Lancaster: Lancaster University and University of Sheffield, pp. 541–8.

Ravenscroft, A. (2004) 'Towards highly communicative e-learning communities: developing a socio-cultural framework for cognitive change', in R. Land and S. Bayne (eds) *Education in Cyberspace*, London: Routledge, pp. 130–45.

Ravenscroft, A. and McAlister, S. (2006a) 'Digital games and learning in cyberspace: a dialogical approach', *E-learning Journal*, 3 (1): 38–51.

Ravenscroft, A. and McAlister, S. (2006b) 'Designing interaction as a dialogue game: linking social and conceptual dimensions of the learning process', in C. Juwah (ed.) *Interactions in Online Education*, Oxford: Routledge, pp. 73–89.

Ravenscroft, A., McAlister, S. and Baur, E. (2006) *Development, Piloting and Evaluation of InterLoc: An Open Source Tool Supporting Dialogue Games in Education,* final report to UK JISC, June 2006, Bristol, UK.

Ravenscroft, A., Cook, J., Boyle, T. and Clay, J. (2005) 'What makes e-learning work? A selective review of successful new media innovations', in *Proceedings of ED-MEDIA 2005 (World Conference on Educational Multimedia, Hypermedia and Telecommunications)*, Montreal, Canada, June 2005, pp. 302–10.

Soller, A. and Lesgold, A. (1999) 'Analyzing peer dialogue from an active learning perspective', *Proceedings of the AI-ED 99 Workshop: Analysing Educational Dialogue Interaction: Towards Models that Support Learning*. Online. Available www.lscl-research.com/Dr/documents/Soller-Lesgold-AI-ED-Workshop.pdf (accessed 26 January 2007)

Vygotsky, L. (1978) *Mind and Society: The Development of Higher Psychological Processes*, Cambridge, MA: Harvard University Press.

Part III

Resources

Appendices

In the Introduction we promised a range of conceptual tools that could be used and adapted for different contexts of learning. Part III is where we have collected these. We hope they will illustrate the practical relevance of the ideas discussed in the book, as well as offering tested tools to support design in practice. Each of these resources is also an appendix to one of the book's chapters, and is prefaced with a brief introduction describing its place in that chapter, as well as its potential application and use.

Many of these resources were developed in the course of work funded by the UK Joint Information System Committee's programme in e-learning and pedagogy. Further resources, including downloadable versions of some of these tools, can be accessed from the JISC 'Effective Practice' web site at: http://www.jisc.ac.uk/pedagogy_resources/.

Original findings and reports of the e-learning and pedagogy programme can also be downloaded from the same web address.

We hope you find them helpful.

Appendix I: How people learn, and the implications for design

This appendix, based on Mayes and de Freitas (2004), is the first of the practical tools offered in conjunction with Chapter 2. It illustrates key features of the three theoretical approaches outlined in Chapter 1, and can be used as a starting point or retrospectively to help evaluate a particular approach.

	Associative	Constructive (individual)	Constructive (social)	Situative
Learning is understood as	building concepts or competences step by step	achieving understanding through active discovery	achieving understanding through dialogue and collaboration	developing practice in a particular community
The theory	People learn by association, initially through basic stimulus-response conditioning, later by associating concepts in a chain of reasoning, or associating steps in a chain of activity to build a composite skill. Associativity leads to accuracy of reproduction: for example when safety-critical skills are learned, or factual material is committed to memory. Mnemonics are essentially associative devices. Associative theories are not concerned with how concepts or skills are represented internally, but in how they are manifested in external behaviours, and how different training/instruction regimes manifest themselves in observable learning. However, all formal learning relies to some extent on external evidence (behaviour) as an index of what has been learned.	People learn by actively exploring the world around them, receiving feedback on their actions, and drawing conclusions. Constructivity leads to integration of concepts and skills into the learner's existing conceptual or competency structures. Learning can be applied to new contexts and expressed in new ways. Experimentation or experiential learning (Kolb's cycle) are typical constructive approaches. Constructive theories are more concerned with how knowledges and skills are internalized than how they are manifest in external behaviour. As in associative approaches, attention will be paid to how learning opportunities are presented so as to allow progressive discovery of relevant concepts/skills.	Individual discovery of principles is heavily scaffolded by the social environment. Peer learners and teachers play a key role in development by engaging in dialogue with the learner, developing a shared understanding of the task, and providing feedback on the learner's activities and representations. Collaborative work is typical of social constructive approaches. Social constructive theories are concerned with how emerging concepts and skills are supported by others, enabling learners to reach beyond what they are individually capable of (learning in the zone of proximal development). Attention is paid to learners' roles in collaborative activities, as well as the nature of the tasks they undertake.	People learn by participating in communities of practice, progressing from novice to expert through observation, reflection, mentorship, and 'legitimate peripheral participation' in community activities. Like social constructivism, situativity emphasizes the social context of learning, but this context is likely to be close – or identical – to the situation in which the learner will eventually practice. Work-based learning, continuing professional development, and apprenticeships are typical examples of situated learning. The authenticity of the environment is at least as significant as the support it provides: much less attention is paid to formal learning activities.

Key theorists	Skinner Gagné (Instructivism and Instructional Design)	Piaget Papert Kolb Biggs	Vygotsky (Social Development) Laurillard and Pask (Conversation Theory)	Lave and Wenger (Communities of Practice) Cole, Engström and Wersch (Activity Theory)
Implications for learning	• Routines of organized activity • Progression through component concepts or skills • Clear goals and feedback • Individualized pathways matched to performance	• Active construction and integration of concepts • Ill-structured problems • Opportunities for reflection • Ownership of the task	• Conceptual development through collaborative activity • Ill-structured problems • Opportunities for discussion and reflection • Shared ownership of the task	• Participation in social practices of enquiry and learning • Acquiring habits, attitudes, values and skills in context • Developing identities • Developing learning and professional relationships
Implications for teaching	• Analysis into component units • Progressive sequences of component-to-composite skills or concepts • Clear instructional approach for each unit • Highly focused objectives	• Interactive environments and appropriate challenges • Encourage experimentation and the discovery of principles • Adapt teaching to existing concepts/skills • Coach and model meta-cognitive skills, e.g. reflection	• Collaborative environments and appropriate challenges • Encourage experimentation, and shared discovery • Draw on existing concepts/skills • Coach and model skills, including social skills	• Create safe environments for participation • Support development of identities • Facilitate learning dialogues and relationships • Elaborate authentic opportunities for learning
Implications for assessment	• Accurate reproduction of knowledge or skill • Component performance • Clear criteria: rapid reliable feedback	• Conceptual understanding (applied knowledge and skills) • Extended performance • Processes as well as outcomes • Credit varieties of excellence • Develop self-evaluation and autonomy in learning	• Conceptual understanding (applied knowledge and skills) • Extended performance • Process and participation as well as outcomes • Credit varieties of excellence • Develop peer-evaluation and shared responsibility	• Credit participation • Extended performance, including variety of contexts • Authenticity of practice (values, beliefs, competencies) • Involve peers

←———— more formally structured learning tasks | more authentic contexts for learning ————→

Example pedagogic approaches	• Guided instruction • Drill and practice • Instructional design • Socratic dialogue	• Cognitive scaffolding • Experiential learning (based on Kolb's learning cycle) • Experimental learning • Constructivist learning environments • Problem-based learning • Research-based learning	• Reciprocal teaching • Conversational model • (Computer-supported) collaborative learning	• (Cognitive) apprenticeship • Situated learning • (Legitimate peripheral) participation • (Continuing) professional development • Work-based learning

All approaches emphasize:

In learning

- The central importance of *activity* on the part of the learner
- The need for *integration* across activities, e.g.
  - associatively (building component skills and knowledges into extended performance)
  - constructively (integrating skills and knowledges, planning, reflecting)
  - situatively (developing identities and roles)

In teaching/assessment

- *Constructive alignment* of activities with outcomes, and outcomes with assessment criteria
- The importance of *feedback* (intrinsic or extrinsic)

They differ in:

- The *authenticity* of the activity →
- The *formality* of activity structures and sequences ←
- The role and importance of *other people* in mediating the activity →
- The emphasis on *retention/reproduction or reflection/internalization*
- The *locus of control* (tutor, learner or peers)

Reference: Mayes, T. and de Freitas, S. (2004) 'Review of e-learning theories, frameworks and models. Stage 2 of the e-learning models desk study', Bristol: JISC. Online. Available www.jisc.ac.uk/uploaded_documents/Stage%202%20Learning%20Models%20(Version%201).pdf (accessed 30 March 2006).

Appendix 2: Learner differences and their implications for design

As discussed in Chapter 2, in any given context of learning design only a few of these differences are likely to be relevant. For relevant differences, it may be necessary only to know the *range of variance* a learning design should accommodate, or it may be important to discover individual learner differences in order to support them effectively. The latter approach will have implications for the resources of teaching and support staff. Collaborative learning, if properly designed and supported, can make a strength of learners' different aptitudes and approaches.

General metrics

1 *Age*
Ensure materials and tasks are age-appropriate

2 *Gender/cultural background (e.g. ethnicity)*
Ensure no gender or cultural bias in learning materials, unless subject matter specifically requires attention to gender or cultural issues

Access

1 *Transport time/cost to place of learning*
Consider distance and blended learning approaches; distance learners should not be disadvantaged in terms of quality of materials and support

2 *Preferred communication media (e.g. visual, auditory, written text, physical action)*
Consider providing materials, setting tasks and accepting assessment outcomes in a range of different media

3 *Preferred language (e.g. English/other OR level of spoken and written English)*
Consider whether materials need to be provided in non-English language variants; ensure appropriate standards of written and spoken English are used

4 *Preferred information-gathering style (e.g. visualizer/verbalizer)*
Consider providing materials, setting tasks and accepting assessment outcomes in both visual and verbal formats

5 *Preferred information organising style (e.g. serialist/holist)*
Consider providing materials in a range of different formats

6 *Preferred learning style (e.g. meaning directed/application directed/ reproduction directed)*
Focus on encouraging appropriate learning style(s) for type of outcome; OR allow learners to use their preferred style

7   *Autonomy in learning (e.g. preference for tutor support, cohort support or self-paced learning)*
    Likely to be determined by the context of learning: but consider providing options (e.g. group work, solo work) to suit different needs

8   *Other access needs (e.g. dyslexic, dyspraxic, visual impaired, hearing impaired etc.)*
    Ensure materials, tasks and assessment outcomes are adapted to meet specific access needs; consider whether some learners require more time or support with specific tasks; consider using adaptive technology to ensure all learners have choices

Competences

1   *Communication (cf. Preferred communication media; Preferred language)*
    Application of number
    ICT (cf. Preferred communication media)
    Working with others (cf. Autonomy in learning)
    Improving own learning and performance (cf. Autonomy in learning)
    Problem solving
    Ensure materials, tasks and assessment criteria are appropriate for learners' existing skills and competences.
    If learners are expected to extend their competences, ensure this is made explicit in the learning outcomes and assessment criteria
    Consider providing additional materials and tasks for learners on either side of the competency 'norm' (i.e. both remedial and advanced)
    Allow multiple opportunities to practice new skills without the pressure of assessment

Qualifications

1   *Highest educational level attained*
    Relevant qualifications (academic, vocational and professional)
    Attainment in course pre-requisites (qualifications and competences)
    Ensure materials, tasks and assessment criteria are appropriate for learners' existing level of skill and understanding
    Consider providing additional materials and tasks for learners on either side of the 'norm'

Appendix 3: A typology of digital tools and resources for learning

This tool maps types of mediating technology onto the tasks they can help to support. Note that the advantages are potential only, and will depend on learners and context. The media typology is based on (Laurillard 2003).

Laurillard media type	Tasks supported or mediated	'Traditional' examples	Electronic and mobile examples
Narrative	**Tasks involving representation** Much formal learning depends on interaction with representations rather than with the 'real world', e.g. text, mathematical notation, diagrams Narrative systems can be used for *assimilation* of images, sound, text, etc. – or for *(re)production* of new images, sound, text etc. Since learning requires activity, learners should not be on the receiving end for too long without producing some representations of their own, e.g. in response to *comprehension* tasks (notes, mind maps, class presentations or answers to comprehension questions) Narrative tools can be shared between teachers and learners to enable group representation and collaboration, for example blackboards, whiteboards, wikis **Potential advantages of e- and m-technologies for assimilation and comprehension** Access at a time and in a place to suit the learner Overcoming physical/sensory access problems (e.g. adaptive systems) Information presented in more than one medium (e.g. text plus image) is recalled better by learners Supporting – or challenging – learner preferences about how they access information (e.g. serially or holistically, visually or textually) Multiple paths through information give learners greater autonomy and insight into their own learning process	*Assimilative:* books, journals, hand-outs, slides, diagrams *Productive:* traditional writing and drawing tools *Both:* blackboard, whiteboard, drawing board **Potential risks of e- and m-technologies for assimilation and comprehension** Information overload Need for a wider repertoire of information skills Ease of production and distribution can mean loss of quality control (e.g. Internet) Some media encourage passive rather than active reception, e.g. cut and paste rather than note-taking	*Assimilative:* on-screen text, image, video files, PowerPoint slides, DVDs, web pages, animations, hot potatoes … *Productive:* web and multimedia authoring tools, word and image processing tools, PowerPoint, audio and video capture and editing tools … *Both:* electronic whiteboards, wikis, blogs, shared write/draw systems …

	Potential advantages of e- and m-technologies for (re)production	Potential risks of e- and m-technologies for (re)production	
	Potential advantages of e- and m-technologies for (re)production More professional outcomes: can be motivating for many learners Outcomes easily distributed to others (e.g. for marking, collaboration, reflection, peer review) Learners encouraged to be confident and creative with new technologies Transferable skills for the world of work Draws on range of learner preferences and skills for articulation.		*Synchronous:* chat, video conferencing, mobile phones, instant messaging . . . *Asynchronous:* email, text, discussion boards, JISC mail lists, blogs, wikis, video and audio messages . . .
Communi-cative	**Tasks involving communication between individuals and groups** Valuable because dialogue is central to learning, whether it takes place through speaking, writing, drawing, gesture or other channels Asynchronous communication can be used to promote reflective learning and allow ideas to be built collaboratively over time. Synchronous communication has the benefits of immediacy and high motivation. Learners tend to find communication tools easy to adopt and use.	*Synchronous:* face-to-face speech and gesture *Asynchronous:* written feedback, written messages, noticeboard	
	Potential advantages of e- and m-technologies for communication tasks: synchronous Learners have to communicate and take turns more explicitly Draws on different skills from spoken communication Dialogues easily recorded for later reflection and review Learners have to think on their feet and respond quickly to others Immediate feedback is inspiring and motivational Good for building shared understanding in collaborative tasks	*Potential risks of e- and m-technologies for communication tasks: synchronous* Demand for rapid response can be intimidating to some	
	Potential advantages of e- and m-technologies for communication tasks: asynchronous Access at a time and place to suit the learner Access to wider range of dialogical resources and opportunities, e.g. remote experts, learners in other institutions/countries Communication disabilities can be overcome with adaptive technologies Learners have time to reflect on what they want to say – some evidence this leads to more equitable participation, e.g. between the genders Dialogues easily recorded for later reflection and review Supports long-term collaborations such as project work	*Potential risks of e- and m-technologies for communication tasks: asynchronous* Lack of immediacy is demoralizing for many learners	

Laurillard media type	Tasks supported or mediated	'Traditional' examples	Electronic and mobile examples
Interactive	**Tasks that return information based on user input** Valuable for developing information skills and supporting *research* tasks. Make learners more active in relation to narrative resources, by requiring them to seek and select. A special class of interactive tools are computer-assisted assessment (CAA) tools, e.g. quizzes, where the input is usually a student answer and the information is appropriate feedback. Another emerging interactive capability is position-awareness	Indexes, reference texts, catalogues, libraries	Search engines Gateways and portals Quizzes and other CAA Position-aware systems e.g. GPS
Productive	**Tasks that involve manipulation of data** Valuable for supporting skills of *analysis* and application In practice many interactive interfaces make use of a productive (data-driven) engine. The distinction is useful when designing learning activities, because productive technologies allow learners to manipulate data consciously and explicitly, using their own parameters and protocols	Subject-specific analytical tools and protocols, e.g. log tables, textual analysis grids . . .	Spreadsheets and other statistical tools Databases of all kinds, e.g. for reference management Qualitative analysis tools Subject-specific tools, e.g. concordancers, calculators
Adaptive	**Tasks that depend on continuous adaptation to user input** Valuable because learners receive intrinsic feedback in response to their actions. Complex interactive and productive systems will be experienced as adaptive, particularly if they have some element of sensory realism (e.g. graphical interface). Such environments can support *experimental* and *experiential* learning tasks and the development of higher order learning skills (e.g. problem solving, evaluation, research) with relatively low cost and risk	Real environments (field, lab, workplace, etc.) in which learners can interact with materials	Virtual worlds Simulations Models Computer games Interactive tutorials (incorporating CAA and feedback)

	Potential advantages of e- and m-technologies for interactive tasks	Potential risks of e- and m-technologies for interactive tasks	
	Learners gain information handling and management skills	Learners need complex information and data handling skills, which are often not supported within subject programmes	Portfolios, learning logs, learning contracts/ plans
	Where routine tasks are automated, focus can be on higher order tasks	Simulations and data models cannot *substitute* for real-world experience	Watches, calendars, timetables
	Tasks can be carried out in a safe, reliable and supportive environment (e.g. fieldwork and laboratory simulations)	Skills associated with traditional technologies will be lost if not practised separately	Paper-based records
	'Real-world' complexity can be modelled in the classroom	Automated feedback may be less motivating and personal to learners than person-to-person feedback	
	Learners can receive immediate and meaningful feedback		
	Evidence that interactivity improves motivation		
	Data analysis and modelling increasingly necessary in a wide range of occupations		
Integrative	**The management of learning activities**	**Potential risks of e- and m-technologies for managing learning activities**	E-portfolios
	A relatively new class of technologies that support the management of learning sessions and activities, allow recording of achievements, and enable learners to review their progress and make action plans. Although they do not take part directly in learning activities, integrative technologies allow learning activities to more easily be organized, managed, captured, and presented for review. Complex assessment systems are probably best regarded as integrative rather than simply interactive.	Require basic ICT skills before learners can access core facilities and services	Virtual learning environments
		Focus on system integration and administrative efficiency can be at the expense of pedagogical considerations	Task and time management software
		Institutional identity may come to be defined around IT systems	'Learning Design' systems
		How learners are represented as users may not acknowledge all their relevant differences and needs	Assessment management systems
			Learner records systems
	Potential advantages of e- and m-technologies for managing learning activities		
	Efficiency gains in learner and class management – can be passed on to learners		
	Can help learners with time and task management		
	Integrated systems foster sense of 'belonging' to the institution when learners sign on		
	Improved monitoring of learners can be used to pick up on difficulties		
	Learner access to and ownership of their own learning history		
	Enhanced fairness and reliability of assessment systems		

Reference: Laurillard, D. (2003) *Rethinking University Teaching: A framework for the effective use of educational technology.* 2nd edn, London: Routledge.

Appendix 4: Learning activity design: a checklist

This appendix summarizes the design considerations from Chapter 2.

Learning outcomes: considerations for design

1   What is the purpose of this learning session or opportunity?

2   What new knowledge, skills and/or attitudes do learners need to gain? (*Learners will be able to . . .*)

3   Open or closed learning outcome(s) (i.e. how far is the verb-for-learning qualified, for example with a level of attainment, a context of application, or an indication of the method to be used)?

4   How will learners know when they have achieved the outcome(s), and how well they are doing?

5   How will they finally be assessed? Are the assessment criteria clear and relevant?

6   How could the learning process be captured to support progression and reflection?

Learner differences: considerations for design

1   Are there a range of activities (especially remedial activities and extension activities) to meet the needs of learners with different capabilities?

2   Do learners have choices about how they carry out a task? About how they participate with others?

3   Are learners' differences valued, e.g. by setting collaborative tasks, by rewarding innovation as well as accuracy?

4   How are support and feedback adapted to individual learners' needs?

5   How are learners being involved in the design process? (Consider not only individual choices within the learning situation, but how learners' views can be canvassed before and/or after participation.)

Digital resources, tools and services: considerations for design

1   What resources will learners have access to? What resources could they find themselves? What advantages do they have?

2   What content-based activities (research, comprehension, analysis) best support these resources?

3   What technologies (tools, services) will learners have available for use? What technologies of their own could they use? What advantages do they have?

4   What activities do these technologies support effectively? How do these help learners to meet the outcomes?

5   What support will learners (and teachers/facilitators) need to use these technologies effectively?

6   Do learners have functional access to these technologies? How will their access needs and developing skills be supported?

Learning dialogues: considerations for design

1   What is the role of the tutor in this activity? Is there a role for other experts or mentors?

2   How will learners interact with one another? What use is being made of their different aptitudes and experiences? What are the opportunities for peer learning and collaboration?

3   How are dialogues structured, guided and supported?

4   Who will give feedback to learners on their progress? Have you considered the possibility of self- and peer-assessment?

5   What other people could be brought into the learning situation e.g. members of support services, subject experts, learners at other institutions . . .?

General theoretical considerations for design

People learn more effectively when . . . So it makes sense to:

1   *They are active*
Base learning around tasks with the emphasis on learner activity

2   *They are motivated and engaged*
Communicate desired outcomes clearly
Relate these to learners' long-term goals
Where appropriate, allow choice over elements of the learning activity

3   *Their existing capabilities are brought into play*
Revisit prior knowledge and skills at the start
Recognize and exploit learners' existing capabilities, e.g. in collaborative work, shared knowledge-building

4   *They are appropriately challenged*
Aim for learners' *zone of proximal development*
Provide support and *scaffolding* (peer, tutor or resource-based)
Give options for learners with different capabilities and preferences

5   *They have opportunities for dialogue*
     Establish opportunities for dialogue with tutors, mentors and peers during the task
     Recognize and reward collaboration as well as autonomy

6   *They receive feedback*
     Provide feedback on *all* tasks and outcomes
     Design tasks to give intrinsic feedback if possible
     Consider peer feedback as an alternative to tutor feedback
     Foster skills of self-evaluation

7   *They have opportunities for consolidation and integration*
     Encourage further practice
     Record outputs *and processes* of learning where possible, so learners can see how they perform
     Promote skills of reflection and planning (e.g. through portfolios, action planning)

Appendix 5: Course design checklist

As discussed in Chapter 3, this checklist has been used by the OCSLD, Oxford Brookes University, UK, as an exercise to support curriculum design by practitioners working with digital technologies. The aim of the exercise is to describe the broad scope of a course: why it exists, why it is special, how students and teachers will experience it. Participants use it to structure their thinking on the way to producing a programme level storyboard.

1 *Course title and level*

2 *Purpose or main aims of course*

3 *Learning outcomes*

4 *Main strengths of current course, which you would not like to lose*

5 *Main weaknesses of the course, which need to be addressed*

6 *Number of students*

7 *Number of staff*

8 *Main characteristics of the students as they affect teaching and learning methods*: (e.g. you may describe two or three students who describe a range of types that may be on your course, or you may just describe a range in each of several characteristics, like prior learning, diversity, their expectations, their likely access to technology, etc.)

9 *Teaching and learning methods* (e.g. online lectures, discussion, individualized self-paced learning, small group work, projects, problems, presentations, portfolios, etc.)

10 *Assessment methods* (both formative, e.g. quizzes, assignments, exercises, problems, seminars, presentations, etc. and summative, e.g. exam, coursework, portfolio, etc.)

11 *Technology requirements* (any special technologies that staff need to develop this course, or students/staff need to study/teach it)

12 *Resources* (other than those noted in technology above, e.g. text books, printed materials, etc.)

13 *Administration* (roles responsibilities, tasks)

14 *Support* (how will students be supported on this course?)

Appendix 6: Storyboard exercise

This exercise, referred to in Chapter 3, helps participants on a course design programme to review each other's storyboards. It was developed by the OCSLD, Oxford Brookes University, UK.

Questions on the checklist are used to prompt discussion between course designers, to draw out advantages and potential difficulties of their proposals, and to help them think of alternative solutions.

Critics' checklist

A suggested structure for your conversations with course designers:

1   *Student experience*: Ask how a typical student might experience their progress through the course, from start to finish.

2   *Course design*: Find out which aspects of this course design are particularly novel and interesting (give designers a chance to showcase their work before you start being too critical!).

3   *Student support*: Clarify how students will be supported in their learning. What aspects of the teaching, learning and assessment process might be new to them? How has support for this been built into the course design? If you see holes in the student support issues, point them out.

4   *Outcome audit*: Ask the designer(s) to take one learning outcome and follow through how students will become familiar with it and its related content, have opportunities to practice their developing skills, gain feedback on their learning, and finally, demonstrate their learning related to that outcome in assessment.

5   *Diversity*: How does the course design proactively accommodate diversity in the student body?

6   *Staffing*: Who will teach/tutor on the course? What additional skills/facilities might the staff need? What would make teaching on this course intolerable to you?

7   *Technology*: How much of the technology incorporated in the plan is already available and accessible? What additional technological requirements does this course have?

Appendix 7: Taxonomy of learning activities

As discussed in Chapter 6, this taxonomy provides detailed descriptions of the nature of tasks that students will undertake as part of a learning activity to achieve the intended learning outcomes.

Context	

Context	*Aims*
	Pre-requisites
	Subject
	Environment
	    Computer-based, Lab-based, Field-based, Work-based, Audio-based, Simulator, Video, Lecture-based, Seminar-based
	Time
	Difficulty
	Skills
	    Creativity, Critical analysis, Critical reading, Group/team work, IT, Literacy, Numeracy, Oral communication, Practical, Problem solving, Research, Written communication, Ability to learn, Commercial awareness, Computer literacy, Criticism, Data modelling, Decision making, Foreign languages, Information handling, Information literacy, Interpersonal competence, Management of change, Negotiating, Planning and organizing, Self-management, Self-reflection, Synthesis, Study skills, Critical analysis and logical argument, Writing style, Library, E-literacy, Listening and comprehension, Making notes, Oral presentation, Reading, Referencing, Research reading, Inference and synthesis of information, Selecting and prioritizing information, Summary skill, Time management and organization

Learning outcomes	*Cognitive*
	Knowledge
	    State, Recall, List, Recognize, Select, Reproduce, Specify, Draw, Finding out/discover, Pronounce, Recite
	Comprehension
	    Explain, Describe reasons, Identify causes of, Illustrate, Question, Clarify, Identify, Understand
	Application
	    Use, Apply, Construct, Solve, Select, Hypothesize, Infer, Calculate, Investigate, Produce, Construct, Translate, Assemble, Demonstrate, Solve, Write
	Analysis
	    Break down, List component parts of, Compare and contrast, Differentiate between, Predict, Critique, Analyse, Compare, Select, Distinguish between
	Synthesis
	    Summarize, Generalize, Argue, Organize, Design, Explain the reasons for
	Evaluation
	    Judge, Evaluate, Give arguments for and against, Criticize, Feedback, Reflect, Affective, Listen, Appreciate, Awareness, Responsive
	Aesthetic
	    Appreciation, Commitment, Moral awareness, Ethical awareness
	Psychomotor
	    Draw, Play, Make, Perform, Exercise, Throw, Run, Jump, Swim

Pedagogical approaches	*Associative* Instructional system design, Intelligent tutoring systems, Elaboration theory, Didactic, Behaviourist, Training needs analysis *Cognitive* Active learning, Enquiry-led, Problem-based, Goal-based scenarios, Reflective practitioner, Cognitive apprenticeship, Constructivist-based design *Situative* E-moderating framework, Dialogue/argumentation, Experiential learning, Collaborative learning, Activity theory, Apprenticeship, Action research, Reciprocal teaching, Project-based learning, Vicarious learning
Task taxonomy	
Type (What)	*Assimilative* Reading, Viewing , Listening *Information Handling* Gathering, Ordering, Classifying, Selecting , Analysing, Manipulating *Adaptive* Modelling, Simulation *Communicative* Discussing, Presenting, Debating, Critiquing *Productive* Creating, Producing, Writing, Drawing, Composing, Synthesizing, Re-mixing *Experiential* Practising, Applying, Mimicking, Experiencing, Exploring, Investigating, Performing
Technique (How)	*Assimilative* *Information handling* Concept mapping, Brainstorming, Buzz words, Crosswords, Defining, Mind maps, Web search *Adaptive* Modelling *Communicative* Articulate reasoning, Arguing, Coaching, Debate, Discussion, Fishbowl, Ice breaker, Interview, Negotiation, On the spot questioning, Pair dialogues, Panel discussion, Peer exchange, Performance, Question and answer, Rounds, Scaffolding, Socratic instruction , Short answer, Snowball, Structured debate *Productive* Artefact, Assignment, Book report, Dissertation/thesis, Drill and practice, Essay, Exercise, Journaling, Presentation, Literature review, MCQ, Puzzles, Portfolio, Product, Report/paper, Test, Voting *Experiential* Case study, Experiment, Field trip, Game, Role-play, Scavenger hunt, Simulation
Interaction (Who)	Individual, One to one, One to many, Group-based, Class-based

Roles (Which)	Individual learner, Group leader, Coach, Group participant, Mentor, Supervisor, *Rapporteur*, Facilitator, Deliverer, Pair person, Presenter, Peer assessor, Moderator

Tools and resources	*Assimilative*
	      Word processor, Text, image, audio or video viewer
	Information handling
	      Spreadsheet, Database, SPSS, NVIVO, Bibliographic software, Microsoft exchange PDAs, Project manager, Digital image manipulation software, Mind-mapping software, Search engines, Libraries
	Adaptive
	      Virtual worlds, Models, Simulation, Modelling
	Communicative
	      Electronic whiteboards, Email, Discussion boards, Chat, Instant messaging, Voice over IP, Video conferencing, Access grid, Blogs , Wikis
	Productive
	      CAA tools, VLEs

Assessment	Not assessed, Diagnostic, Formative, Summative

Appendix 8: Evaluation framework for learning design tools

As discussed in Chapter 8, this is an evaluation framework for learning design tools. These questions are designed to provide insight into not only the features and capabilities of each software tool but also its intended purpose and its target user group.

1 *Intended purpose of the software and scope*
   Has the software been designed specifically to support learning design or is it intended for a more general purpose (e.g. VLEs)? Some of the tools in this area are authoring or editing environments, some are runtime environments also known as players. Yet others do both.
      Some tools are intended to support single-learner electronic delivery, others are intended for handling multiple-learner and blended learning situations.

2 *Who is the system for? Who else is involved?*
   Some of the tools are intended for use by 'end' users, i.e. teachers and learners, others are intended for use by software developers or instructional designers with a high-level of technical expertise. It is important to be aware of the difference as it is ultimately a key requirement that learning design software be produced that assists teachers in creating and adapting learning designs.

3 *How are units of learning represented in the software?*
   What is the base model of a Unit of Learning (UOL) in the software? Is it a course, a lesson or a more abstract entity such as a UOL?

4 *How are activities represented in the software?*
   The concept of an 'activity' is at the heart of learning design. Does the software incorporate a model for activities or does it only handle content resources?

5 *How is workflow represented in the software?*
   Similarly workflow is an important concept. So it is important to find out about the model of workflow. Is it simple sequencing or are more complex workflows possible?

6 *Can the software represent a variety of pedagogical models?*
   A key concept in learning design is the support of a variety of pedagogical approaches. How does the software provide support for implementing different pedagogical models?

7 *Does the software support sharing and reuse of learning designs?*
   How easy is it for a learning design created within the software to be exported for reuse in other contexts? Can the design be represented in a platform-independent way?

8   *Is the learning design adaptable at run-time?*
A criticism of the IMS Learning Design specification is that Learning Designs have to be engineered in advance and cannot be easily adapted at run-time.

9   *What form is the software in (web-based, stand-alone app, etc.)?*
What sort of software is it? Will it run on a variety of platforms, etc?

10 *Integration*
Some of the software tools are designed to be used independently of any other application; others are designed to work as part of a wider suite of tools or environment. Can the software integrate with other tools?

11 *Does the software implement the IMS Learning Design specification? (If so, at what level: A, B or C?)*
A simple question. If it doesn't, then is it intended that it should in the future?

Appendix 9: E-learning practice evaluator – reflecting on a learning activity in a technology-rich context

This evaluator was designed for the Joint Information Systems Committee (JISC) Effective Practice workshops and adapted with feedback from participants. It can be used to evaluate an e-learning activity once it has been carried out by learners.

Descriptive questions

1   *What did you ask learners to do (learning task)?*
    Did they do what you expected?
    Did this help them achieve the learning outcomes?
    Were there alternatives for learners to choose, and did you notice any patterns in their choices?

2   *How did learners interact?*
    What kinds of dialogue took place between yourself and the learners, among learners working collaboratively, and with other support staff?

3   *What resources did they use?*
    Did these prove useful and relevant to learners?
    Were they accessible and available to all learners?
    Were there any interesting patterns of use/non-use?

4   *What technologies did they use?*
    Were these accessible and available to all learners?
    Did learners have the skills to use them effectively?
    Were equipment and support adequate?

5   *What was the e-learning advantage?*
    What advantages were there to using electronic resources or technologies?
    Consider: accessibility, inclusion, participation, personalization.
    Or: what challenges did this help you to meet?

6   *How did learners receive feedback on this activity?*
    Did feedback come from learners (self or peer), from you, or was it intrinsic to the activity itself?
    Was the feedback part of a formal assessment?

7   *(Optional) How did this activity support your rationale?*
    How did it express your preferred approach to teaching and learning (ideals, values, beliefs)?

Reflective questions

1   *What was the experience like for learners?*
    Did they meet the learning outcomes?
    Did they enjoy the experience?
    Were they motivated and involved?
    Have there been any unexpected benefits?
    Use any formal or informal feedback, e.g. conversations, feedback forms, observations etc.

2   *What was the experience like for you?*
    Were there any costs to you of taking this approach?
    Were there any benefits? Did you enjoy it?
    Did it involve working with other staff, and how was this experience?
    Use your own reflections and any evidence you have gathered.

3   *What do you think has worked well?*

4   *What would you have done differently?*

5   *How did your approach meet the challenges presented?*

6   *What advice would you give to another teacher working in a similar context to your own?*

Appendix 10: Template for describing a case study in e-learning practice

The following template can be used as a guide for collecting information about examples of e-learning practice. It was developed in collaboration with several of the UK Higher Education subject centres. Fields included were those considered useful or essential by most subject centre staff who took part in a survey. Fields in italics were considered useful by a smaller number of staff.

To tailor the template to the needs of your own subject centre, department or institution:

1   Decide why you are collecting case studies. Who are the end users and what information do they really need? Remember that baseline information, while it may seem boring, can be important in helping users to find case studies from a database or collection, and to understand the context in which an activity was carried out.

2   Decide how much time and commitment you are likely to have from the people whose practice you are collecting.

3   Decide how you will collect these examples of practice. Will somebody interview the practitioner(s) involved and write up the case study afterwards? Will you ask practitioners to complete case studies themselves, following your guidelines? In the second case you will need to give more explicit guidance on completing the pro forma and you may have to consider incentives (e.g. payment).

4   On the basis of 1–3, decide which fields in the template you need to include. There may be one or two fields you need to add to meet your requirements.

5   Prepare the template for delivery as either an interview pro-forma or guidelines for writing up. In the first case, you need to brief the interviewer about the kinds of response you might expect, and how to prompt for more information. In the second case, include subject-specific or local examples to help people understand what you are looking for.

6   Pilot the pro-forma with one or two naive users. You may find that you need to change the order of fields to help them tell their story in a more natural way. You may find that the wording used in this template is not appropriate for your participants, and you need to change it (though if you change the names of any fields, please make a record of this so that different case study collections can be mapped to the same original template). You may also find that you need to include more examples to help users make sense of what is being asked.

I Curriculum and intended learning outcomes	
Field	*Example(s) and guidance*
Subject/discipline area	General subject area, which may be indicated by the name of the department delivering the programme, or the name of the qualification studied e.g. English literature, statistics, woodworking, mechanical engineering
Topic/domain	A phrase to describe the content of this specific UOL, whether a whole module, a learning session, or a single activity e.g. *Jane Eyre*, normal distribution, mitre joints, beam deflection
Mode of delivery	How the UOL was delivered and how learners engaged with it, e.g.: • self-paced or cohort learning? • autonomous or tutor-supported learning? • face-to-face, distance or blended mode?
Intended learning outcome(s)	Learning outcomes, copied from the written curriculum or devised for this UOL. Include all outcomes that are relevant to the UOL being described e.g. Learners will be able to: specify beam parameters for a given deflection e.g. Learners will be able to: compare a psychoanalytical and a socio-historical approach to the study of *Jane Eyre*
Context/level of study	*Context (e.g.): further education, higher education, continuous professional development, vocational education, community education* *Level (e.g.): GCSE (year 1), A/S level (year 2), NVQ (level 4), Bachelor degree (year 3), Masters degree (year 1) . . .* *Context and/or level may be used. Full-time, part-time or 'sandwich' study could also be recorded*
Prerequisites	*Any other units of study that learners needed to complete before embarking on this unit of study, or any prerequisite qualifications or skills* *e.g. E1004 Background to the English Novel* *e.g. GCSE Maths grade 'C' or above* *e.g. Learners should be able to: make and finish a butt joint; make drawings to scale*
2 Activity	
Field	*Example(s) and guidance*
General approach	Brief description of the educational approach taken, i.e. any general theoretical or practical models informing the practitioner's choice of activities e.g. 'problem based learning' e.g. focus on collaboration and developing learning communities

Learning task(s)	The tasks or activities defined by the practitioner for the learner(s) to carry out (i.e. *what* learners are asked to do) e.g. read hand-out on uses of mitre joints e.g. practise calculating the area under the curve in the following examples e.g. compare extracts (a) and (b): what do they reveal about the characters of Jane and Rochester?
Technique	*For some tasks you may want to say more about how learners carried out the task:* *e.g. Socratic dialogue technique* *e.g. discussion in pairs and reporting back* *e.g. multiple choice questions*
Feedback	*How learners received feedback on the activity or task. This may be intrinsic, i.e. it may have arisen in the course of the activity itself, or it may have involved somebody (e.g. the tutor, other learners, or the learners themselves) making an explicit judgement about performance* *e.g. observed changes in the experimental system* *e.g. grade and comment* *e.g. verbal feedback in small groups*

3 People involved

Field	Examples and guidance
Number of learners	e.g. 29 in class; 4–5 in each group
Learner characteristics	Characteristics of individual learners or the learning group that influenced the choice of learning tools, resources and activities. You might consider:
	Access: issues relating to disability, language preferences, technical and media preferences e.g. two learners assessed as dyslexic: allowed more time for written work; remembered to use coloured backgrounds!
	Qualifications: actual attainments of learners in prerequisite and other courses e.g. around one-quarter of the class had not taken the recommended foundation module: had to revise key concepts
	Competence: actual attainments of learners in key skill areas e.g. previous tutor says learners often need help with basic numeracy skills (measurement, multiplication)
Other people involved	*The role of the tutor (if any) and any other people involved in the learning activity* *e.g. lecturer provides feedback and corrects mistakes* *e.g. technician sets up equipment and supporters learners in using it* *e.g. learning support team introduce key web sites and search techniques*

4 Environment for learning

Field	Example(s) and guidance
Physical setting	Where the learning activity took place e.g. Lecture Room 11 e.g. workplace: general office with access to networked computer e.g. field: data gathering in the covered market
Social setting	Group size and roles assigned to the participants e.g. individual activity, one-to-one mentoring session, small group tutorial, group collaborative activity, one-to-many (large lecture)
Tool(s)	All physical and virtual tools (hardware, software, networks) used by practitioners and learners in preparing and carrying out the learning task(s) e.g. kar2ouche running on networked computers in computer lab e.g. RealPlayer version 2.0 e.g. one laptop running ICQ per four learners
Resource(s)	Content resources sourced or designed for use with this learning task e.g. hand-out with joint diagrams and assembly instructions e.g. Bronte's home page e.g. Virtual Deflector package available via intranet
Support issues	*What support was needed to set up the environment, its tools and resources?* *e.g. technician to set up data projector in Room ST12* *e.g. ICT officer to be available during drop-in session* *e.g. media services to transfer transparencies to CD-ROM*
Access issues	*What specific access needs did learners have? Include not only physical access to tools and resources but any learner skills and literacies that needed to be addressed* *e.g. learners were already familiar with use of the VLE from induction in semester 1* *e.g. some learners needed revision of information skills – online tutorial available*

5 Outcomes for learners

Field	Example(s) and guidance
Learner feedback	Outcomes of any evaluation, formal or informal, carried out with learners, including feedback from module evaluation forms, student reps, etc.
Learner observations	Report from any observations, formal or informal, carried out during the learning, including anecdotal evidence from professionals involved
Assessment scores	*Grades or other formal assessment outputs for the learner(s) involved* *e.g. mean grade of 72.5 as compared with 67 in parallel module* *e.g. essays showed greater range of references and depth of analysis than in previous years*

6 Reflections	
Field	*Example(s) and guidance*
Aims and rationale	Main aims in delivering this activity, and rationale for choices of tools, resources, etc. e.g. the focus may have been on specific learner needs, on enhancing a skill, on covering a tricky area of the curriculum, on making use of a particular technology, etc.
Benefits and opportunities	Assessment of what worked well and/or what the benefits were in taking this approach
Problems and risks	Assessment of what worked less well and/or what the risks were in taking this approach
Advice	Advice you would give to another practitioner planning to deliver a similar activity or use a similar technology or approach
Other reflections	*Any other reflections on the process of planning and delivering this activity, on further developments that might be undertaken, and on what the practitioner has learned*

Appendix 11: A typology of effective interventions that support e-learning practice

As discussed in Chapter 9, the typology presents a number of characteristics of effective interventions and illustrates how these characteristics might operate in the context of working with resources, individuals and groups or wider change.

Principles of effective interventions ('Interventions' include a combination of resources, tools and services)	Representing and sharing knowledge Supporting well-informed approaches to the use of e-learning	Developing staff Enabling individuals or groups to do something new or differently	Developing organizations Supporting change in the structure and processes of organizations
Usability To be usable, interventions need to be available, relevant and understandable by a tightly defined audience, e.g.: • be known of by their audience • be available and accessible to their audience • take account of the language, values, culture and priorities of their particular audience	Representations of knowledge are made more usable by: • being easily sourced, e.g. The LTDI Evaluation cookbook available as PDF, interactive html or print • being free or reasonably priced • being in a media and format familiar to that particular community, e.g. law academics are familiar with textual information • using accessible and meaningful language • ensuring that the resources themselves do not present users with technical problems	Where developers are working with individual practitioners, the process of building relationships is facilitated where developers work hard to make their expertise accessible. Staff can be enabled to use tools to change practice by providing support in the form of workshops or one-to-one mentoring	To be usable, organizational interventions need to ensure that their target audience are aware of what the service offers, how the service works and how to access it. Good examples are those that: • are conceptually simple enough so users can grasp what they are offering • offer training or support in how to use the service • have a tightly defined audience and speak in the language of that audience
Contextualization Practitioners continue to favour tools and resources	Representations can be contextualized by:	Contextualized working with individuals might involve:	Organizational development can be supported by contextualizing

that have either been contextualized for them and/or that they can create or adapt for their context. For educators this is likely to include: • acknowledging the realities of the educational setting • tackling pertinent, real life issues • relevance to the discipline • allowing practitioners to create, adapt, reuse or repurpose their own resources	• encouraging the sharing of authentic scenarios through e.g. case studies, show and tells, stories, narratives • offering facilities that allow for personalization, e.g. the Virtual Learning Space allows users to create their own profile and personalized space • offering multiple versions of resource for different disciplines, e.g. RDN Virtual Training Suite • presenting ideas from a variety of subject areas, e.g. ScotCit Effective Lecturing project • being sufficiently small to be adapted, but large enough to be educationally useful • using repurposable media and formats	• establishing common ground between developers and practitioners (e.g. common discipline) • establishing and maintaining an ongoing dialogue with staff to identify what they perceive their needs to be • a better understanding of the realities of practitioner's work, e.g. actual course design processes at work, the inequalities of the workplace or the changes in working practice • tools that provide an obvious solution to a problem • supporting staff to develop information literacy, e.g. how to source, retrieve, use, repurpose, organize and share learning resources	development through a concerns-based approach to staff development involving, e.g. • offering a broad repertoire of approaches to support staff throughout an organization • undertaking a user requirements analysis, e.g. Connect • reducing the time lag between analysis of user need and setting up of the service • exploiting national and institutional policies, e.g. TechDis or JISC Legal Info Service • explaining the relevance of the support for particular groups
Professional learning Changing practice requires practitioners to learn, specifically to alter their conceptions of teaching and learning through, e.g. • opportunities to construct their own meanings • learning from experience through reflection	Representations can support the professional learning process through • engaging the learner through the use of activities • those that allow people with different learning approaches to engage with concepts • being able to contribute to a resource embraces	Work with individuals and groups can support their learning through • allowing practitioners to reach their own conclusions rather than presenting predefined solutions • requiring assumptions to be made explicit and open to discussion and critique	Effective services are organized around problems that teachers encounter. Long-term effectiveness requires staff to understand new practices (rather than have it done for them) Caution that informal learning may perpetuate historical prejudices, short-cuts or misinterpretations Evaluations of toolkits show they are most effective when used as

• informal learning • problem-based learning • action learning • peer supported learning.	constructivist principles, e.g. *Journal of Interactive Media in Education*, wikis, weblogs Effective toolkits are those that recommend a range of suitable approaches, which the practitioner uses to make their own informed choices, e.g. pedagogical toolkit, Media Advisor, evaluation toolkit. E-portfolios may be the next step to support reflection, e.g. JISC PETAL project	• suggesting options that practitioners may not have considered • using toolkits to prompt and support peer conversations • opportunities for sharing and discussing practice One to one support with, e.g. learning technologists is effective, but costly	part of a staff development programme
Communities There may be real advantages to working within the existing communities where practitioners are already based	Practitioners from different communities are likely to choose specific types of resources. Ownership is increased in resources that can be contributed to e.g. JIME or repurposed, e.g. ELICIT modules. Involving communities in resource creation and maintenance to promote ownership and use, e.g. SNAS project creating resource lists for new lecturers. Practitioner commentaries on use of resources could be fed back into their communities.	In designing curricula, academics are strongly influenced by their discipline and academic backgrounds Approaches that focus on disciplinary identity are more likely to be effective than those that seek to instruct in 'alien' processes. Curriculum design is a political and cultural process. Academics are aware of these process and forms of support that recognize these constraints should be easily adopted. Examples of attempts to create and use communities of interested staff, e.g. the Virtual Learning Space and conferences	Where a service is working with just one community, it is much easier for that community to feel a sense of ownership. Services set up in competition may find it difficult to work well together Services need to be sensitive to the working practices of the department, e.g. using the Media Advisor tool with course teams or whole departments to make explicit the communities language, culture and practices. A key attribute of successful staff development services is the involvement of the end user community, e.g. Ferl uses ordinary teaching staff as authors and CETIS, which has built a strong community

		of practice around the service that they offer	Institutional quality assurance processes and policy may be used to promote aspects of effective learning design
Learning Design Practitioners need to be supported in engaging with a process that starts with the educational approach. Effective interventions are those that are used to support student learning and are dependent on our understanding of the learning design processes	There are tools that explicitly help practitioners to make theoretically informed decisions, e.g. LAMS, DialogPlus, the pedagogical toolkit and Media Advisor. Potential to extend generic in built support and guidance with a pedagogical focus, e.g. PowerPoint wizards or VLE tutorials Lesson plans are well used in school and further education and have been shown to positively influence the effective adoption of e-learning in this sector Case studies, and other representations, should clearly illustrate the pedagogical strategy adopted	such as Online Tutoring Skills e-workshop and Ferl's 'VLEs Beyond the Fringe' Curriculum design is experienced by academics as re-design rather than rational process of designing from scratch Where the production process is a dialogue, this enables the development of the academic's repertoire of approaches to teaching Practitioners need to be supported in combining representations, e.g. combining an activity with a learning resource	

Author index

Subject index

Note: Page numbers referring to figures, tables and boxes are shown in italics.

eBooks – at www.eBookstore.tandf.co.uk

A library at your fingertips!

eBooks are electronic versions of printed books. You can store them on your PC/laptop or browse them online.

They have advantages for anyone needing rapid access to a wide variety of published, copyright information.

eBooks can help your research by enabling you to bookmark chapters, annotate text and use instant searches to find specific words or phrases. Several eBook files would fit on even a small laptop or PDA.

NEW: Save money by eSubscribing: cheap, online access to any eBook for as long as you need it.

Annual subscription packages

We now offer special low-cost bulk subscriptions to packages of eBooks in certain subject areas. These are available to libraries or to individuals.

For more information please contact webmaster.ebooks@tandf.co.uk

We're continually developing the eBook concept, so keep up to date by visiting the website.

www.eBookstore.tandf.co.uk